HAND COLOURING BLACK & WHITE PHOTOGRAPHY

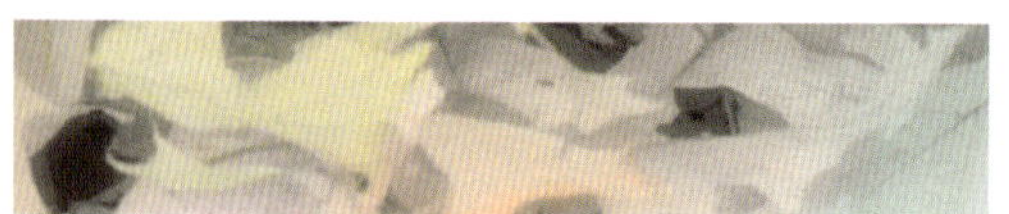

First published in Great Britain
2000 by Argentum, an imprint of
Aurum Press Ltd
25 Bedford Avenue,
London WC1B 3AT

A catalogue record for this book is available from the British Library.

ISBN 1 902538 07 2

10 9 8 7 6 5 4 3 2 1
2004 2003 2002 2001 2000

Design: The Design Company
Layout: SYP Design & Production
Cover Photographs: Laurie Klein
Photographs of materials (page 10) and presentation artwork (pages 16–17) by Kevin Thomas

Berg Color Tone box appears with permission from Berg Color Tone Inc., 72 Ward Road, Lancaster, New York, 14086.

Printed in China

HAND COLOURING BLACK & WHITE PHOTOGRAPHY

An introduction and step-by-step guide

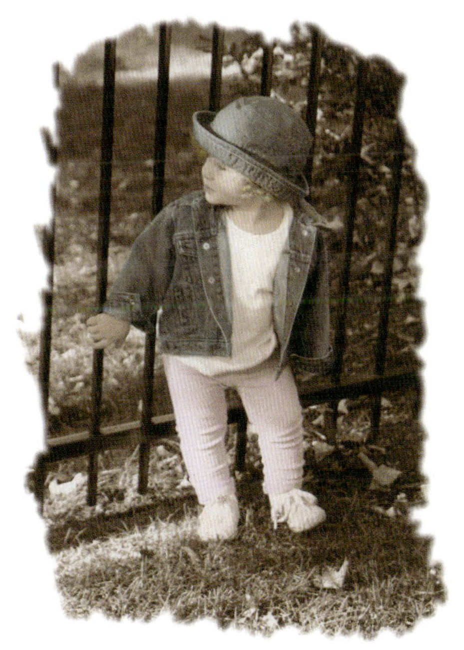

Laurie Klein

All Step-by-Step Photography by Laurie Klein

Argentum

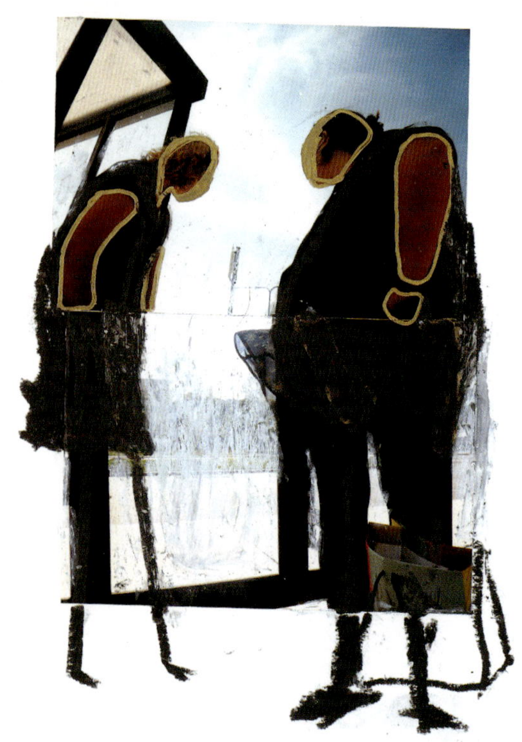

CONTENTS

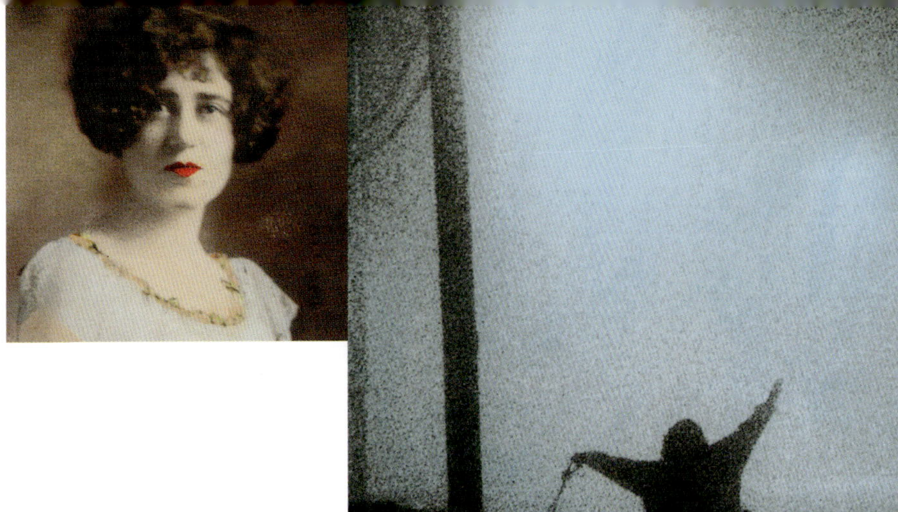

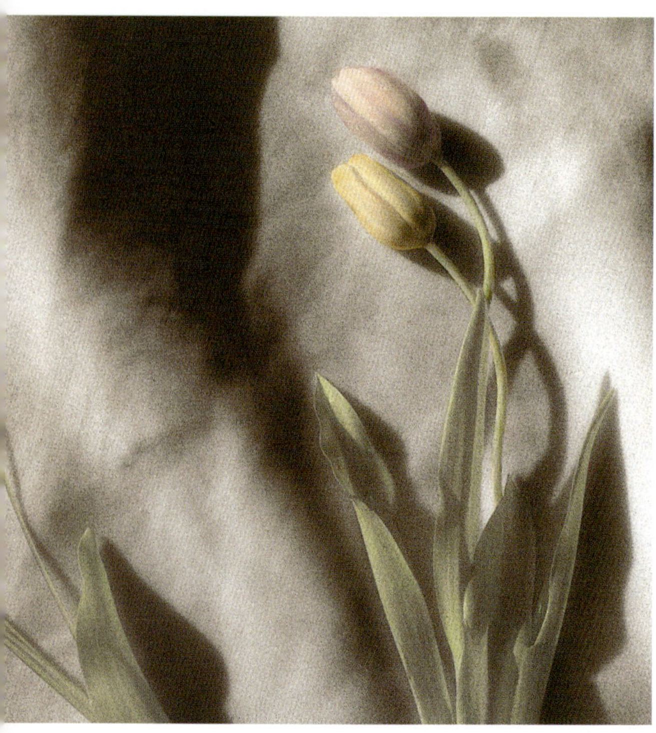

△ Hand colour to give a photograph a "painterly quality."

INTRODUCTION

Can you paint or draw? I can't! I'm intimidated by a paintbrush, and sketching has never been my strong suit. And yet I am regarded as a leader in hand colouring photographs. How do I do it? Well, in addition to having a good eye for composition and a technique that works wonders for me (as it will for you), I think of each photograph I'm going to hand colour as a page out of a colouring book—and I colour within the lines!

I have been a fine-art photographer for twenty-five years and a photographic educator for over eighteen years. I have taught hand colouring to photographers, artists, and craftspeople and to children as young as kindergarten age. Many of my students who had prior experience in hand colouring said they found the process to be relatively complicated. The method I use, however, is very easy and produces beautiful results. And the materials needed are readily available—you probably have most of them already.

Hand colouring photographs was popular in the early years of this century, and recently I have observed a resurgence in this art form. Perhaps it is due to the popularity of memory books. Our photographs of family and friends represent our personal history. Hand colouring these photographs results in a unique and timeless piece of artwork. In my commercial wedding and portrait photography business, many of my clients come to me because my images are a marriage of photography and a "painterly quality" created by hand colouring. Indeed, hand-coloured photos are a lasting and creative expression of favourite memories.

Hand colouring is also a great project to do with children. Children are extremely creative, whether they're hand colouring photographs they have taken themselves or that someone else has taken. Let the creative child within you surface, and feel free to experiment. You can't make a mistake, so have some fun.

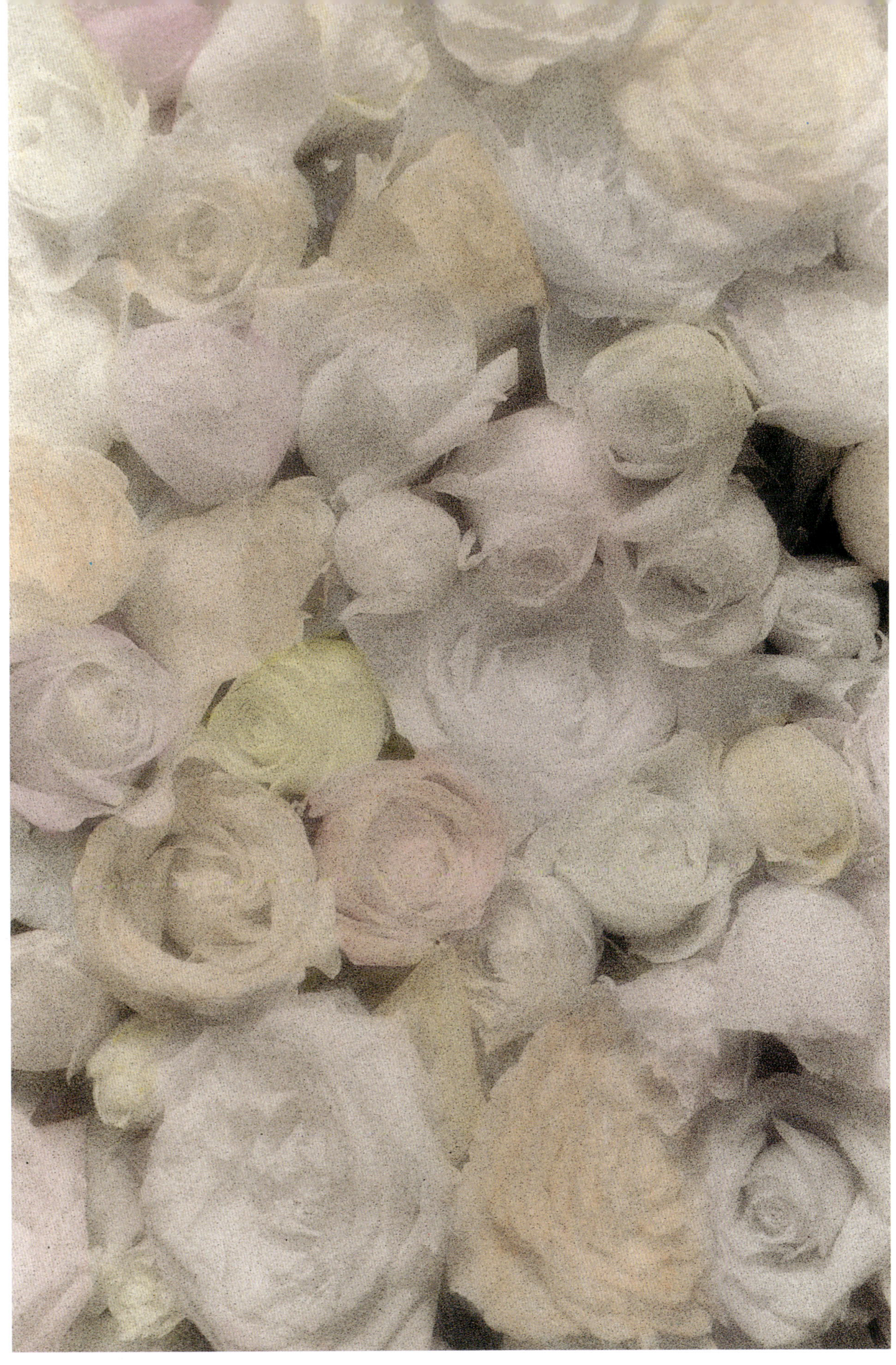

△ Use coloured pencils to enhance the nuances of a complicated image.

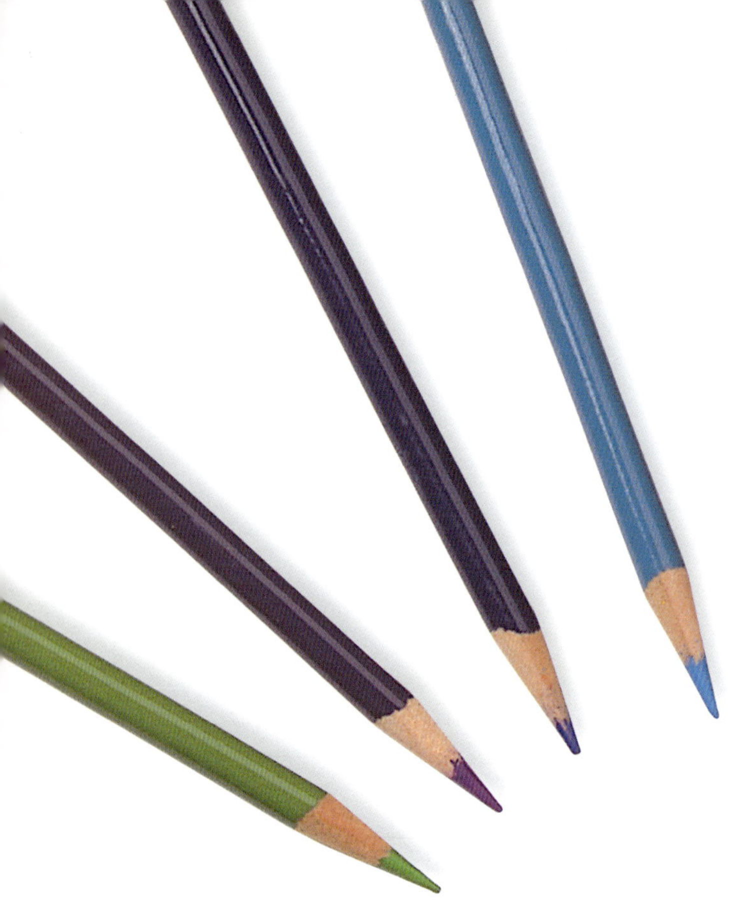

THE BASICS

Sanford's Karisma colour pencils were used in many of the demonstrations in this book. Karisma colour pencils are made in a variety of colours and have a soft lead that will not scratch the surface (emulsion) of the print. Most coloured pencils, however, will work just fine for hand colouring.

Coloured pencils are great for hand colouring photographs because they're not intimidating like a paintbrush can be—you don't need special skills to use them. We've all been using pencils for most of our lives, and you probably even have some coloured pencils around the house. A wonderful part of working with coloured pencils is that mistakes can be removed with a cotton swab moistened with a very small amount of water, making this a very forgiving medium for hand colouring.

In some of the demonstrations, a solution of turpentine and vegetable oil is used as a solvent for the coloured pencils. The solvent is used to create a wash of colour so the pencil strokes are not apparent on the print. Applied with a cotton swab, the oil allows the colour to move around, creating the wash, and the turpentine cuts the oil slick on the print. This technique produces a transparent colour that doesn't obscure the photograph; the colour appears to be a part of the image rather than sitting on the surface of the print. Turpentine-and-oil solution can also be used to remove excess colour. But be careful not to use too much solution. A very little goes a long way, as is explained in this book.

When learning to hand colour, be sure to make multiple prints of the image being hand coloured. This way you can experiment and compare the effects of different procedures and mediums. Keep records of each step so you can duplicate results you like.

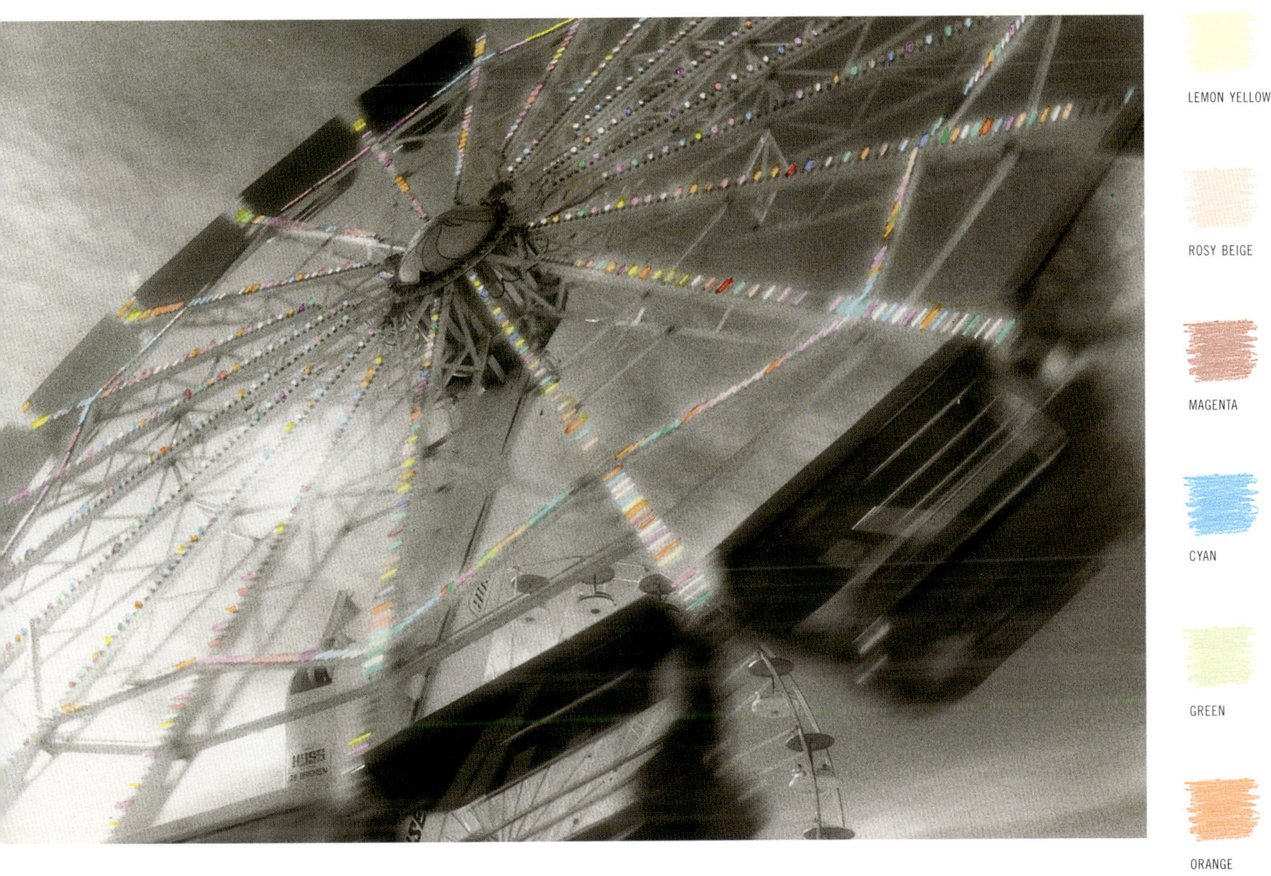

LEMON YELLOW

ROSY BEIGE

MAGENTA

CYAN

GREEN

ORANGE

△ Coloured pencils are ideal for hand colouring because they don't require special skills to use them. And even just a handful of colours, such as the ones shown here, can produce vivid results.

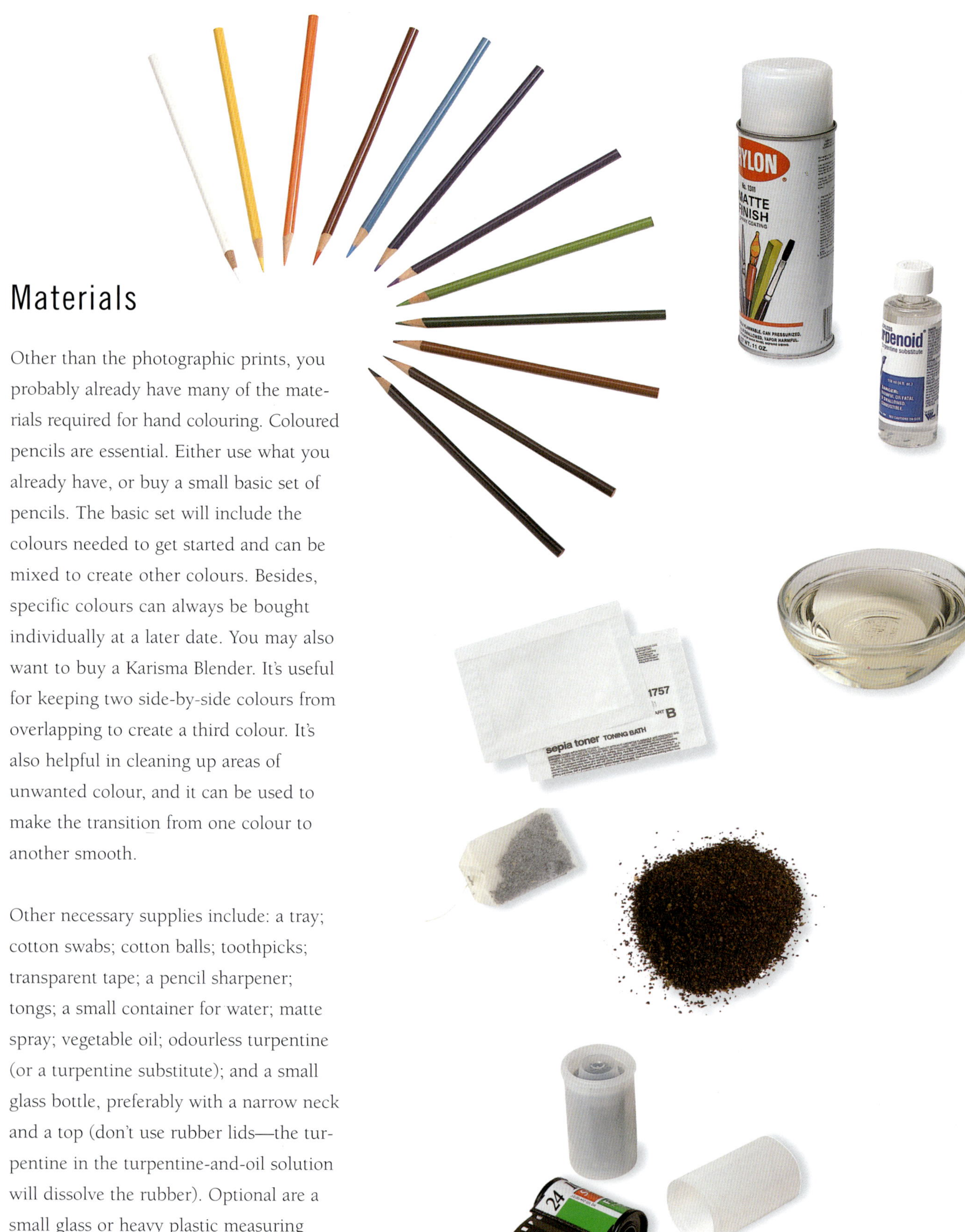

Materials

Other than the photographic prints, you probably already have many of the materials required for hand colouring. Coloured pencils are essential. Either use what you already have, or buy a small basic set of pencils. The basic set will include the colours needed to get started and can be mixed to create other colours. Besides, specific colours can always be bought individually at a later date. You may also want to buy a Karisma Blender. It's useful for keeping two side-by-side colours from overlapping to create a third colour. It's also helpful in cleaning up areas of unwanted colour, and it can be used to make the transition from one colour to another smooth.

Other necessary supplies include: a tray; cotton swabs; cotton balls; toothpicks; transparent tape; a pencil sharpener; tongs; a small container for water; matte spray; vegetable oil; odourless turpentine (or a turpentine substitute); and a small glass bottle, preferably with a narrow neck and a top (don't use rubber lids—the turpentine in the turpentine-and-oil solution will dissolve the rubber). Optional are a small glass or heavy plastic measuring cup, sepia toner, and nylon or soft, lint-free gloves.

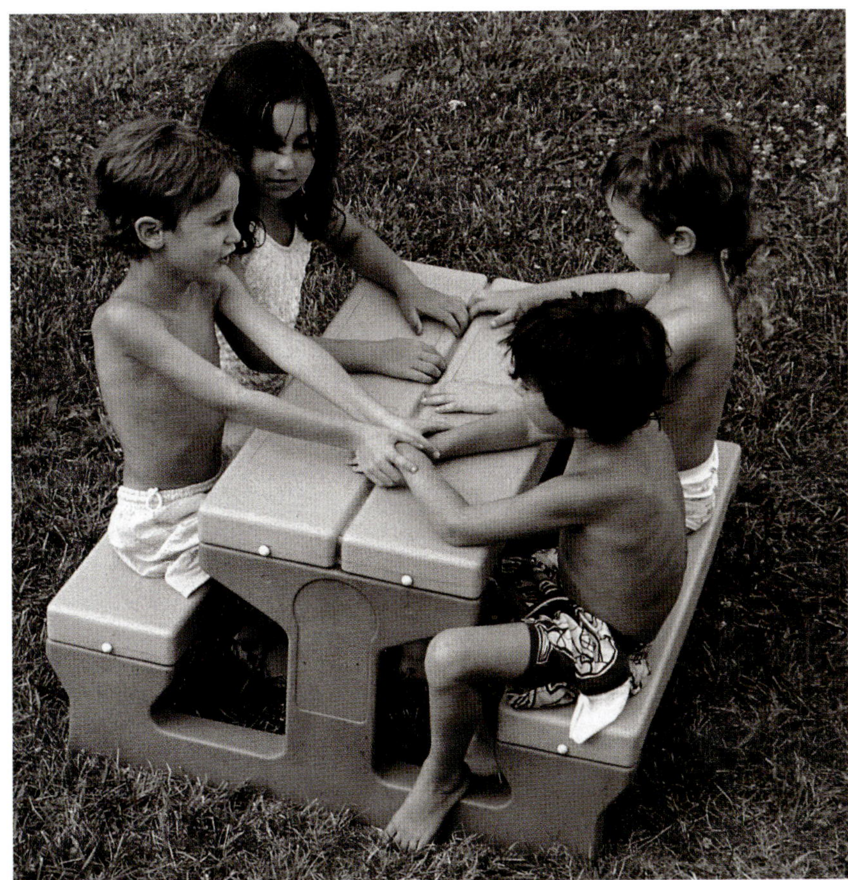

◁ 100-speed film

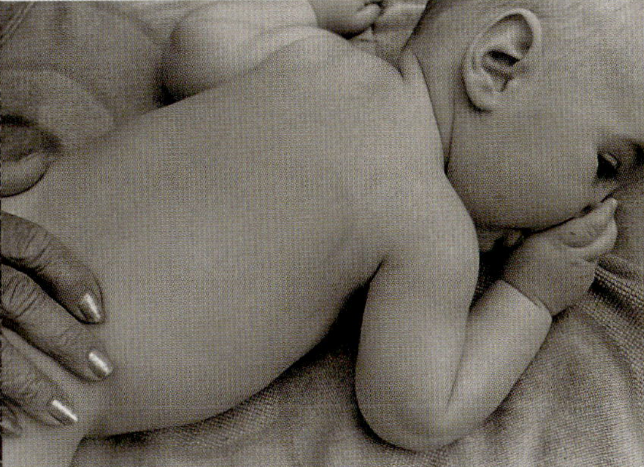

△ 400-speed film

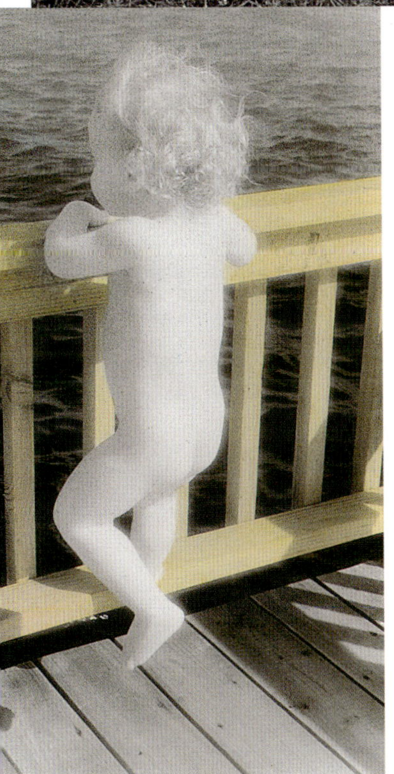

△ High-speed infrared film

Film Types

The majority of photographs that are hand coloured are taken with black-and-white film and are printed on black-and-white photographic paper. (A black-and-white print can be made from a colour negative, but the results will be different.)

The photographs in this book were taken with three different film speeds: 100, 400, and high-speed infrared film. Which black-and-white film to use depends on the subject matter as well as the lighting conditions, the time of year, and whether you are shooting indoors or outdoors. When photographing outside in bright sunlight or even on bright overcast days in warmer weather, use a slower film speed, like 100 or 125. These films have less grain and, in photographs of people, will render soft, smooth skin tones. For overcast, cloudier days, during the winter months, or when inside, use a faster film like 400, which is a bit grainy. In very low light situations without a flash, experiment with high-speed films, such as 1000 and above. Read the data sheet that comes with the film to become familiar with its characteristics.

Different kinds of film yield different effects or can evoke certain moods. For a romantic feel, try using a high-speed infrared film, which will produce a grainy look. Infrared film is a technical film that lends itself beautifully to hand colouring because it produces so many light/highlight tones.

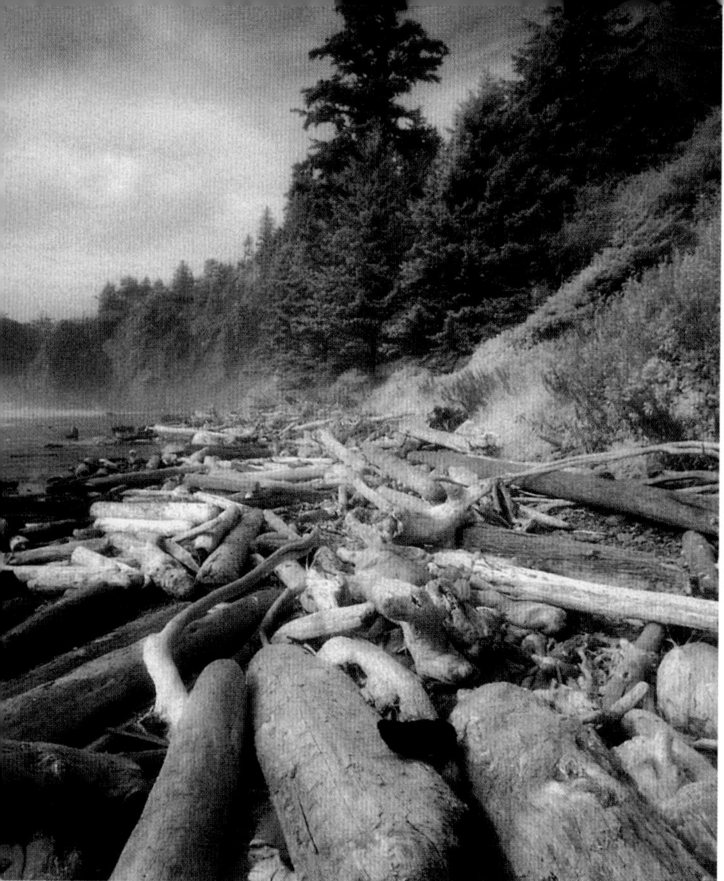

◁ Photographs with a matte surface are ideal for hand colouring.

Print Surfaces

Photographic papers come in a variety of sizes, surfaces, types, and tones. Paper surface should be selected based on the materials being used to hand colour. Matte surfaces, for instance, work the best regardless of the medium, but many materials won't adhere to a high-gloss surface. In fact, if you'll be using pencils, a flat matte surface is required. Oils can be used on a flat or semimatte/pearl surface, and acrylics can be used on any surface. To make a print with a glossy or semimatte/pearl surface suitable for hand colouring, spray it with matte spray to give it "tooth," or texture.

Print sizes vary. The easiest to hand colour, and the size I recommend for beginners, is an 8" x 10" (20 cm x 25 cm) print. Anything smaller than this size will require more detailed work. Plus, larger prints are more expensive and take longer to colour. After mastering hand colouring an 8" x 10" (20 cm x 25 cm) print, try working on a larger print. The results can be spectacular.

Photographic papers are either fibre-based or resin-coated (R/C). Photos printed on fibre-based paper are somewhat easier to hand colour, and coloured pencils appear slightly brighter on them. However, this paper is more expensive, and it takes longer to make a print on it than on resin-coated paper, which should be taken into account if you're doing the printing yourself. Keep track of the kind of paper you're using. Tonal qualities vary by manufacturer. Some papers are warmer or cooler toned, and some have a slight colour cast. These characteristics will affect the results of hand colouring.

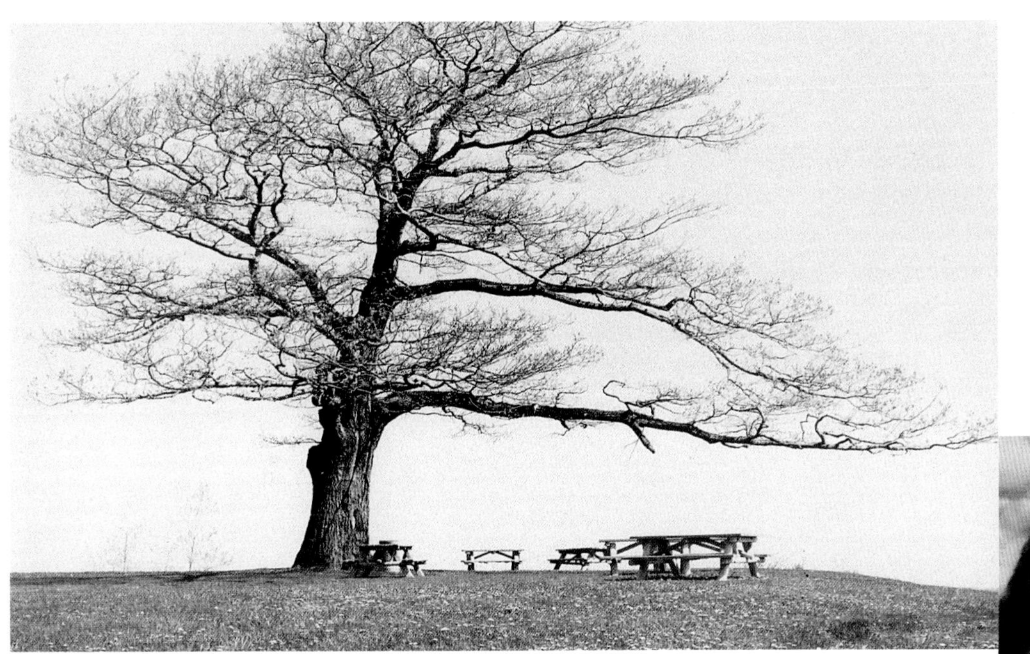

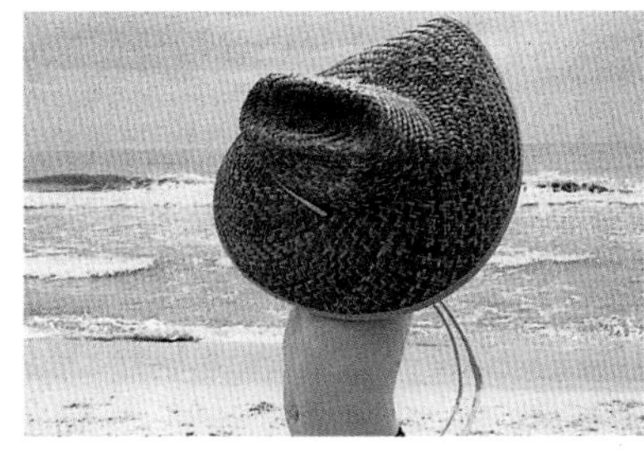

Shooting Images to Hand Colour

Any subject matter and type of photograph can be hand coloured. Landscapes, people, animals, architecture, interiors, vacation photos, or even scenes staged with props and costumes work well. The more you enjoy the subject matter and the photograph, the more fun you will have hand colouring the print.

Keep in mind, though, that the sharper the image, the better defined the potential hand-colouring areas will be. Areas that hand colour the best are the light and highlight areas; colour applied to dark areas of a print won't show up very well. Since the light/highlight areas are the most obvious areas to hand colour, some hand colourists print their photos slightly lighter than usual.

Photographing with black-and-white film is different from using colour film. All colours become a shade of grey, black, or white. If you're posing a shot, use props that are light in colour, and have the subjects wear light-coloured clothing. Since you are the artist, if you want the colour of someone's sweater to be red, then have that person wear a pastel or very light-coloured sweater and then colour it the desired red after printing the photo. Learning how black-and-white film sees reality takes practice. Sometimes squinting or wearing dark sunglasses that are neutral in colour helps simulate how the film read colours.

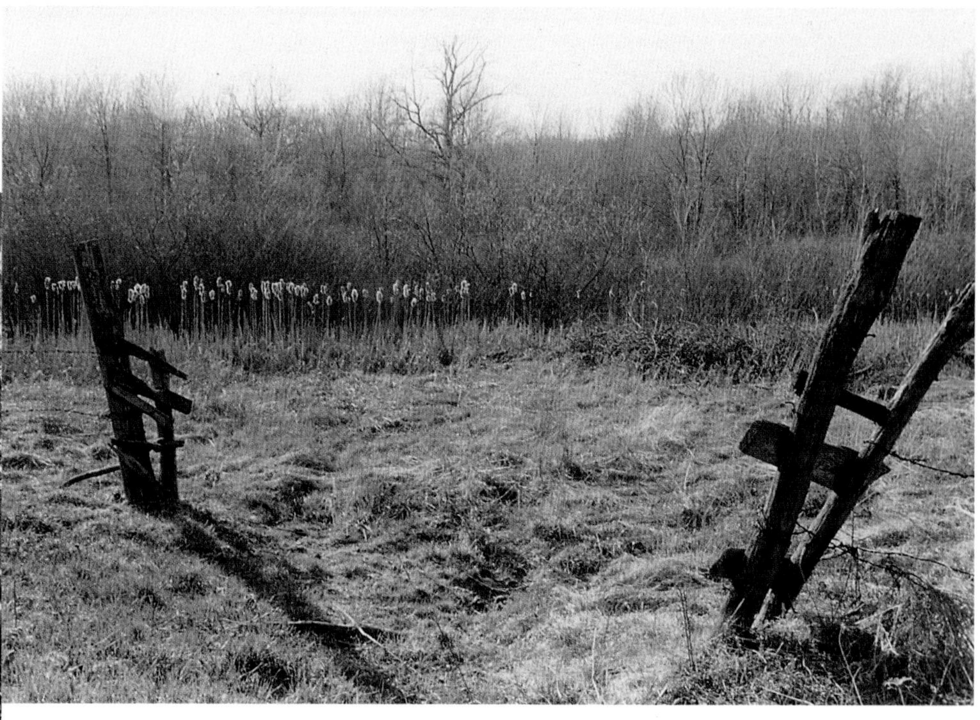

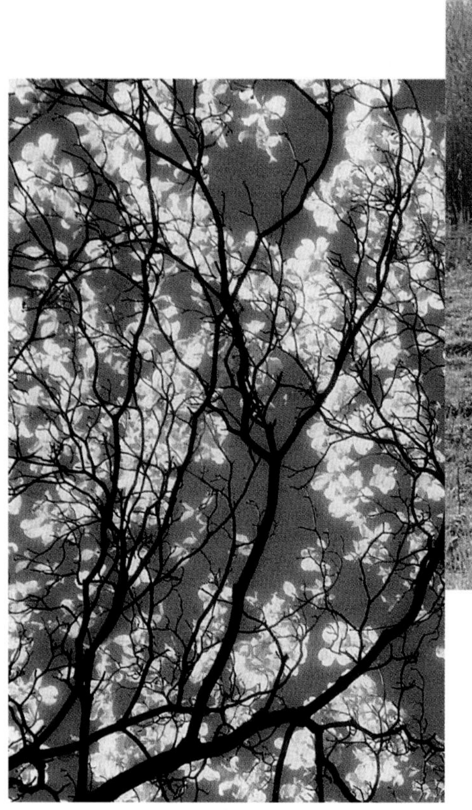

Using Images of Your Own

Test existing black-and-white photographs you'd like to hand colour to see if the surface of the prints will "take" the coloured pencils. Take a bright-coloured pencil and make two marks: one in the white border that surrounds the image and the other on a blank piece of paper. Compare the two marks to see if they look similar. If they do, then the print can be hand coloured. If the pencil barely makes a mark on the print or comes off when rubbed, then the print surface is not suitable. (Remember, the mark can be erased with a small amount of water and a cotton swab.) In the latter case, use matte spray to give the print tooth (see "Print Surfaces"). One note on matte spray: If you overwork a sprayed print or use too much solution on it, the spray can come off in areas, and in those areas the colour will not adhere.

When working with snapshots or vintage photographs, you may not want to use the original print. Instead, go to a lab and have either a copy negative or computer-generated negative made. Then have a black-and-white print made from that on matte-surface paper. You may have to go to a professional lab for this because most colour labs print black-and-white film on colour paper, and the tones and the surfaces will not be good for hand colouring.

Colour prints are also an option. Colour negatives can be printed on black-and-white paper, but the prints will need to be sprayed first if they are not printed on matte-surface paper.

▷ Look for a smooth work surface, such as a drafting table or a regular table covered with a piece of acrylic or smooth mat board.

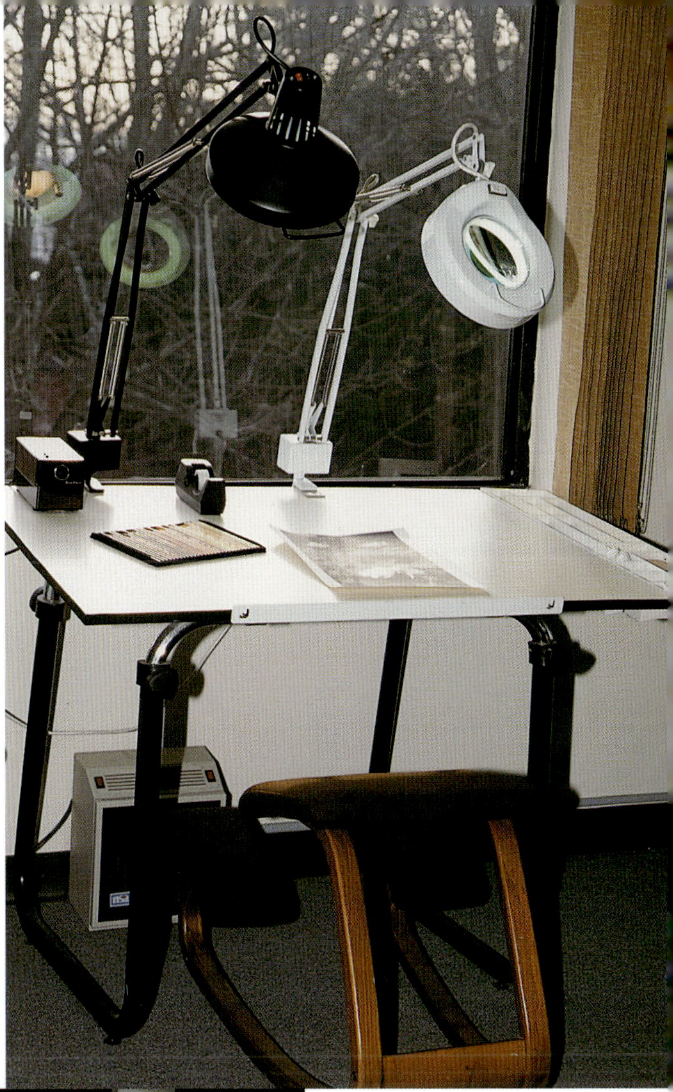

Work Area

Start with a smooth work surface. If it isn't smooth, the print will pick up its texture when it is hand coloured, just as if it were a rubbing of the table. If you like to work at an angle, try a drafting table or a portable drafting table that can be placed on an existing tabletop. Drafting tables, which are adjustable, are available at most office-supply stores. To work on a flat surface, use a piece of acrylic or smooth mat board on a regular table.

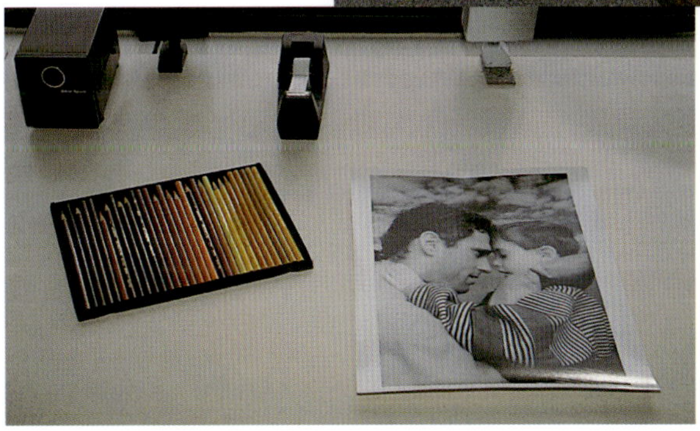

Some of the materials used to hand colour are toxic, so if you're working in your kitchen, be sure to keep your work area separate from food-preparation areas. Ventilation is also something to keep in mind. When using turpentine (in the turpentine-and-oil solution), it's a good idea to use an air purifier or keep a window open. When working outside, avoid bright sunlight because the heat from the sun could curl the prints and make your pencil tips more apt to break.

Good lighting is essential in a work area. Natural light works well, as do lights that have both a fluorescent tube and a tungsten bulb. These lights give a natural, balanced light and are very bright. If working outside, choose a shady area.

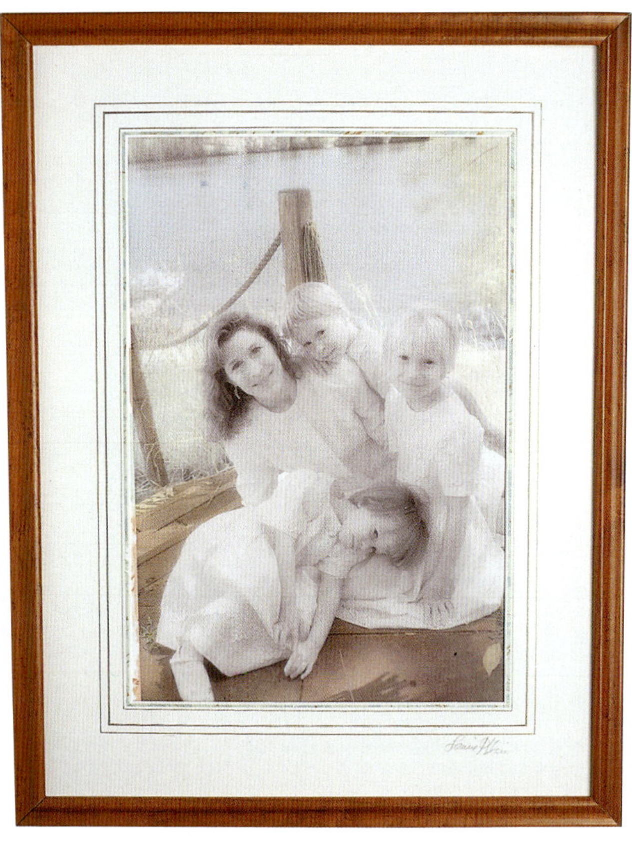

◁ *Joanne, Kelly, Barton, and Stephanie*
by Laurie Klein
This photograph was over-matted with a French mat. Some of the colours used in the photo were also applied to the French mat.

Presentation

I do not recommend spraying a print after it has been toned and hand coloured. The more chemicals (other than toners) that are applied to a print, the greater the chance it will deteriorate. Instead, try framing the photograph. This will protect it from moisture and dust, both of which could ruin the hand colouring that you have spent so much time creating.

Many people don't like the look of matte print paper because it has a dull, flat appearance. But once the print is behind glass, you won't be able to tell whether the photo was printed on matte or semi-matte paper. Also, the small amount of residual oil from the solution or the waxy residue that coloured pencils sometimes leave will not be visible.

Double mat your print, or at least place a mat over it to avoid contact with the glass. If the glass from the frame is flush against the print, the hand colouring will be transferred from the print to the glass. Using an over mat or double mat makes the piece look very professional.

I don't recommend dry mounting the print with a hot or cold press because the heat and rubbing necessary in this process can affect the hand colouring. Don't use an album that has acetate overlays. They can destroy photographic prints over a period of time. Your work of art is one of a kind and therefore irreplaceable. To make copies, either have a colour laser copy made or have a lab make a colour copy negative, from which a colour print can be made.

▷ *Untitled*
by Laurie Klein
This photo is over-matted. The colour of the frame echoes that of the barn.

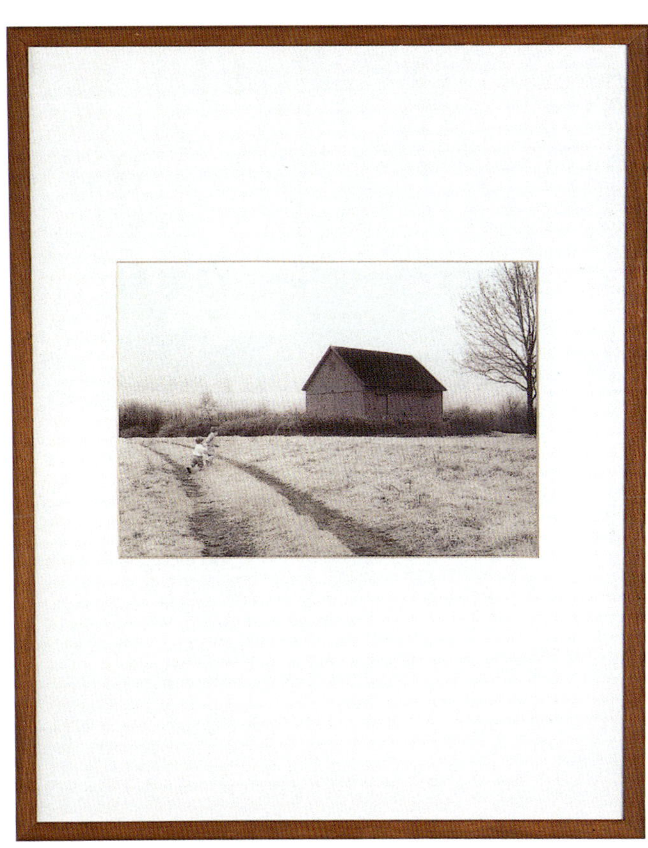

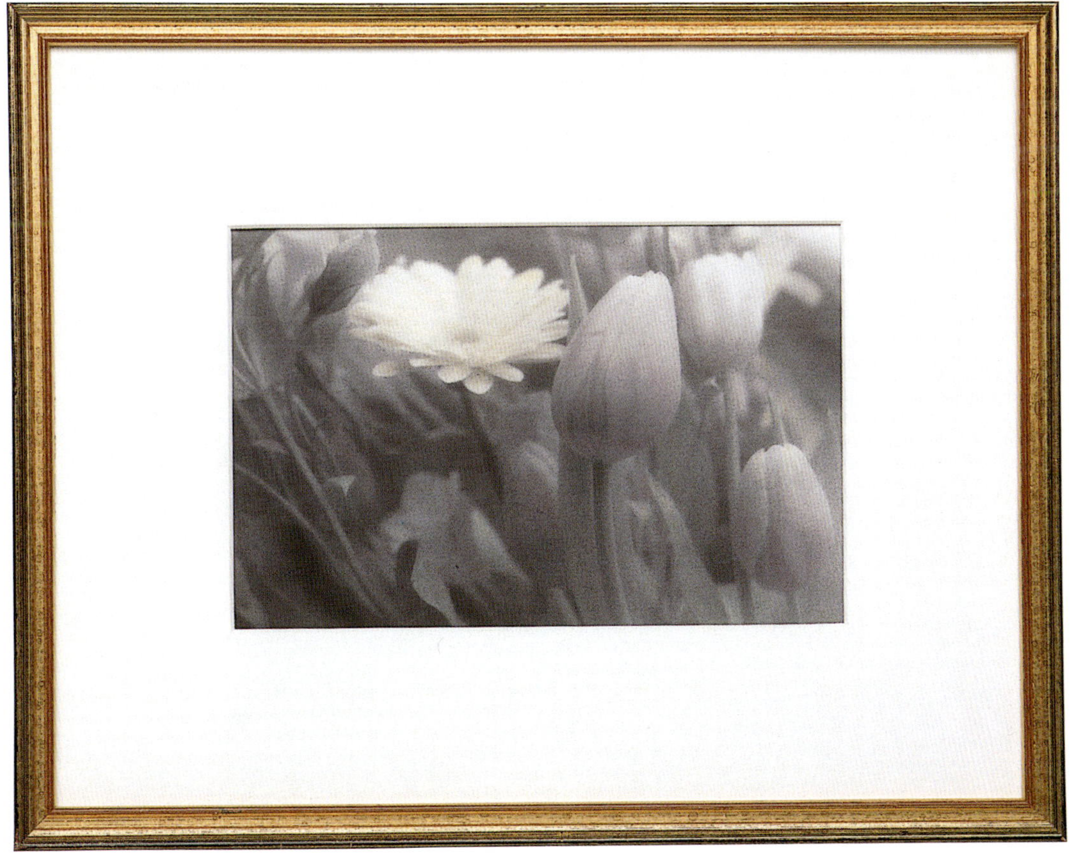

◁ This photo is framed very simply with a bevelled over-mat.

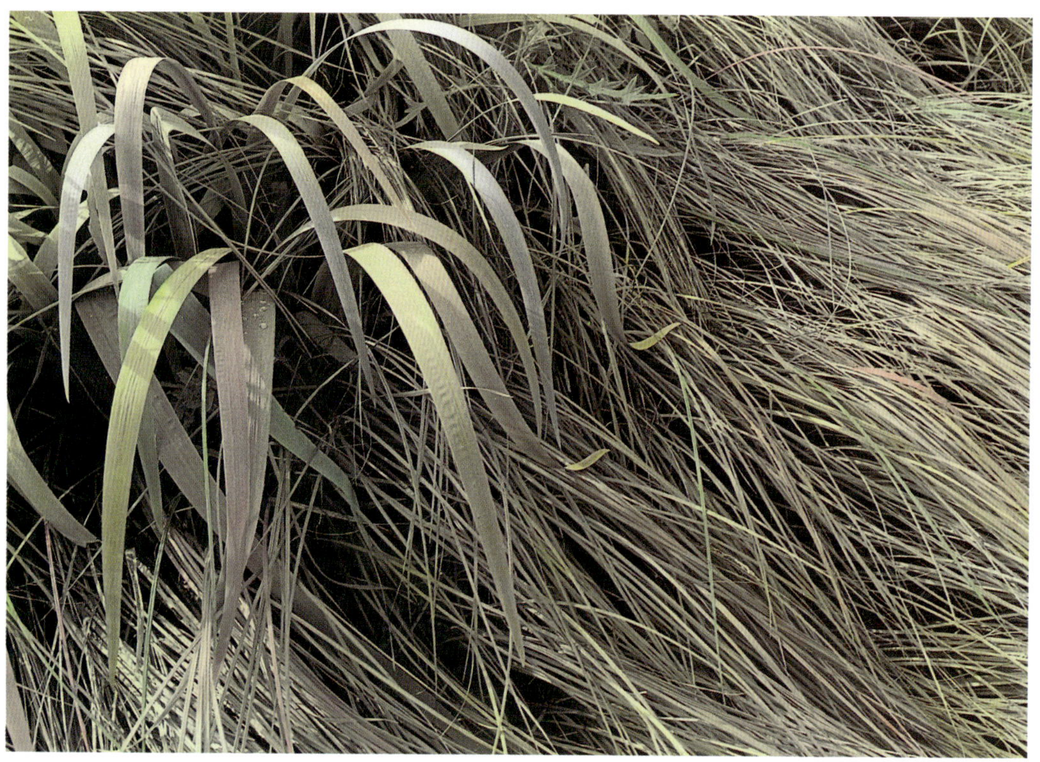

BASIC HOW-TO DEMONSTRATION

MIXING COLOURS

A colour wheel, which can be made or purchased, is helpful in understanding how to mix colours, such as making green out of blue and yellow. Harmonious colours are located next to one another on the colour wheel. For example, red and orange are harmonious colours. Conversely, colours opposite each other on the wheel, such as red and green, are called complementary colours. They create a bold, dramatic feel, which is a much different mood. When complementary colours are mixed together, however, a muddy colour results.

Coloured pencils can be mixed directly on the print or in the white border area of the print. Using the blender, blend the colours where they overlap, producing a third colour. Another option is to use a separate piece of plain white photographic paper as a palette. Mix colours with the turpentine-and-oil solution and then transfer them to the print using a cotton swab.

CHOOSING COLOURS

Choosing colours can be the hardest and yet most enjoyable part of the hand-colouring process. There are so many approaches. A photo can be coloured realistically, interpreted with colours, or made to look surrealistic by using colours that are far from realistic and that allow the imagination to soar. Adding colour to a black-and-white photograph establishes a mood or feeling. Always look at the image and get a sense of what you'd like to communicate. Hand colouring takes an image one step further, and the colours directly affect the message. If the goal is to make the print bold and graphic, for example, use vibrant colours.

It's important to maintain your coloured pencils. Sharpen the end of the pencil that doesn't bear the name or number of the colour so you'll know which one it is when you need to replace it. Also, make sure the tips aren't too sharp or long.

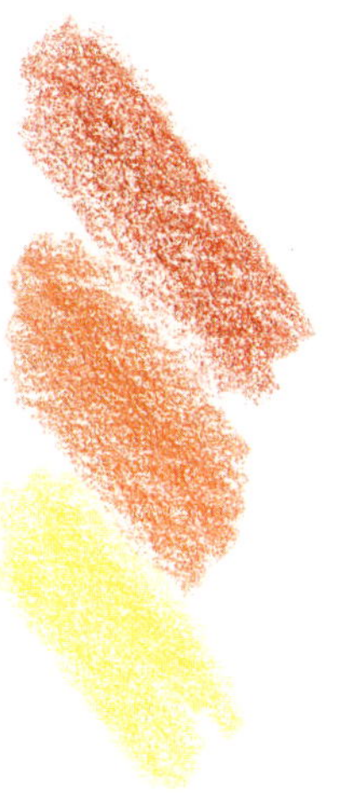

Red, orange, and yellow are warm colours.

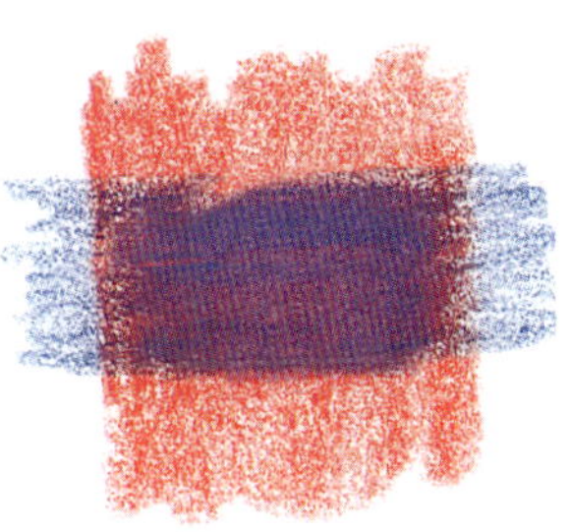

red + blue = purple

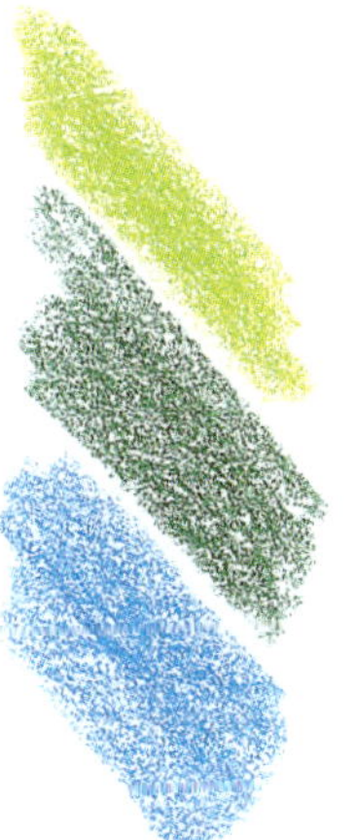

Greens and blues are cool colours.

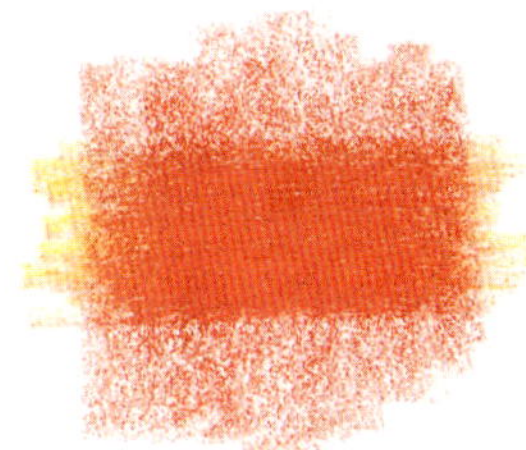

red + yellow = orange

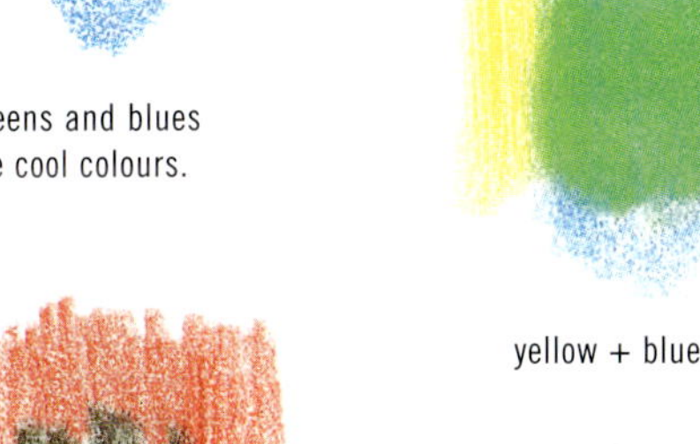

yellow + blue = green

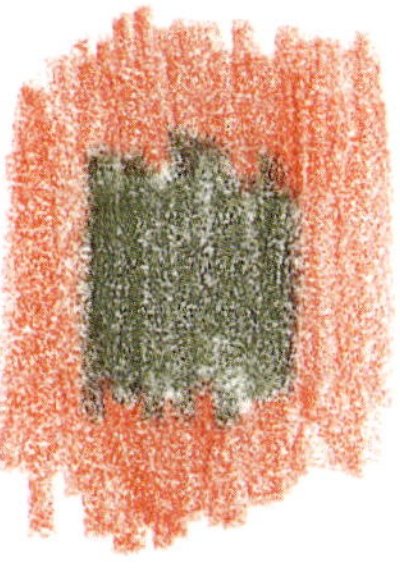

Red and green are complementary colours.

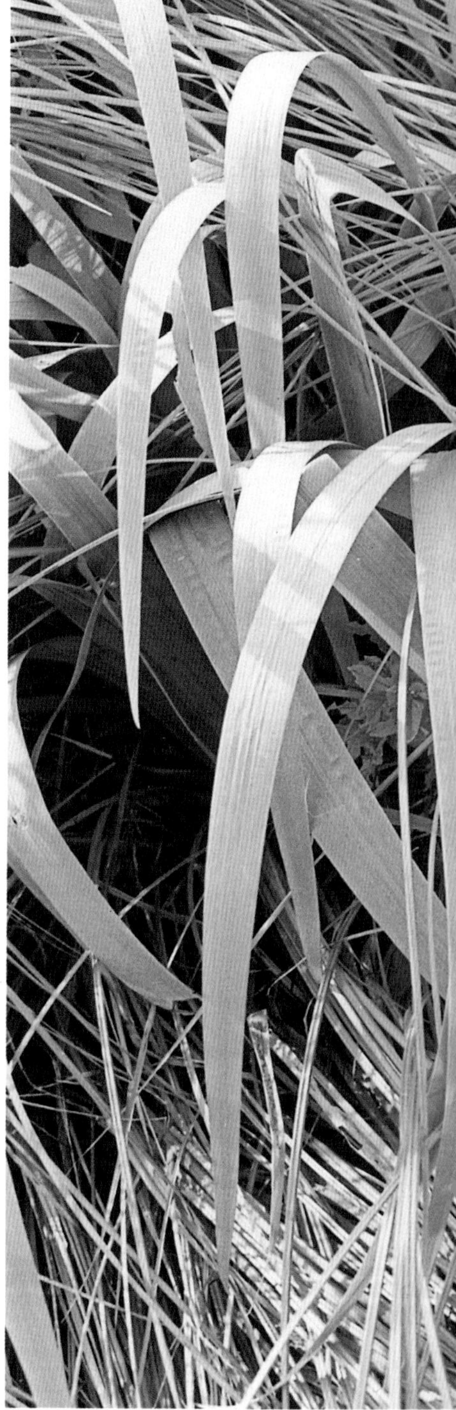

Hand Colouring a Photo

Now it's time to jump in, take a pencil in hand, and actually colour the photograph. But keep it simple. Sometimes the least amount of colour creates the most interesting result. Remember that hand colouring an area changes the composition, so after choosing the first area to hand colour, check the compositional balance. This may influence which area you choose to colour next and how you colour it.

Experiment with a solution that is equal parts vegetable oil and odourless turpentine. It's important to prepare this solution properly. If the print is too oily looking, there's too much oil in the solution; if all the colour comes off, then there's too much turpentine (turpentine removes colour). Store the solution in a small bottle with a lid. It will last for a long time. Don't leave the solution uncovered, though, because the turpentine will evaporate and the mixture will then be out of balance. Use as little solution as possible, and try not to use it too often. In small areas, for example, rubbing the colour with a cotton swab is sufficient to smooth out the pencil strokes and remove waxy buildup.

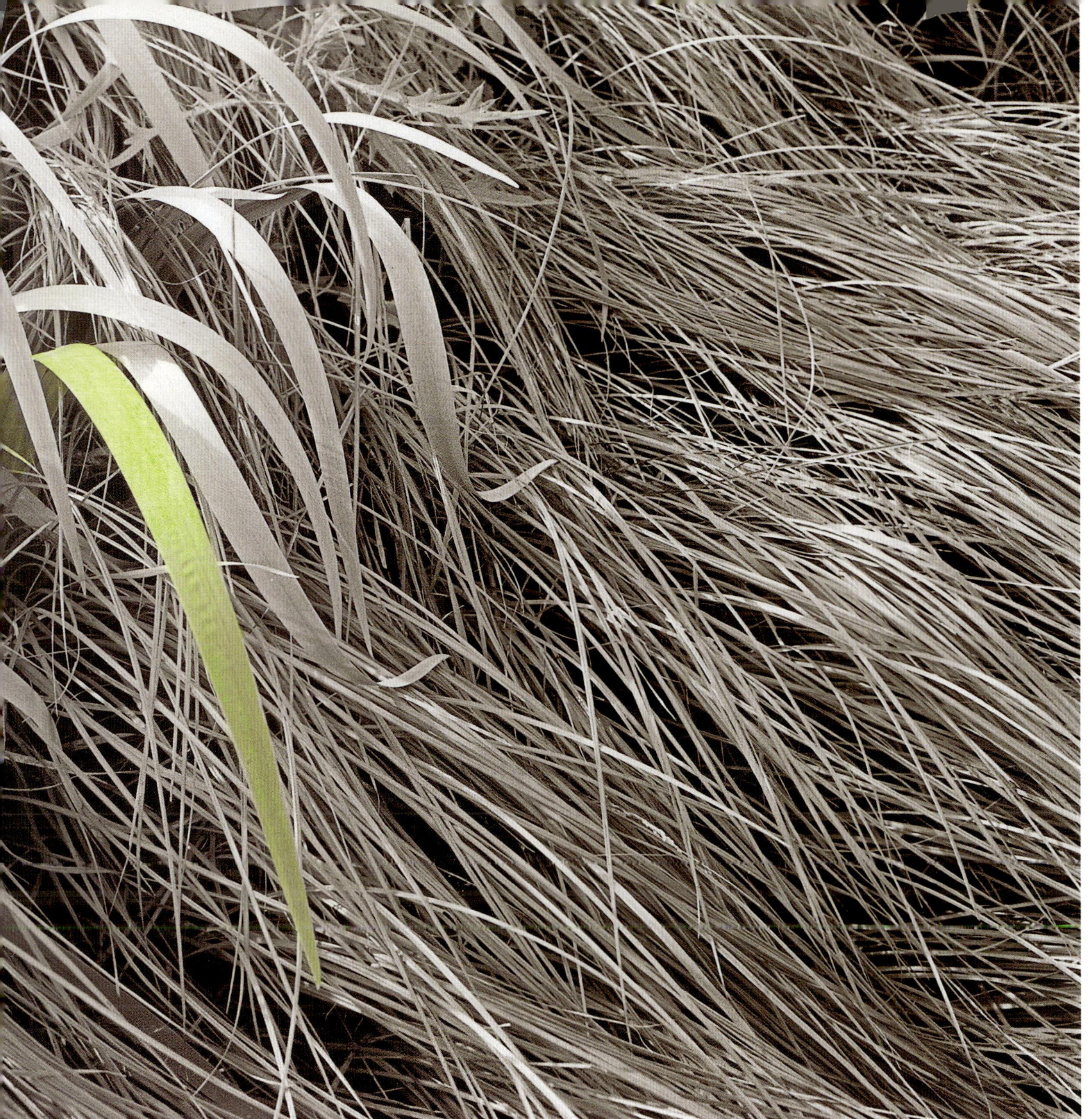

△ This photo was chosen because there is no single focal point; each blade of grass has equal importance. Choose one blade of grass and colour it in using the spring green pencil. (It will not be necessary to use solution.) Now the emphasis is on that one blade of grass.

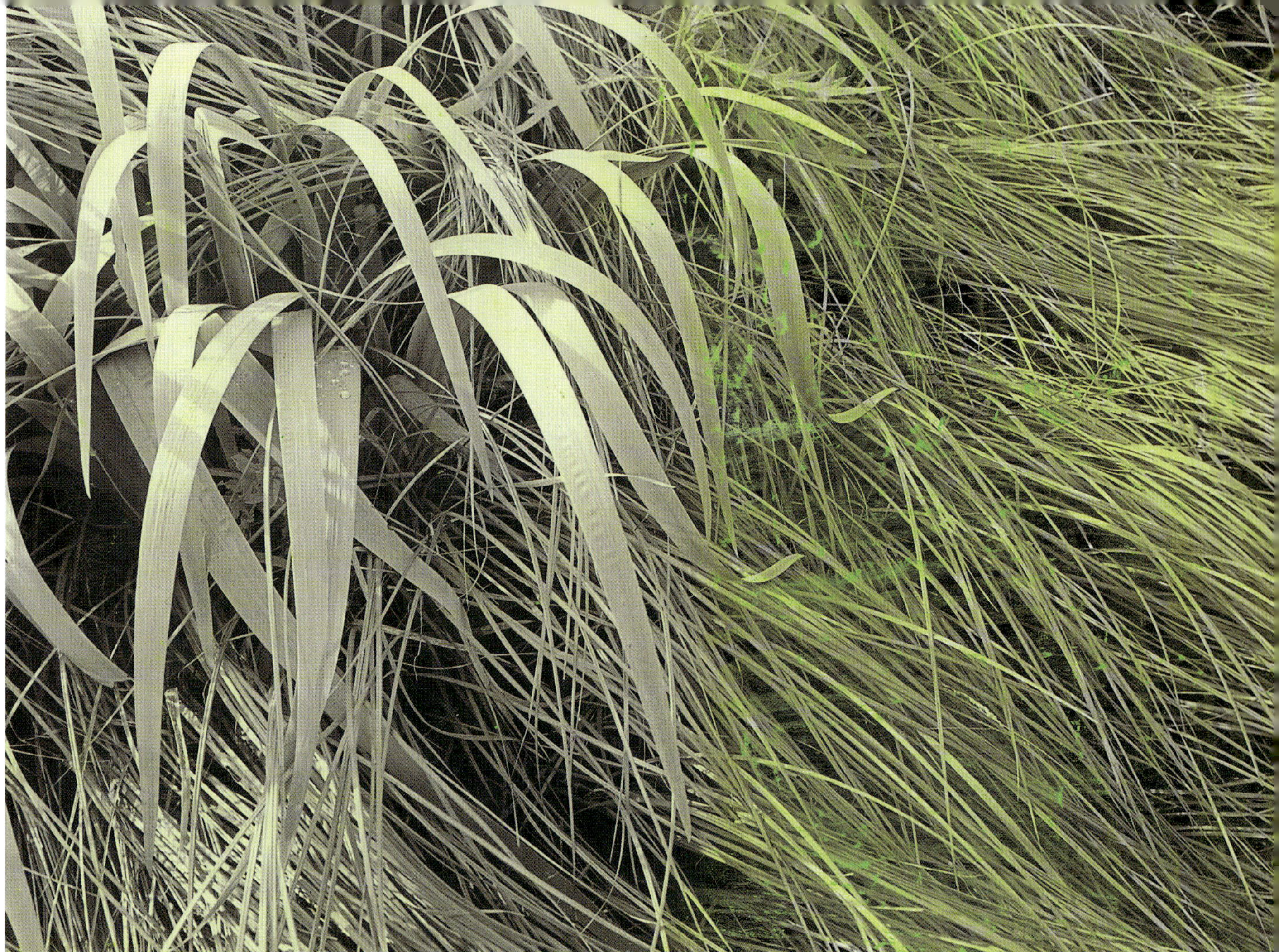

△ Here, the whole image was coloured with the same green pencil. Don't colour each blade of grass individually; it will take too long. Instead, create a colour wash by using a small amount of solution and a cotton ball. Solution was applied to the left side of the photo, whereas the colour on the right side of the photo was not blended and the pencil marks are still apparent. Leaving the marks unblended makes the colour appear to sit on top of the print instead of be a part of it.

No solution

▽ In this photograph, lighter, brighter colours were added to the grass in the foreground to give the image a three-dimensional look. Other greens were used, and pinks and oranges were blended with the spring green to create a warmer green. These variations of green make the image more interesting.

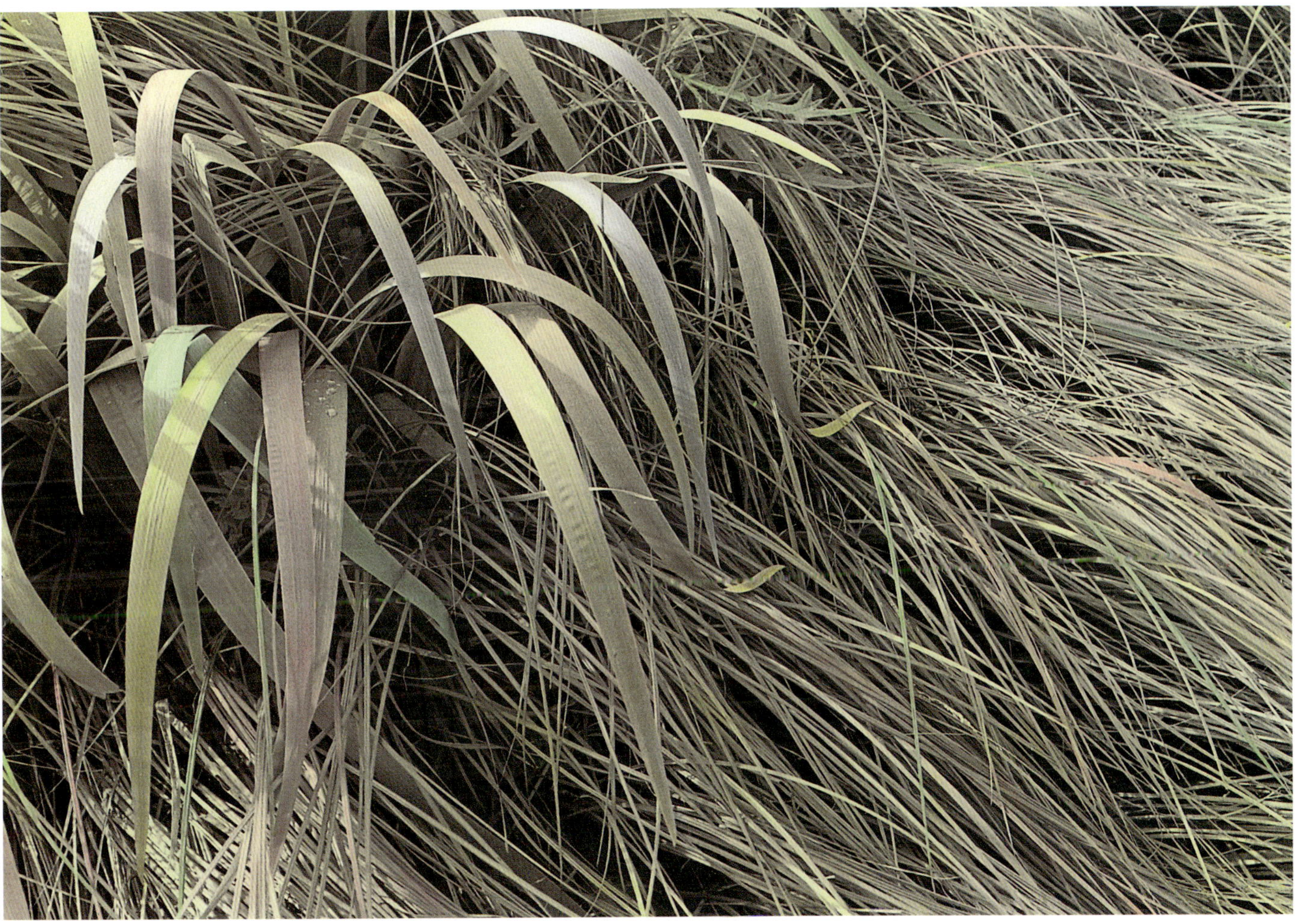

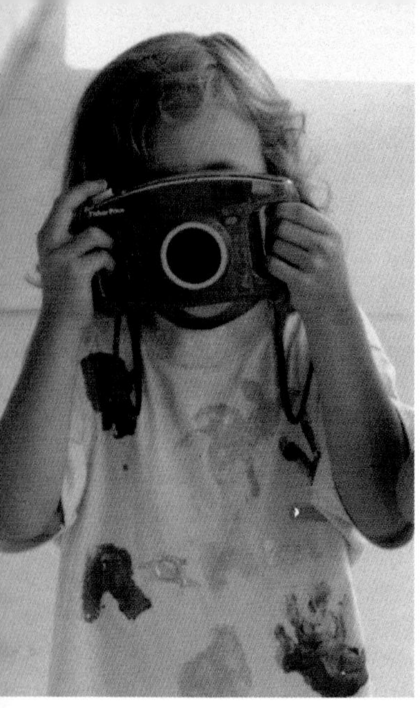

△ Colour to capture the mood.

PEOPLE

Most of the photographs you already have are probably snapshots of family members and friends. You may have a lifetime of memories filed away—family vacations, weddings, birthdays, and anniversaries, or perhaps friends just having fun. Maybe you even have vintage photographs of ancestors. Have you ever wondered what else could be done with these photographs? Hand-coloured photographs make wonderful, personal gifts. Hand colouring a photo gives the image a timeless quality and combines the realism of photography with the artistry of painting. With the popularity of memory albums and scrapbooks, many people are colouring vintage black-and-white and contemporary family photographs to preserve their family history. Chances are, most of your photographs are colour prints or vintage black-and-white prints. Before you start to colour, have "copy negatives" made, so that you can have multiple prints of the same photo and can preserve the original. Use the copies to experiment—try several different applications of colour to achieve different results.

▷ Colour for realism.

▷ Colour photos to remember the moment.

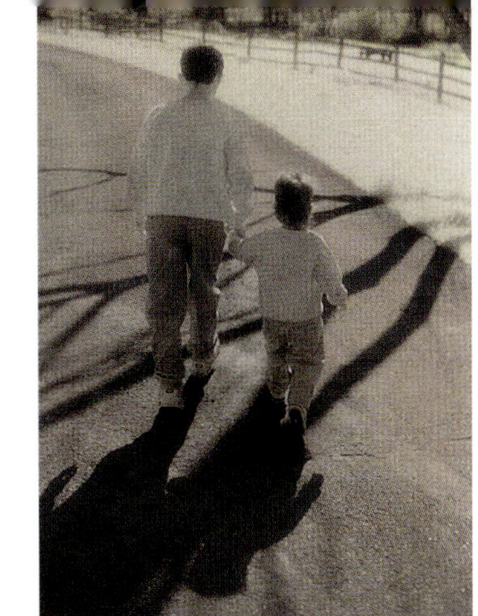

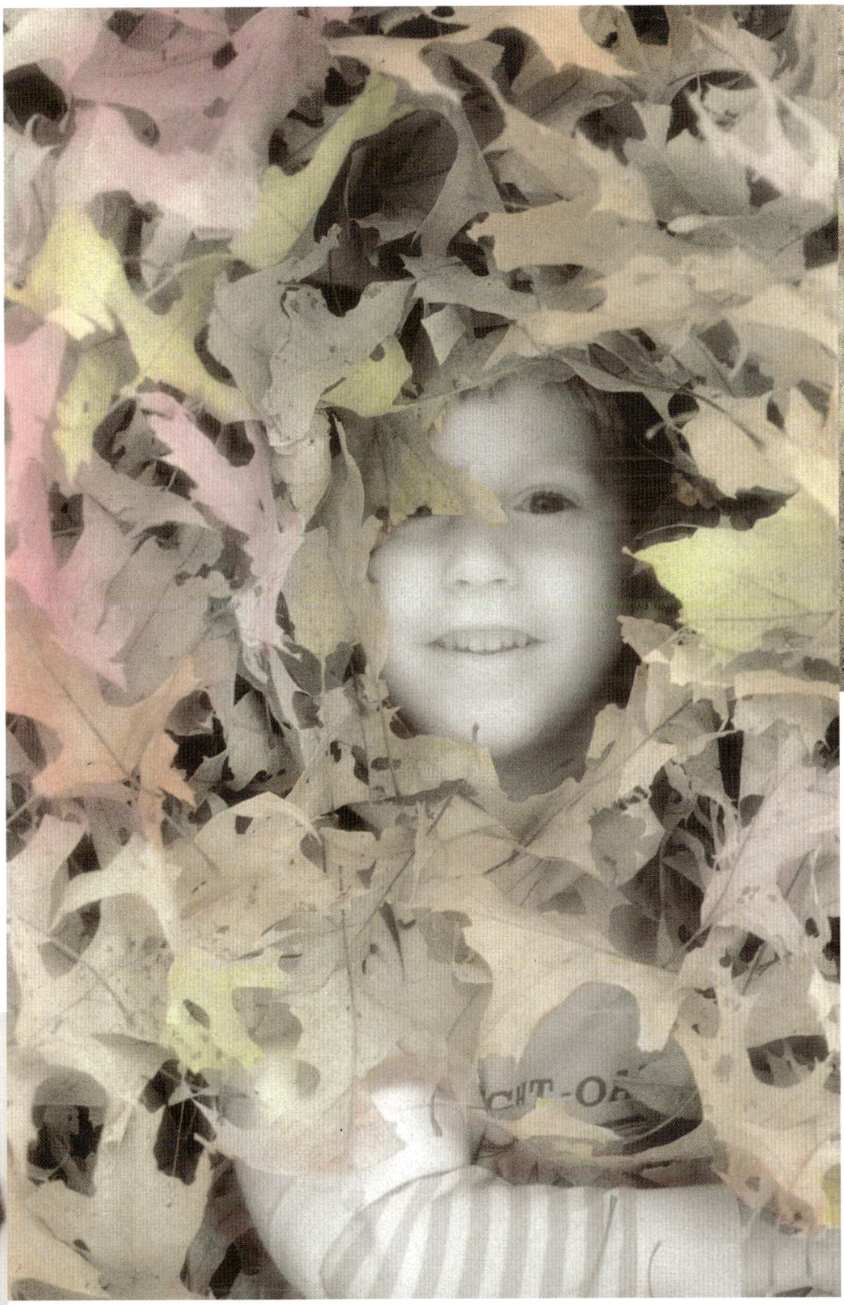

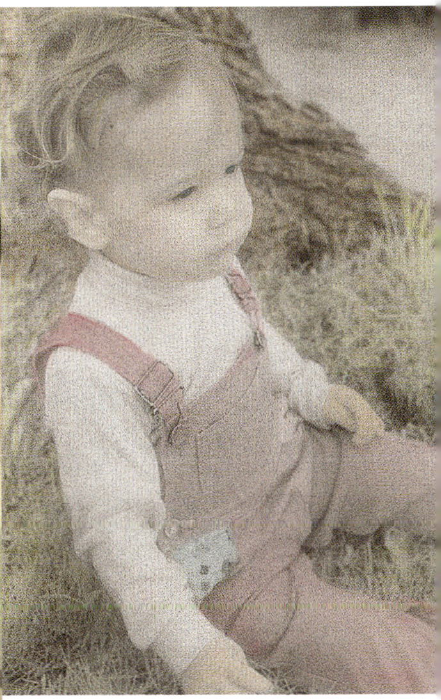

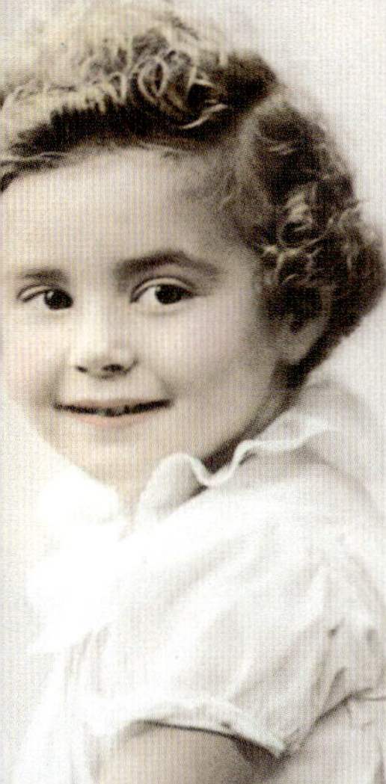

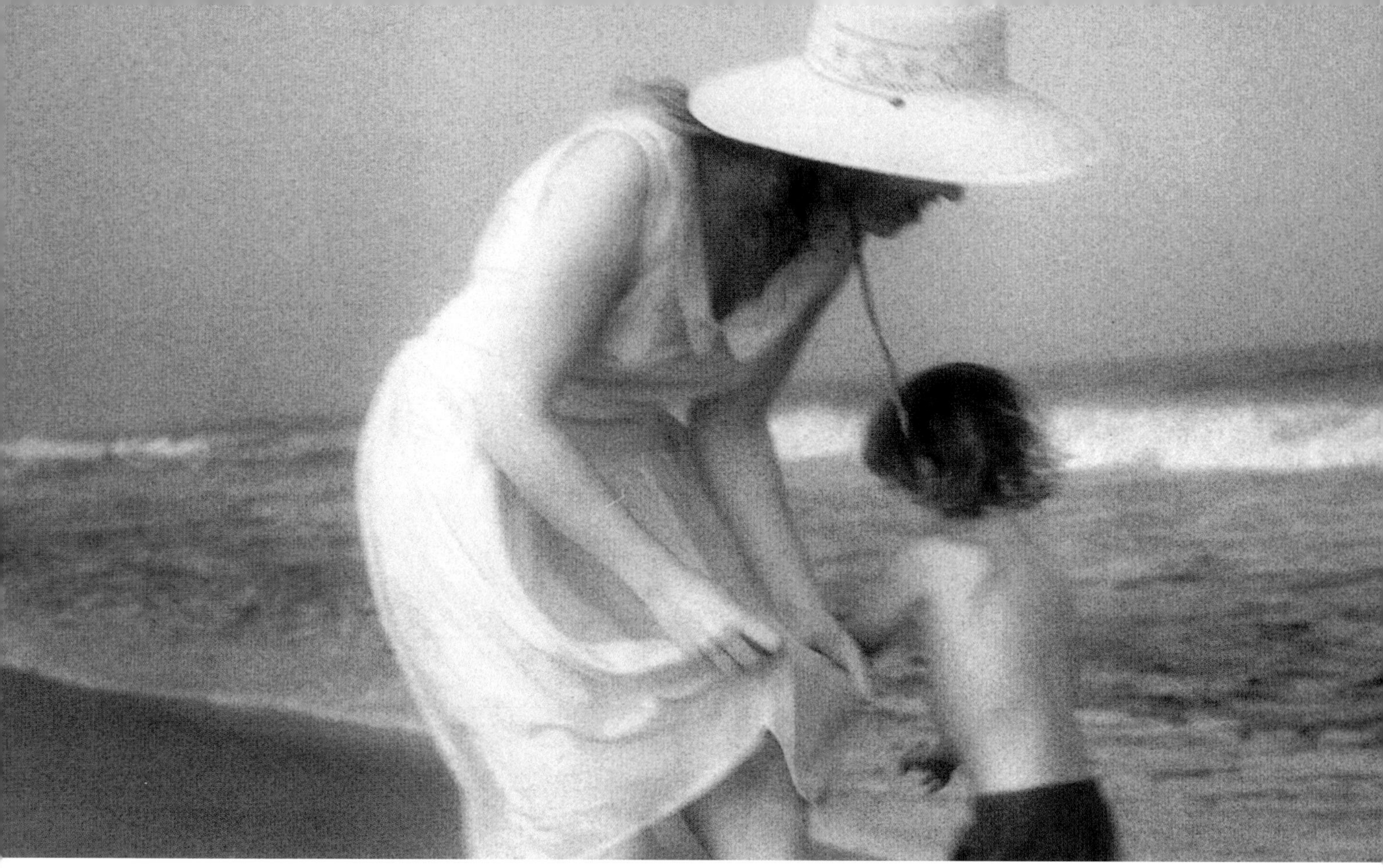

Working with Photographs of People

When selecting a photograph to colour, seek images with a lot of highlight areas (places that show white or a pale tone on the photograph). Images with lots of highlights work best for hand colouring. Selecting an image that is a close-up of someone's face allows you to colour in skin tones or apply colour like makeup. If the colour is applied subtly, you can mimic the appearance of an "old-fashioned portrait." Colour applied more boldly creates a contemporary effect.

Photographs of people in landscapes ("environmental" portraits) give you the opportunity to colour both people and nature. Where you apply the colour is a matter of artistic choice. Start with the part of the image that you feel is most important. It will be easiest to leave small details for last, after applying the main colours.

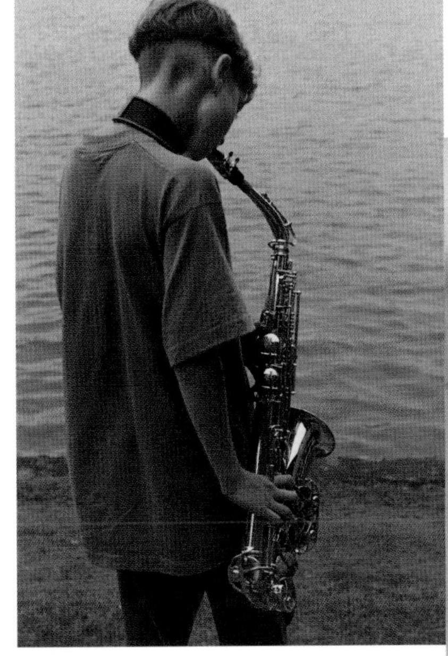

▷ Outdoor photos allow you to colour both people and landscapes.

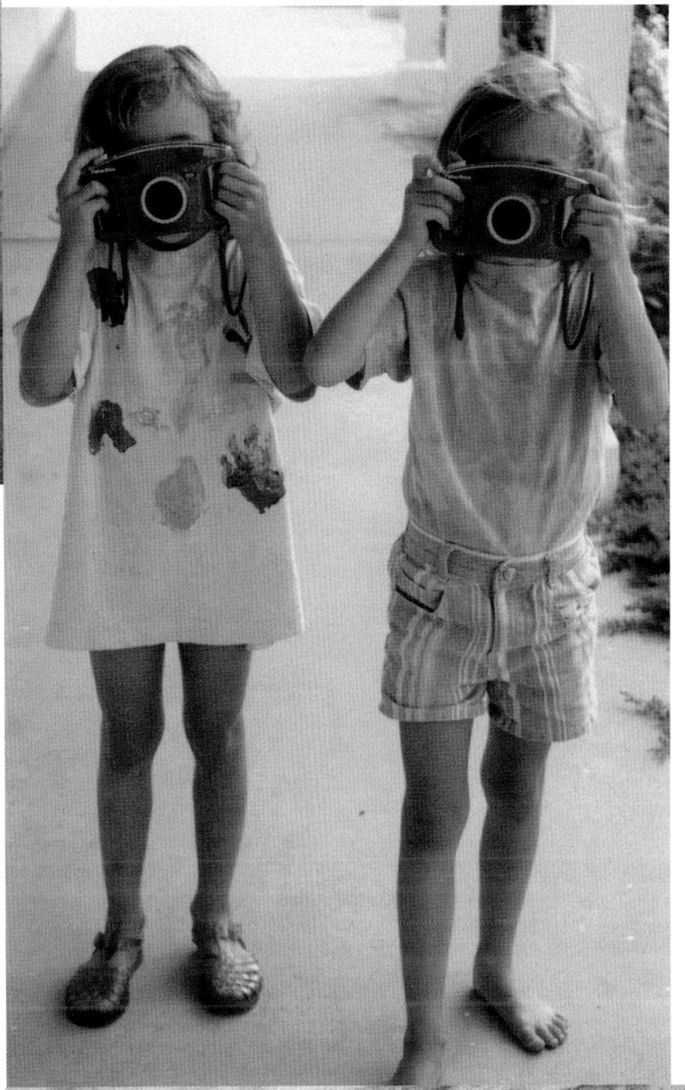

▷ Emphasize the foreground by adding colour.

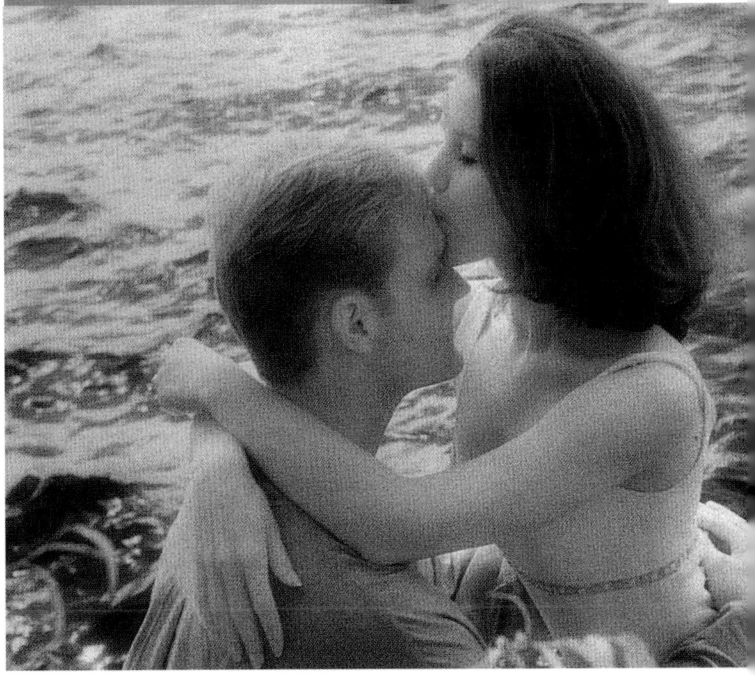

▷ Look for images with a lot of white areas.

Colour is powerful. Even a little colour added to a photo will change it entirely. Different colours create different moods: Reds, yellows, and oranges will make an image warm and inviting, while blues and greens produce a colder, fresher look. Use more than one shade of a colour for a more natural effect. Blending and layering warm or cool colours will add dimension and realism.

If you want an area to stand out, try using a colour that is opposite to the surrounding colour—red against a green background, for example. Conversely, applying heavy layers of colour will flatten the area somewhat, and put more emphasis on colour than on the content of the image, making it less like a photograph and more like modern art.

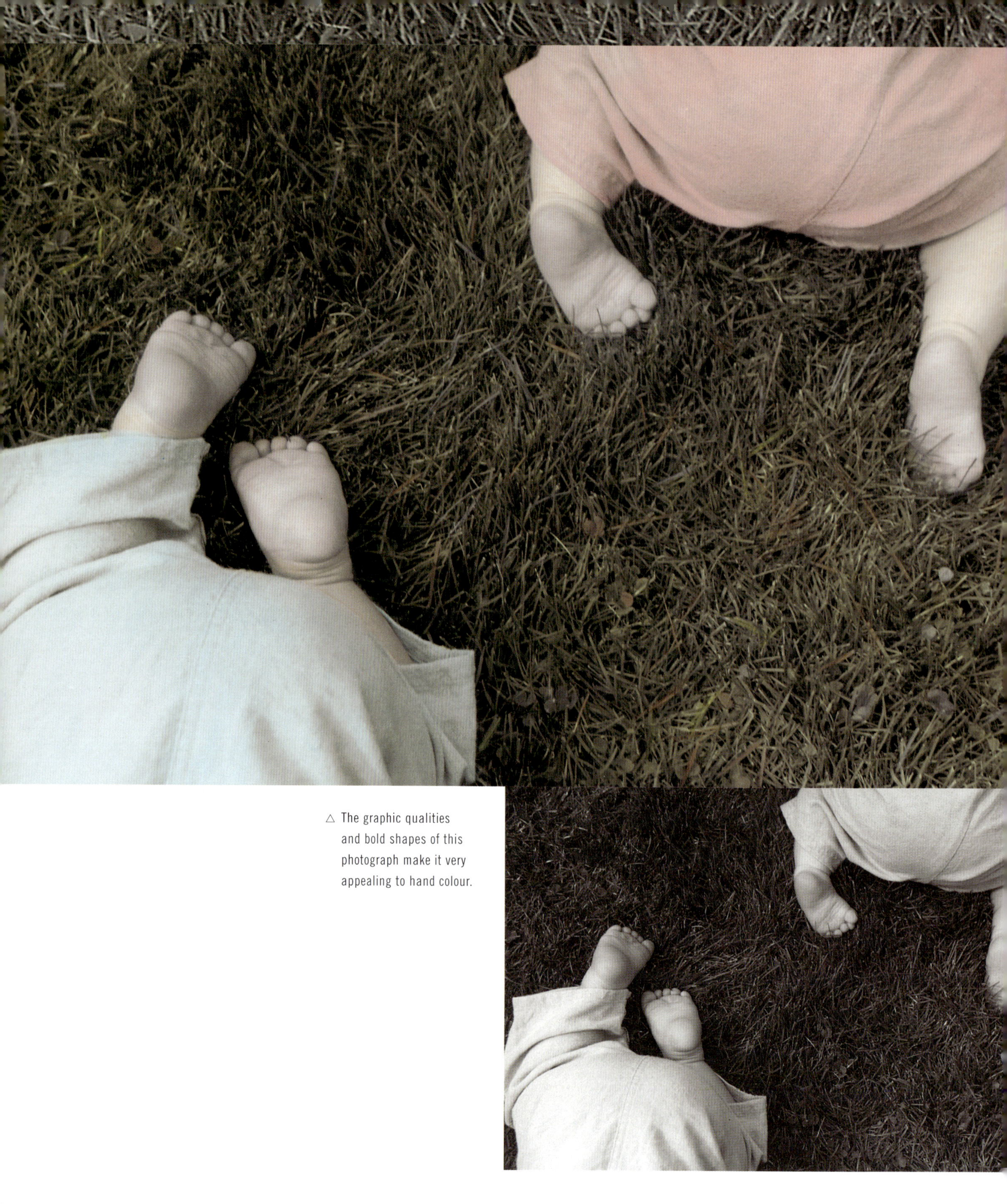

△ The graphic qualities and bold shapes of this photograph make it very appealing to hand colour.

Hand Colouring a Contemporary Photo

GETTING STARTED

Try hand colouring photographs of people that are unique or abstract, as this image is. For example, a people photo without actual faces in it can be interesting and full of feeling. People often assume that when photographing someone, they should place the subject's head in the center of the viewfinder. But feel free to try something different. Play with the whole frame; move in close and place the subject in the corner of the frame. (See "The Basics" for more on shooting images to hand colour.)

MATERIALS

- black-and-white print on matte-surface paper
- coloured pencils: rosy beige, blush, scarlet lake, true blue, olive green, gold, imperial violet, green bice, orange, apple green, lemon yellow, blue violet
- cotton balls
- cotton swabs
- turpentine-and-oil solution

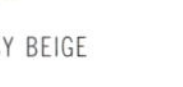
ROSY BEIGE

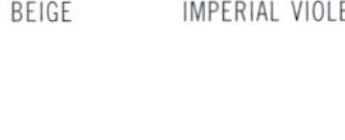
IMPERIAL VIOLET

BLUSH

GREEN BICE

SCARLET LAKE

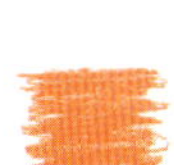
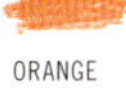
ORANGE

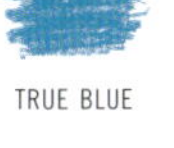
TRUE BLUE

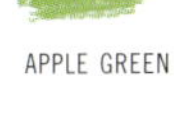
APPLE GREEN

OLIVE GREEN

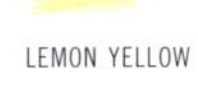
LEMON YELLOW

GOLD

BLUE VIOLET

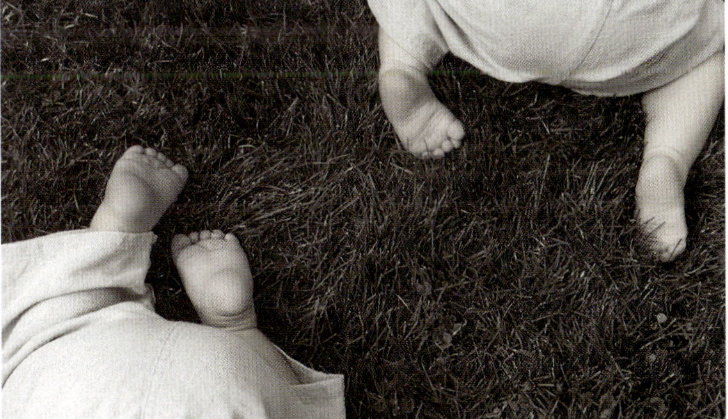

△ **1**

Using the rosy beige pencil, colour both babies' legs. Rub with a cotton swab to smooth in colour (solution won't be necessary). Using the blush pencil, colour the soles of the babies' feet, once again using the cotton swab to smooth the colour in. Now use the rosy beige pencil again, moving from the legs to the soles of the feet, so it is not apparent where one colour ends and the other begins. This is called "feathering."

▷ 2

Colour the outfit on the baby in the upper-right section with the scarlet lake pencil. Use a cotton swab and a small amount of solution to smooth in the colour so that no pencil marks are visible. Using the true-blue pencil, colour the outfit on the baby in the lower-left section. Smooth the colour in with a cotton swab and a small amount of solution, just as with the previous baby. Use a dry cotton swab on both outfits to remove any residual colour or solution. To make the outfits deeper in colour, apply a second coat. Use a dry cotton swab to smooth in the colour.

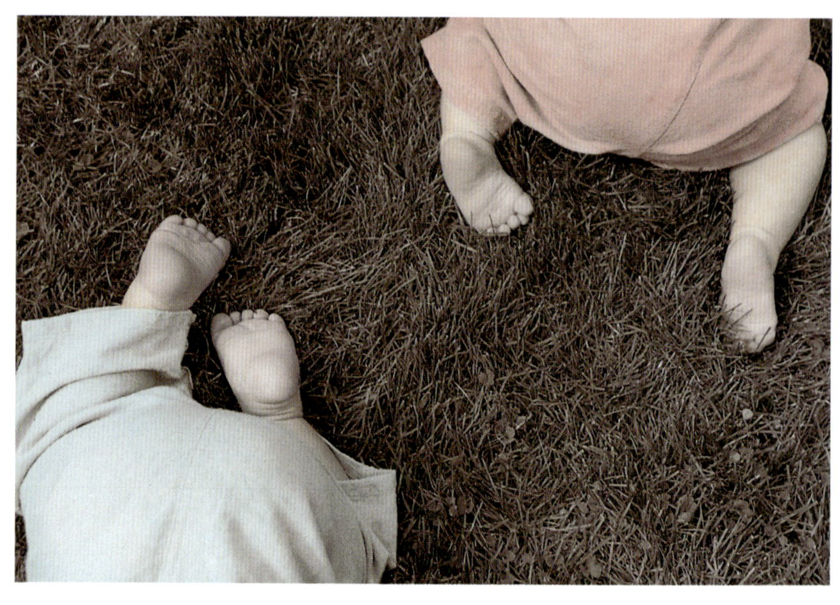

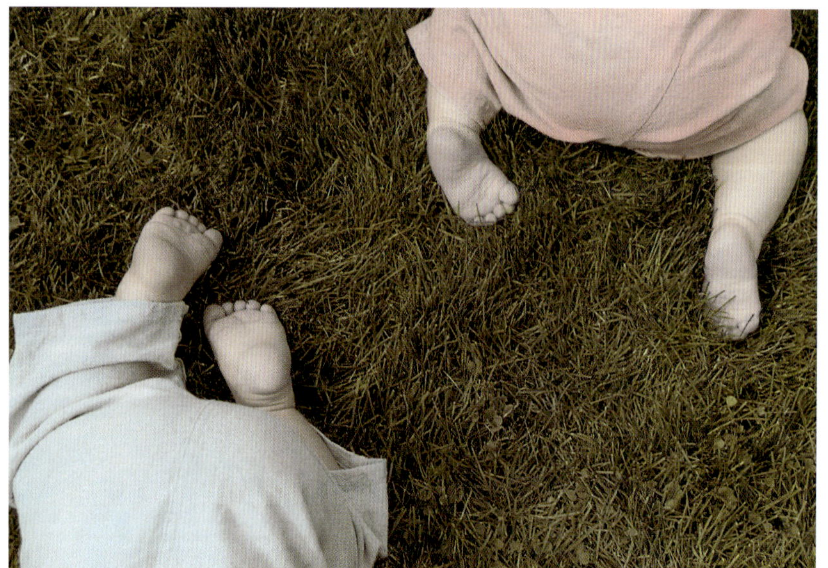

◁ 3

Using the olive-green pencil, colour the grass area. In the areas around the babies' bodies and clothing, use a small amount of solution on a cotton swab to smooth in the colour. For the larger areas, use a cotton ball with a small amount of solution to smooth in the colour. Colour the blades of grass in front of the babies' feet with a sharpened olive-green pencil.

▷ 4

Use the orange, imperial violet, gold, and green bice pencils on the grass to give it more depth. Select a few different blades of grass and colour them individually for a more natural look. Smooth the colour in with a cotton swab.

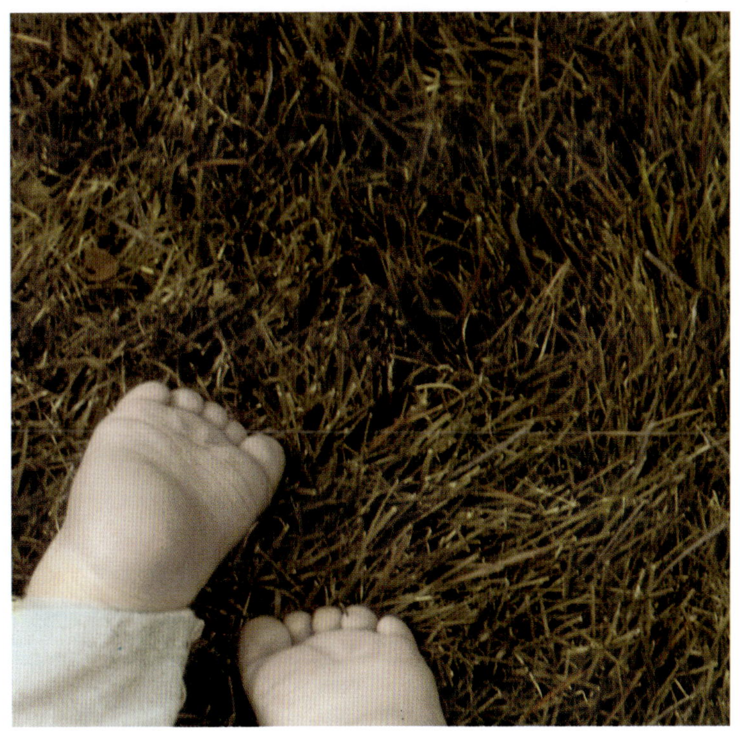

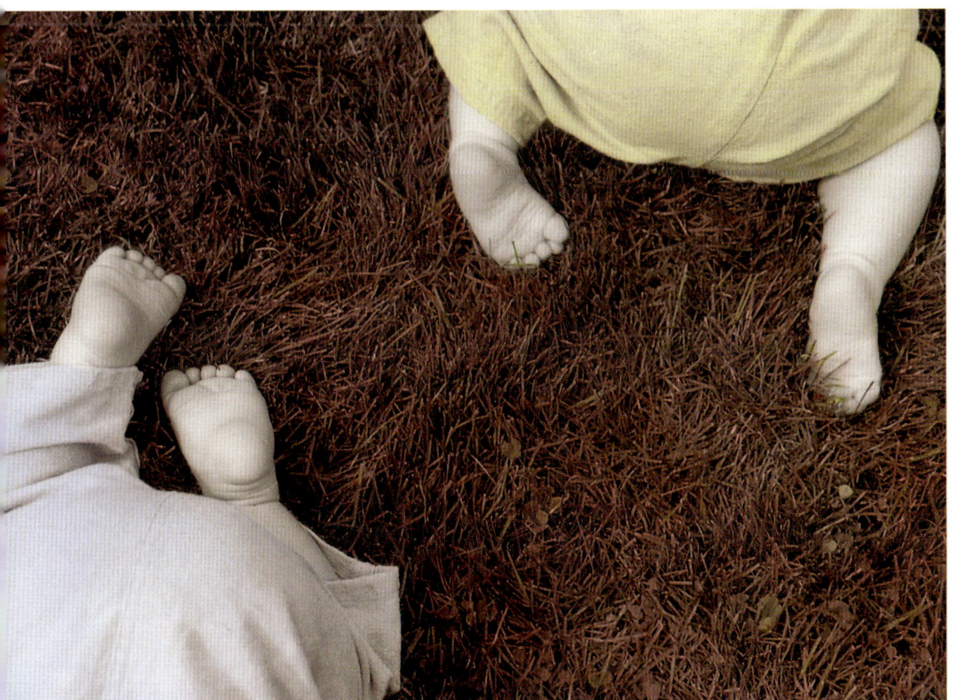

VARIATION

Complementary colours are perfect for making a statement.

1. Don't add any colour to the babies' feet. Use the scarlet lake pencil for the grass to create a surrealistic effect. Use turpentine-and-oil solution on a cotton swab to smooth in the colour.
2. With the apple-green pencil, colour a few select blades of grass. Blend with a cotton swab. The red (scarlet lake) and green, which are complementary colours, add up to a bold statement.
3. Colour the outfit on the baby in the upper-right section using the lemon-yellow pencil. Apply a small amount of solution to a cotton swab and smooth in the colour. Using the blue violet pencil, colour the outfit of the baby in the lower-left section. Use a small amount of solution on a swab for blending.

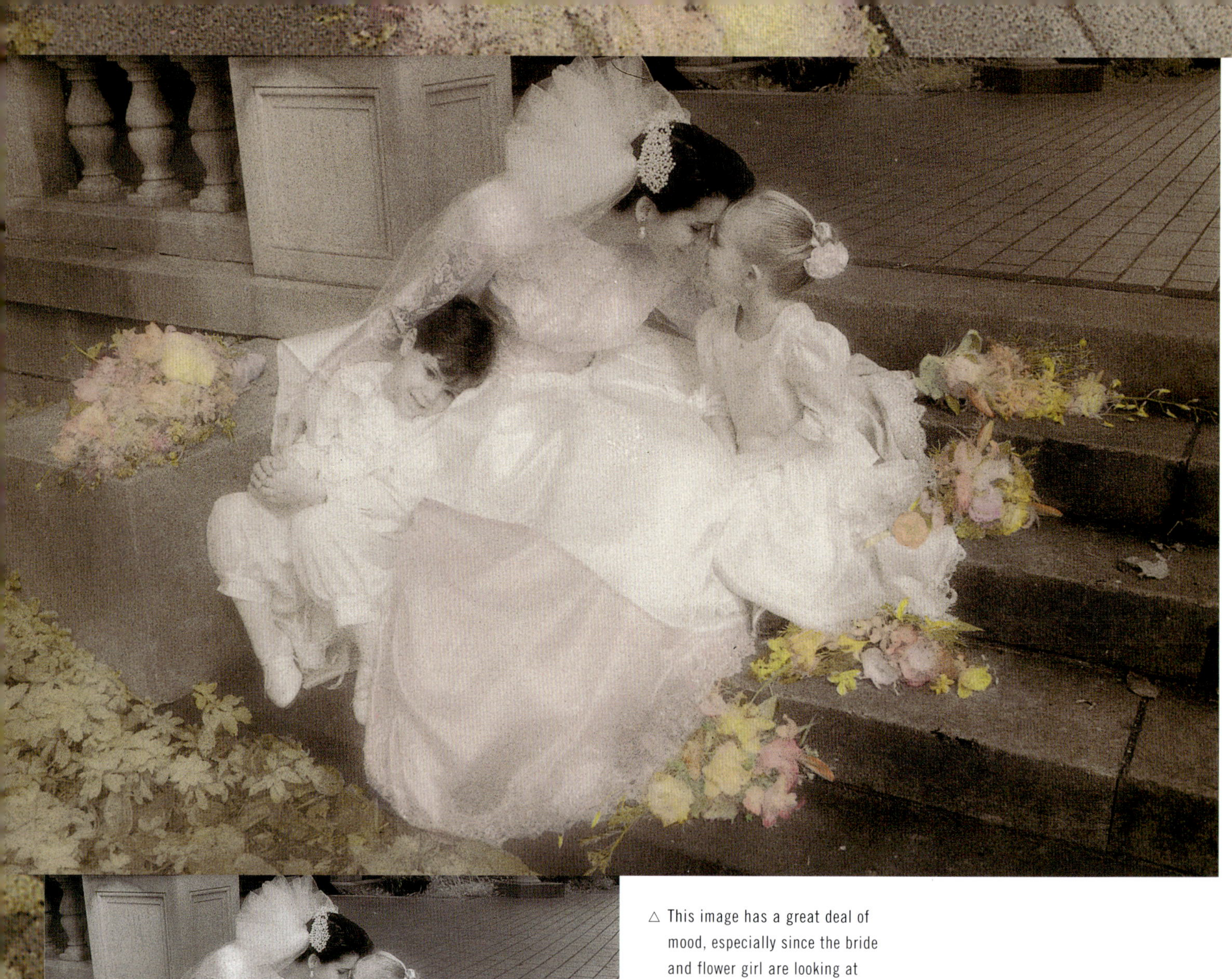

△ This image has a great deal of mood, especially since the bride and flower girl are looking at one another and not directly into the camera.

◁ The way the grey stonework and stairs contrast with the pale tones of the garments and flowers makes this a wonderful image to hand colour.

Creating a Romantic Atmosphere

GETTING STARTED

This photograph was chosen because it is a candid depiction of the bride, ring bearer, and flower girl. They are the main subjects in the photograph, but the flowers and greenery can have as much emphasis if hand coloured. Hand colouring them also strengthens the balance of the composition, echoing the triangular shape made by the bride and the children.

MATERIALS

- black-and-white print on matte-surface paper
- coloured pencils: pink rose, olive green, lavender, warm grey 20%, pink, salmon pink, bright purple, orange, lemon yellow, greyed lavender, true green, pale peach, blush, true blue, raw umber, clay rose, terracotta, sky blue
- cotton balls
- toothpicks
- cotton swabs
- turpentine-and-oil solution
- blender
- sepia toner

PINK ROSE GREYED LAVENDER

OLIVE GREEN TRUE GREEN

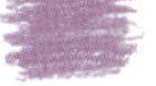

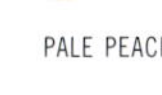

LAVENDER PALE PEACH

WARM GREY 20% BLUSH

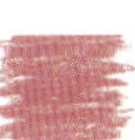

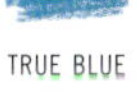

PINK TRUE BLUE

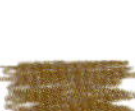
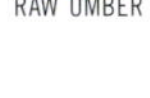

SALMON PINK RAW UMBER

BRIGHT PURPLE CLAY ROSE

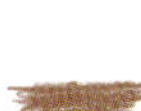

ORANGE TERRACOTTA

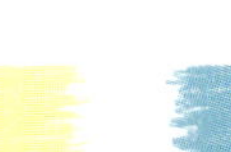

LEMON YELLOW SKY BLUE

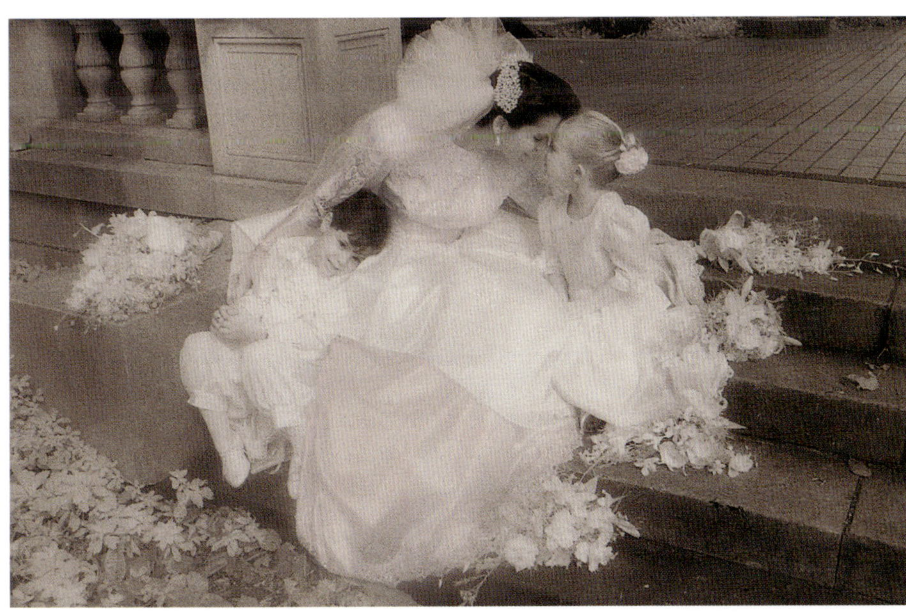

△ 1

Sepia-tone the print. (See "Advanced Techniques.") Use the pink rose pencil to colour the top and bottom of the bride's dress, applying very small amounts of solution to smooth in the colour. Use the same pencil for the flower girl's hairpiece. Smooth the colour in with a fresh cotton swab.

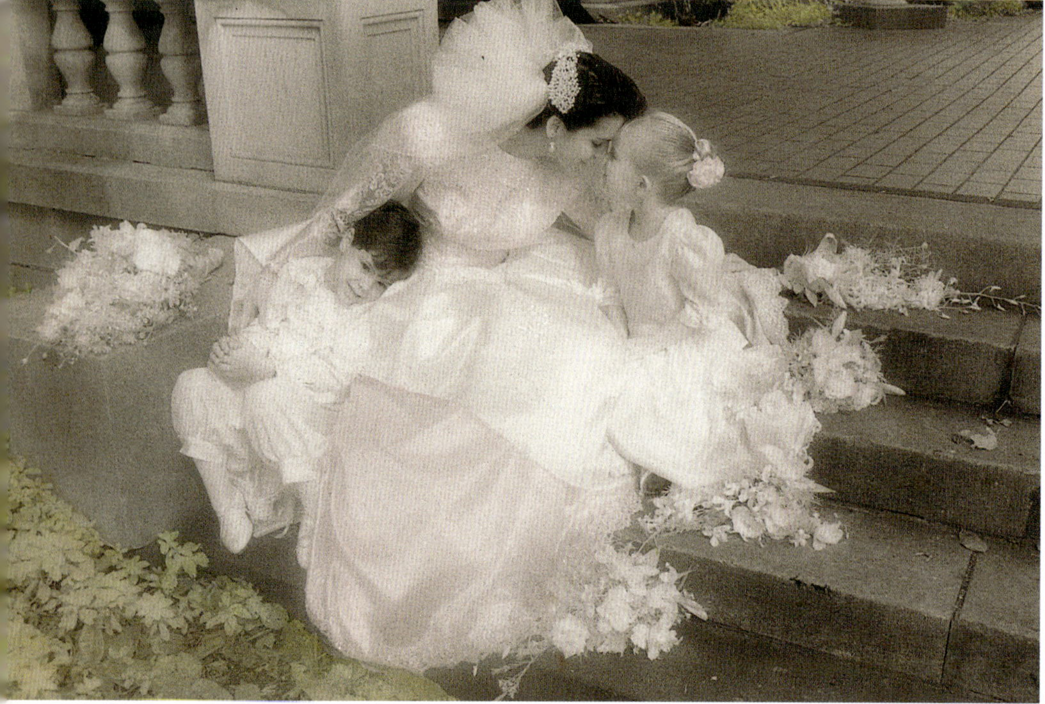

△ 2

Colour the foliage with the olive-green pencil. Use a small amount of solution to smooth in the colour.

TIPS

- To remove a colour, use a toothpick with a very small amount of water on it. Wait a few minutes for the water to dry (the colour won't adhere if the print is wet), and then reapply colour.
- To soften the line where two colours meet, try using the blender.

▷ 3

Using the lavender pencil, colour the satin wrap on the stems of the bouquet. Use the grey pencil to colour the large flower. Also use the grey pencil on select smaller flowers to balance the large flower. Use the pink, salmon pink, and bright purple pencils to colour the remaining flowers. A little solution may be necessary for blending. Use a toothpick wrapped tightly in cotton with some solution for blending small areas, or try using the blender instead. Use the olive-green pencil to colour the darker areas around and within the flowers to add depth.

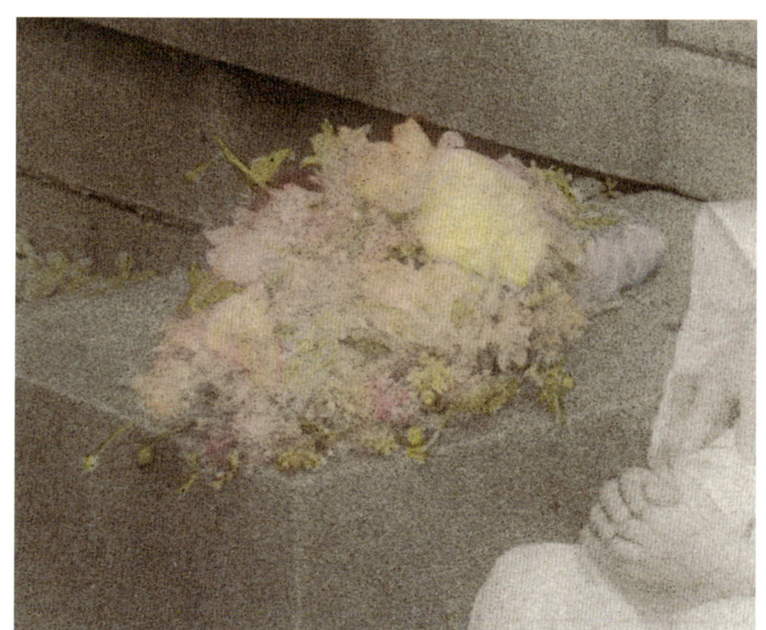

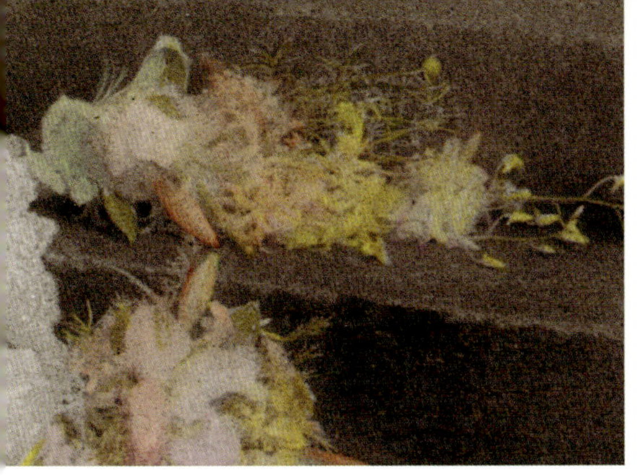

 4

Hand colouring is a way to strengthen or even alter the composition of a photo. Use the grey, lemon yellow, salmon pink, pink, and greyed lavender for the flowers on the steps. Try layering colours, such as yellow over pink. Use the true green for some of the foliage in the bouquets and olive green to add depth between and within the flowers. These colours, which are from a slightly different palette than those used in the bride's bouquet, draw the viewer's attention up and around the steps.

VARIATION

Bold hues can heighten the sense of romance.

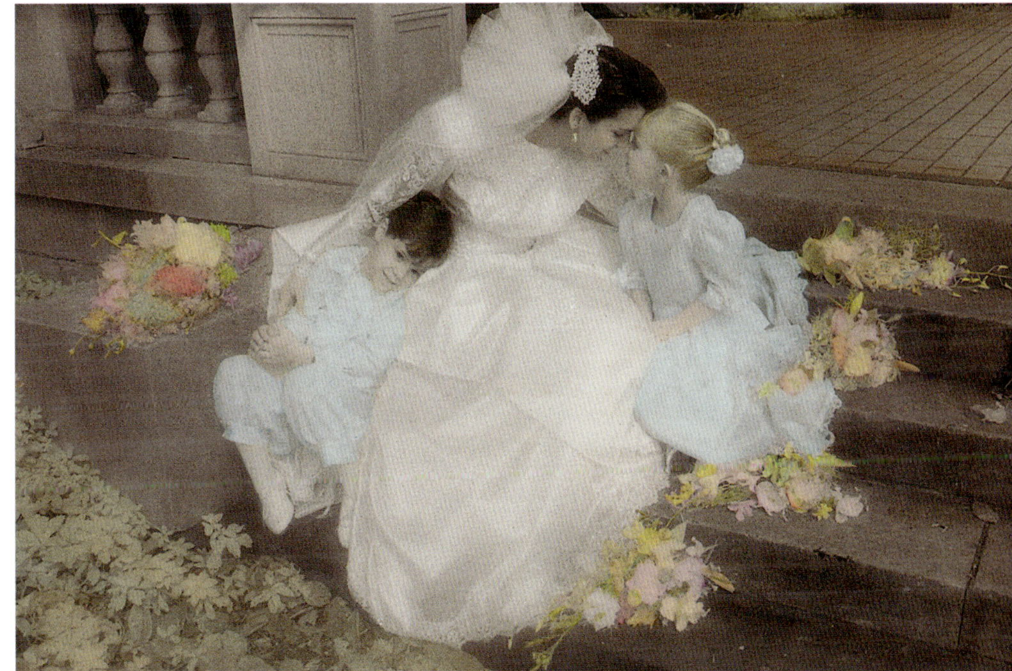

1. Use the pale peach pencil to colour all skin areas. Then, using a very small amount of solution on a toothpick wrapped in a cotton ball, smooth in the colour.
2. Moving the pink pencil in a circular motion, colour the cheek areas. Blend with a fresh cotton swab so the colour doesn't appear to be on top of the skin tone, but rather looks like it's a part of it. Use a sharpened blush pencil to colour in the lips.
3. The true-blue pencil was used on the boy's eyes. The girl's hair was coloured with streaks of lemon yellow in the lighter areas and raw umber in the darker strands of hair.
4. Use the lemon yellow to lightly colour the lighter strands of the boy's hair to highlight and add lustre, creating depth and balancing his hair with the girl's.
5. Colour the bride's earrings with the grey pencil. Use the clay-rose pencil and solution to colour the background stone and steps.
6. Use the olive-green pencil and solution for all the foliage in the lower left and upper right. The terracotta pencil can be used on a few leaves; blend with a dry cotton swab for depth.
7. On the boy's and girl's outfits, use the sky blue. Experiment with different colours in the flowers, using bold complementary colours.

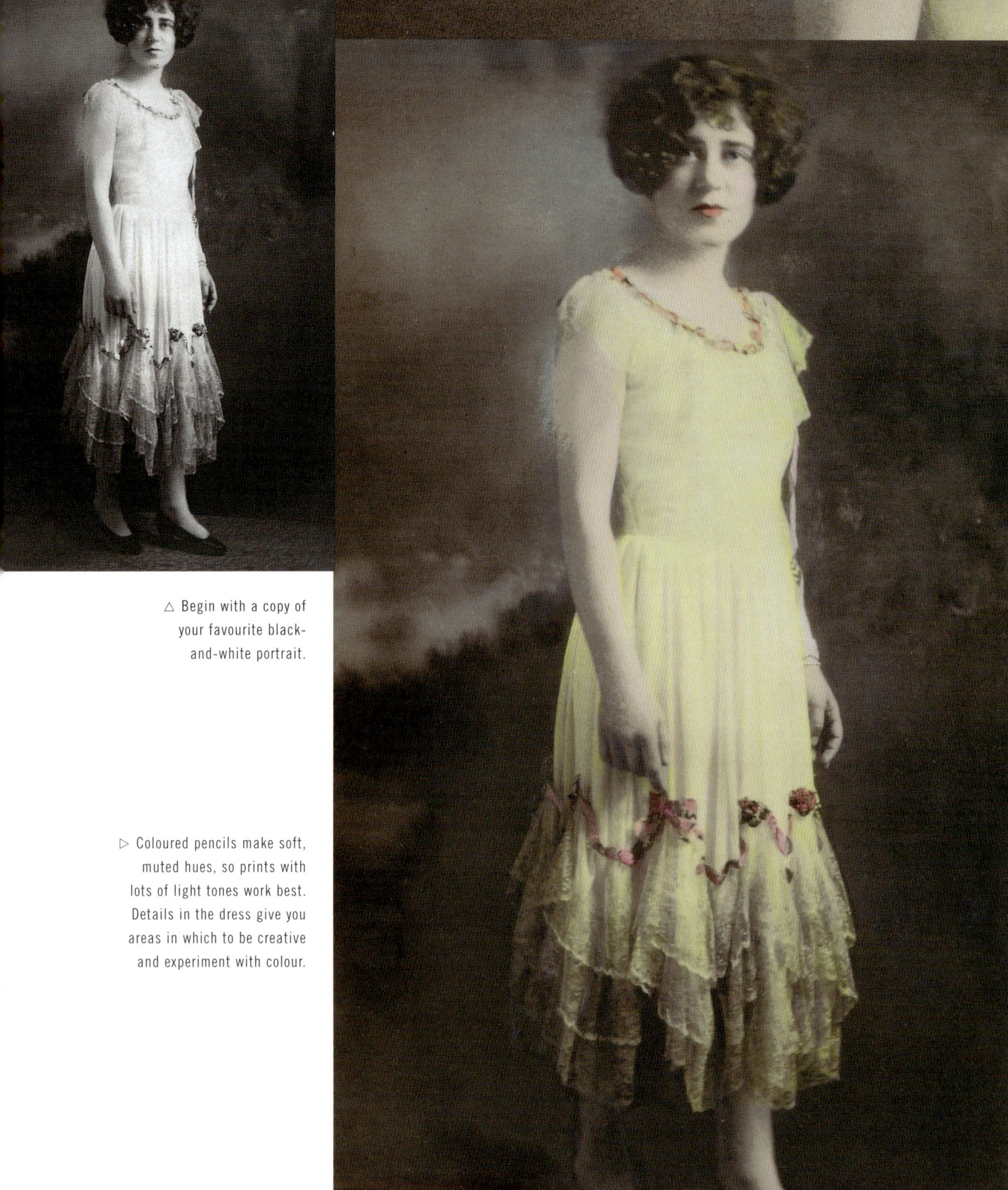

△ Begin with a copy of your favourite black-and-white portrait.

▷ Coloured pencils make soft, muted hues, so prints with lots of light tones work best. Details in the dress give you areas in which to be creative and experiment with colour.

Hand Colouring a Vintage Photograph

GETTING STARTED

Start by choosing a black-and-white print with a matte surface. Any image you have on hand can be used. If all your photographs are in colour, have a black-and-white copy negative made and then printed on matte-surface paper. Most photo labs can easily make one for you. Likewise, if you have selected a vintage black-and-white photograph, it is a good idea to have a copy negative and print made. Then you can work on the re-print rather than colouring the original. Sepia-toning your prints will give them an antique look and can make even the most recent photographs seem vintage. When choosing a photograph to colour, remember that lighter tones will show colours best.

MATERIALS

- black-and-white print on matte-surface paper
- coloured pencils: rosy beige, pink, blush, scarlet lake, true blue, lemon yellow, canary yellow, mineral orange, crimson red, lavender, true green, white, vermilion red, green bice
- cotton balls
- toothpicks
- cotton swabs
- turpentine-and-oil solution
- sepia toner

ROSY BEIGE

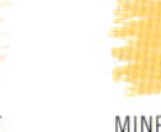

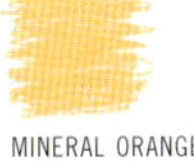

MINERAL ORANGE

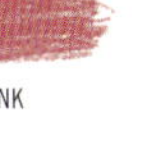

PINK

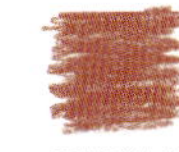

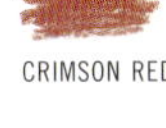

CRIMSON RED

BLUSH

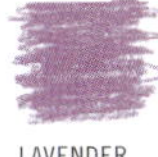

LAVENDER

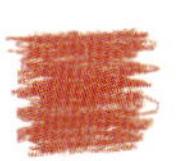

SCARLET LAKE

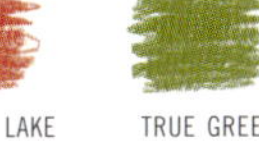

TRUE GREEN

TRUE BLUE

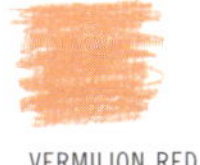

VERMILION RED

LEMON YELLOW

GREEN BICE

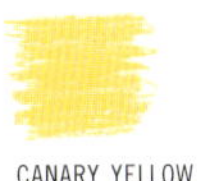

CANARY YELLOW

▷ 1

First, sepia-tone the print. (See "Advanced Techniques.") Then, choose the most important areas and colour these first. For this sepia-toned print, a rosy beige-coloured pencil was used for the skin. Work with a back-and-forth motion to fill the whole area with colour, then gently rub in the colour with a cotton swab. For small areas, use part of a cotton ball wrapped around a toothpick.

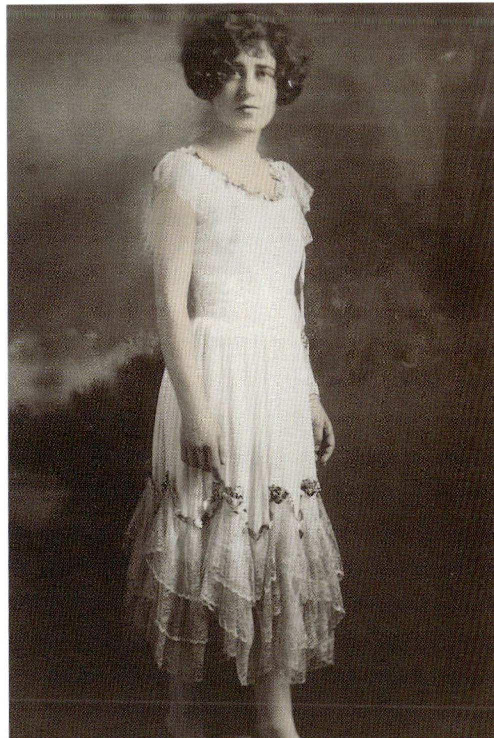

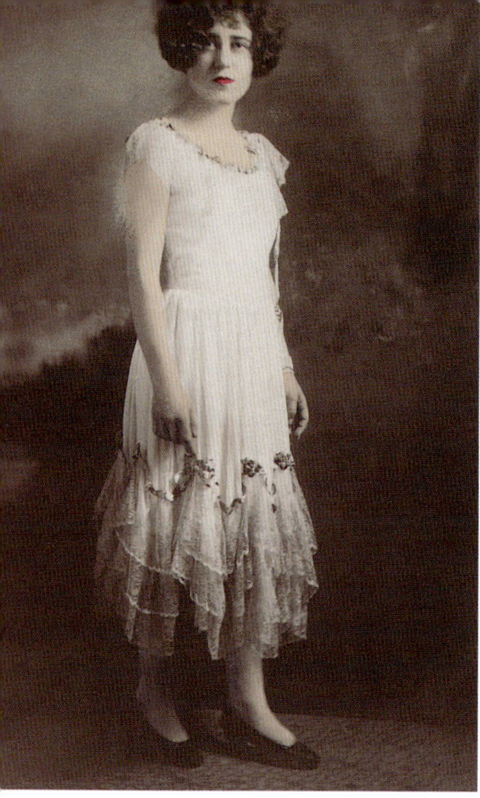

△ 2

A sharpened scarlet lake pencil adds brilliant colour to the lips. A sharp-pointed true-blue pencil accents the eyes. Create contour in the cheek area with the pink pencil, or, if you want a look that is more subtle, you can use the blush pencil. To add accents to the hair, try using the lemon-yellow pencil in the lighter areas. Wipe away any excess pencil wax with a cotton swab.

▽ 3

Using light, even strokes, colour the clothing next. Dab a tiny amount of solution on the print with a cotton swab. With a different cotton swab, use a circular motion to rub in the colour; aim for a uniform, transparent wash.

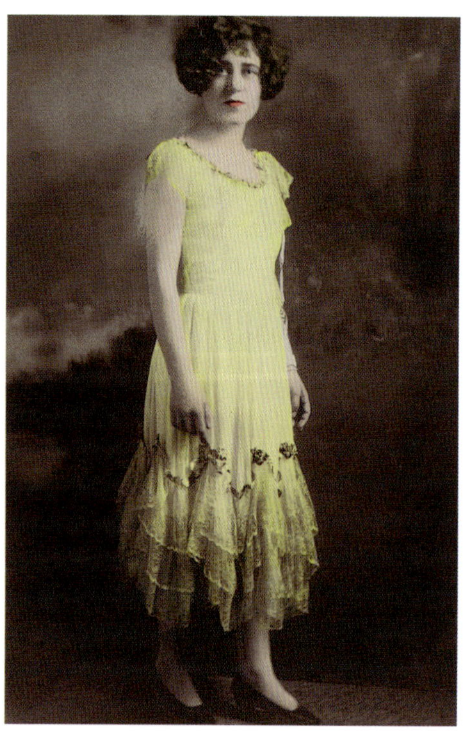

TIPS

- For more vibrant skin tones, mix crimson red and white instead of using the rosy beige.
- Erase mistakes with cotton swabs and small amounts of water.
- Make sure the entire area is filled with colour before rubbing with the swab.
- Go over areas twice to enhance colour saturation. Use a new swab for each colour.
- If dark areas look shiny, swab them with a little water to dull them.

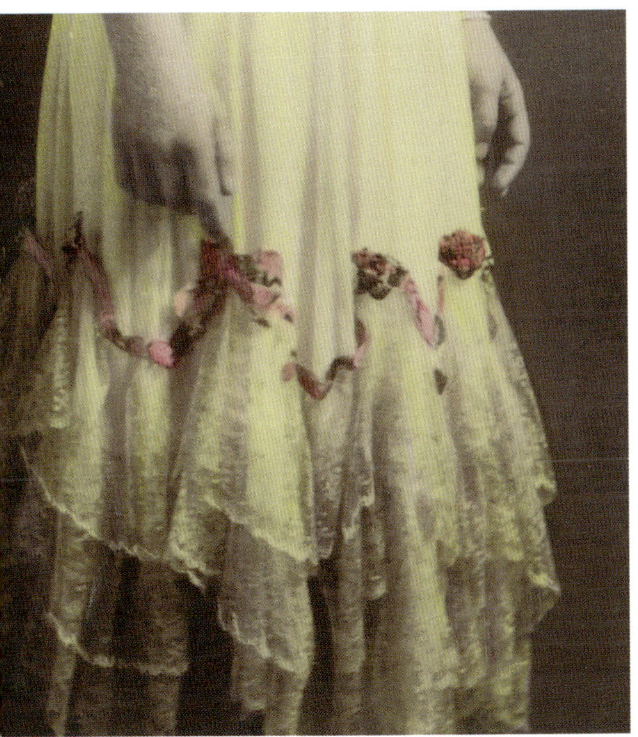

 4

Contour the folds in the clothing with an accent colour, such as mineral orange, to create depth. To finish, use crimson, lavender, and true green pencils on details such as the garland of flowers. The same colours are also used on neckline to give the image harmony. True-blue pencil in the background and scarlet lake hues in the rug complete this hand-coloured photograph.

VARIATION

A different palette creates a completely different mood.

1. Colour skin tones as in step one.
2. Use vermilion red to colour the hair, then accent with canary yellow in the highlight areas for depth.
3. True blue and green bice create heightened contrast in the clothing. Green in the folds of the dress brings the colour up into the bodice for continuity.
4. Use vermilion red on accents, such as the flower trim here.
5. Shade crimson on the background and blend smooth with a little solution on a cotton ball. On the areas close to the body, you may need to use a swab for better control. Canary yellow works well for small highlight areas in the background.

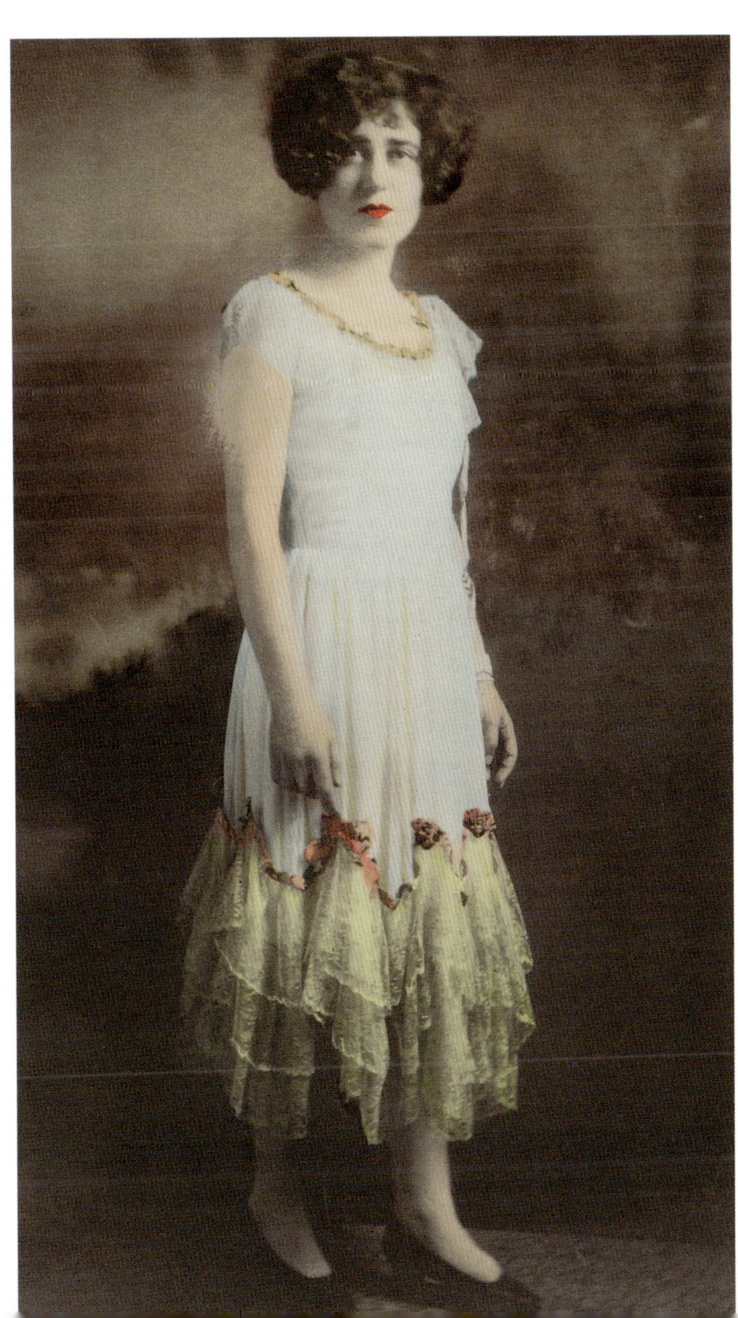

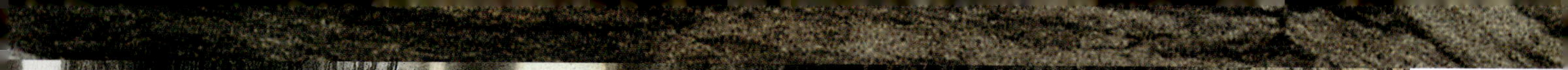

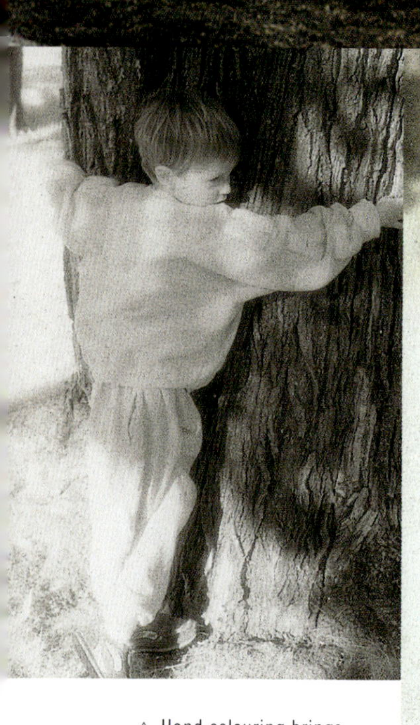

△ Hand colouring brings out the textures.

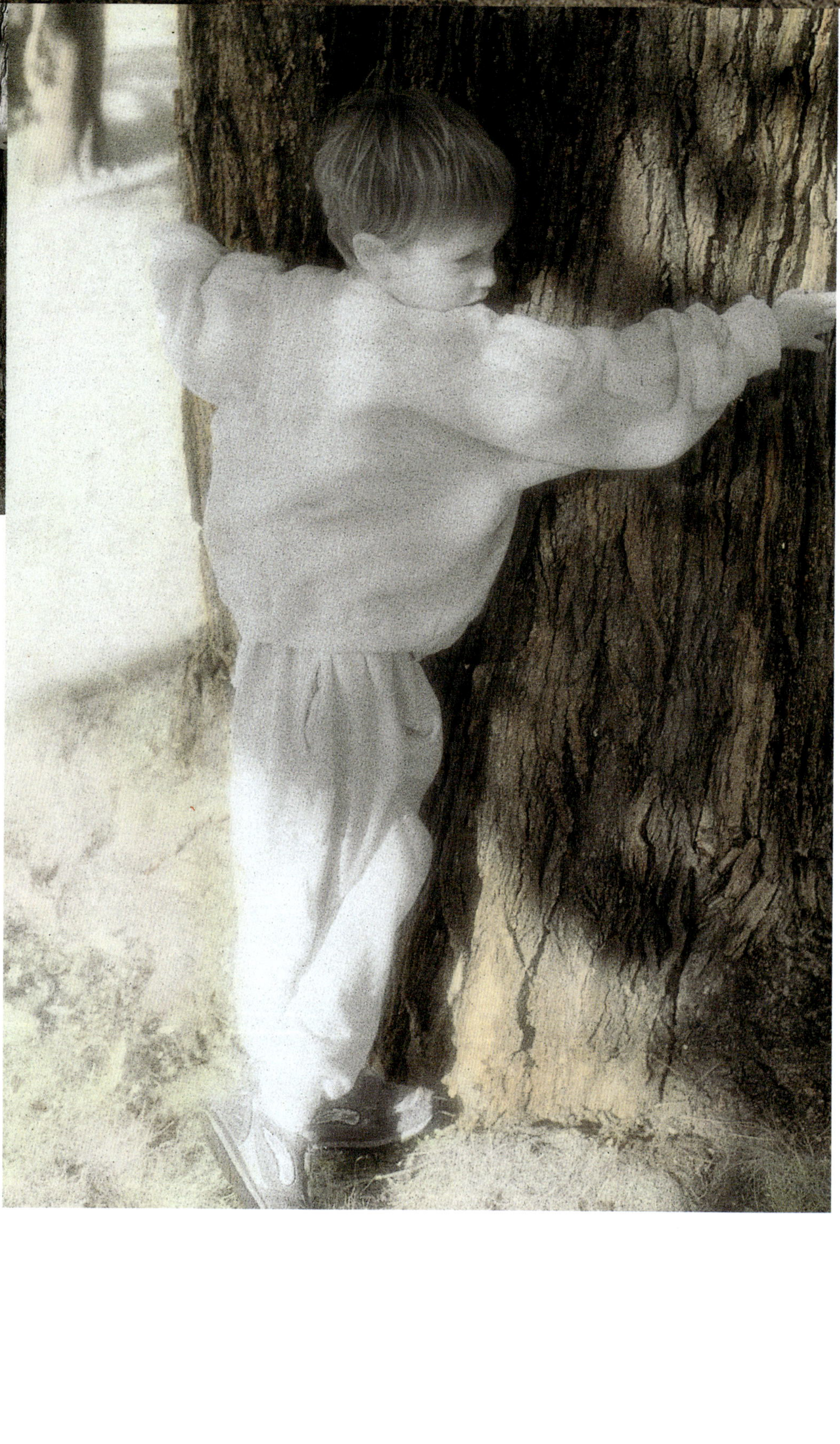

▷ This image had a great deal of mood even before it was hand coloured.

Hand Colouring for Realism

GETTING STARTED

The texture of the tree trunk in this photograph made it an interesting selection to hand colour. Different colours were used to create even more texture. Hand colouring everything except the young boy distinguishes him from the background, which also makes the photo look more three-dimensional.

MATERIALS

- black-and-white print on matte-surface paper
- coloured pencils: apple green, terracotta, sienna brown, pink, canary yellow, scarlet red, gold, carmine red, Copenhagen blue, rosy beige, crimson red, peacock blue, warm grey 20%, blush
- cotton swabs
- turpentine-and-oil solution

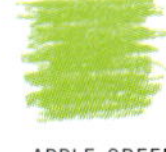
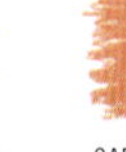
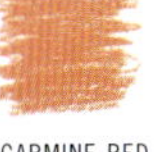

APPLE GREEN　CARMINE RED

TERRACOTTA　COPENHAGEN BLUE

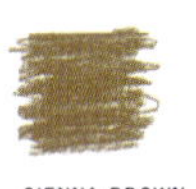

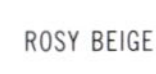

SIENNA BROWN　ROSY BEIGE

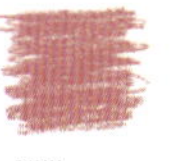
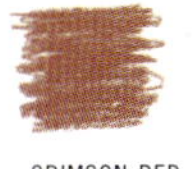

PINK　CRIMSON RED

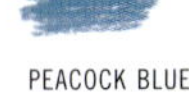

CANARY YELLOW　PEACOCK BLUE

SCARLET RED　WARM GREY 20%

GOLD　BLUSH

▷ **1**

Apply an even wash of apple green on the grass. To create the wash, apply the colour and then smooth it in with a cotton swab soaked in a small amount of solution. Take your time when smoothing in the colour so that it will be consistent throughout the grass. Continue to use fresh cotton swabs until you get an even wash. To clean areas where the colour has bled, use a fresh cotton swab and a small amount of water.

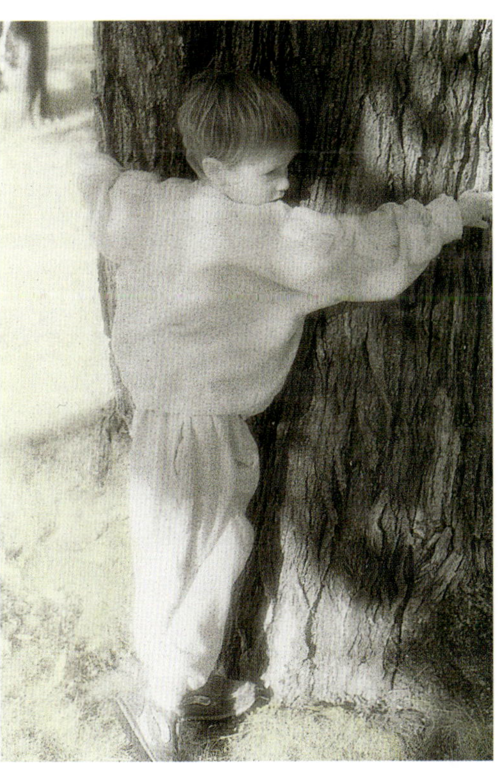

▷ 2

Colour the larger tree using the terra-cotta pencil. Using a small amount of solution on a cotton swab, smooth in the colour. Use the sienna brown for the trees in the background. Blend with a small amount of solution.

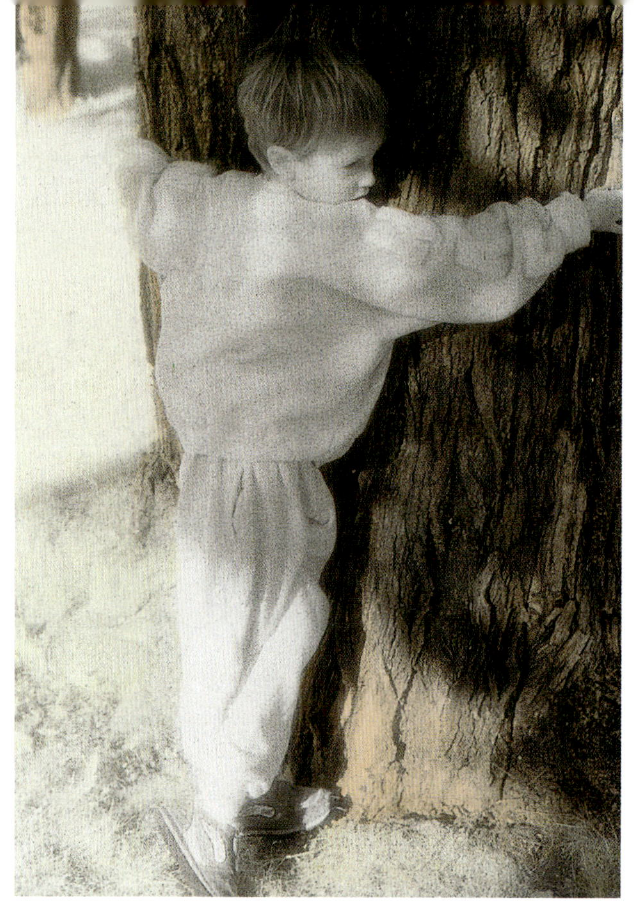

◁ 3

To create more depth, use the pink pencil to colour random areas of the grass. The mixture of the coolness of the green in the grass and the warmth of the pink adds depth. Smooth in the colour with a cotton swab.

TIP

- Use the sunlight in a photograph as a guide when choosing an image to hand colour. In this photograph, for example, it appears to be late afternoon. The shadows are long and angular and create warm sunlight on the tree trunk for contours and depth.

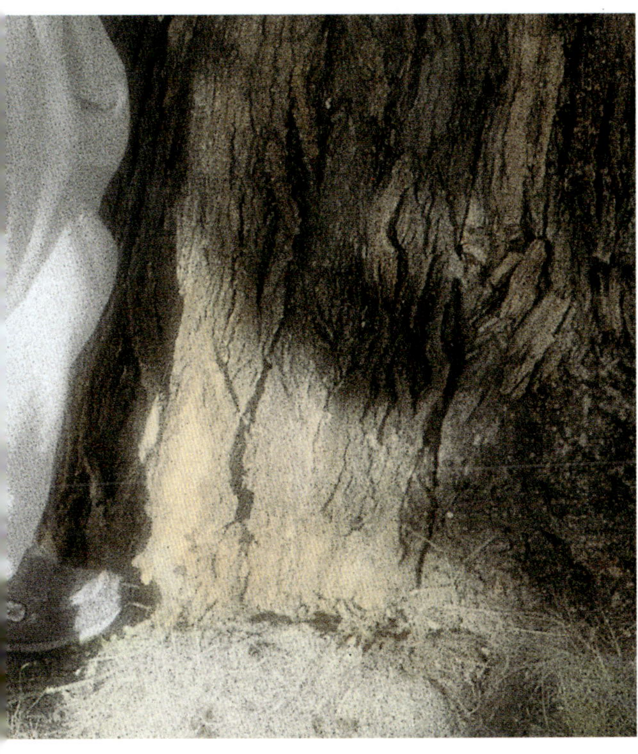

◁ 4

Use the canary yellow and scarlet red pencils to colour the lighter (highlighted) areas of the tree. (Tree bark is never just one colour. Using other colours makes the trunk appear three-dimensional. Blend with a dry cotton swab.) Colour the dirt area in the grass and the other shadow areas with the gold pencil, using a small back-and-forth motion. This adds contrast (by making it darker) and warms up the area. Use a cotton swab to lightly rub the colour in.

VARIATION

Experiment with bold colours on dyed or toned prints.

This photograph was dyed using tea. (See "Advanced Techniques.") Stronger colours are necessary for prints that are heavily dyed or toned.

1. Use carmine red, a warm colour, for the trousers, adding crimson red in the darker folds to show the contours.
2. Colour the sweatshirt with Copenhagen blue, a cool colour. Use peacock blue in the folds.
3. Use the grey pencil for the highlights in the boy's hair. Rosy beige can be used on his face and hand, with blush added on his cheek.

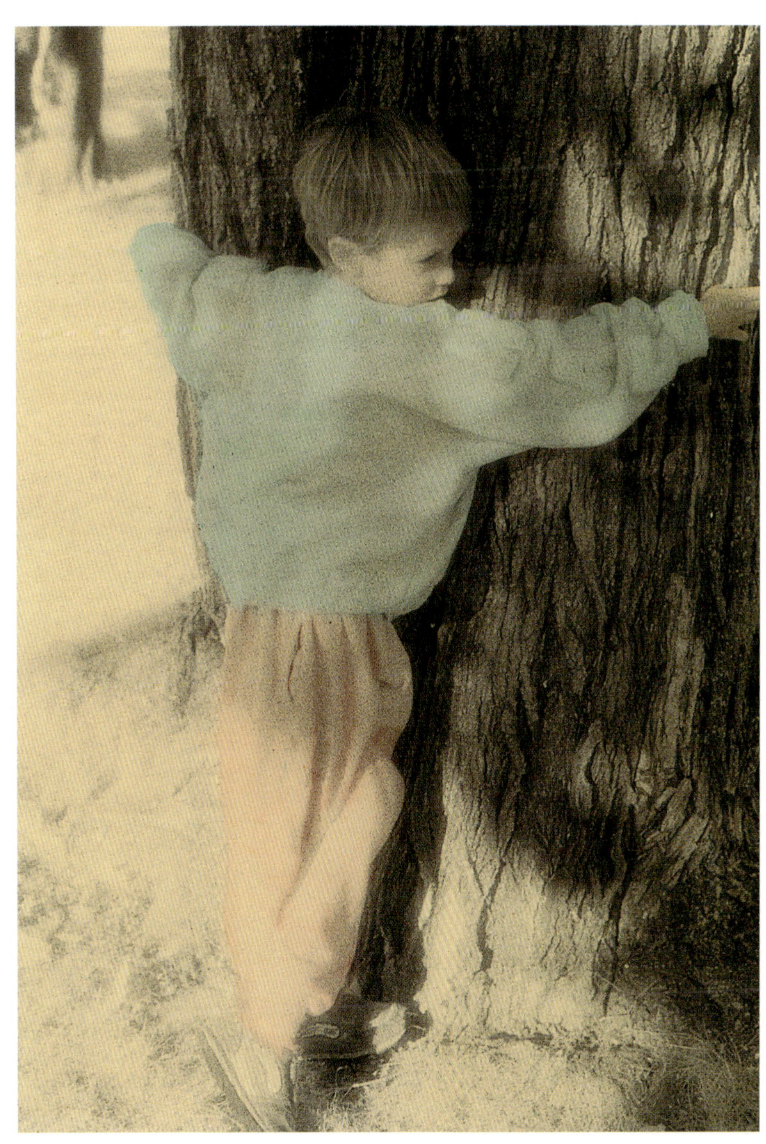

PLACES

Photographs of landscapes and nature are wonderful to hand colour. Black-and-white photographs of sunsets, for example, can be hand coloured to create a romantic or serene feel. Photographs of clouds taken before or after a storm also can be the basis of a dramatic hand-coloured image.

Another advantage of landscapes is that they lend themselves to a three-dimensional look. Use darker and more saturated colours in the foreground and lighter and less saturated ones for objects that appear further away from the viewer. Colouring the sky area blue adds to the effect of distant objects receding. Choose a palette to create the desired mood.

Other possibilities include photographing pets outdoors. Then there are flowers and wild animals, although a macro setting or close-up attachment may be necessary to photograph flowers (many zoom lenses have macro settings as a feature). Try photographing your house and then hand colouring it and sending it as a postcard. Boats and interesting architecture are excellent subjects for hand colouring. Amusement parks, with their bright lights and action, are great to photograph and hand colour. Experiment with slow and fast shutter speeds to capture the energy of the rides, then use vibrant colours to colour the image. It's also fun to hand colour photographs of still lifes arranged using fruit, flowers, and shells.

You may already have these types of photographs at home. Just remember that when picking out prints to hand colour—or when actually photographing images to hand colour—choose one with as many highlight areas as possible, since that is where colour shows up best.

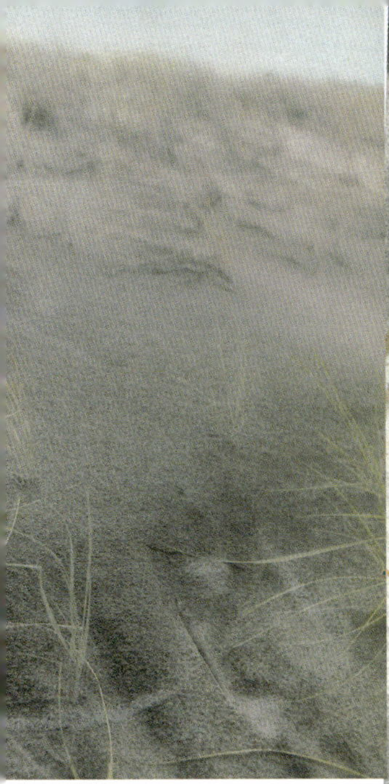

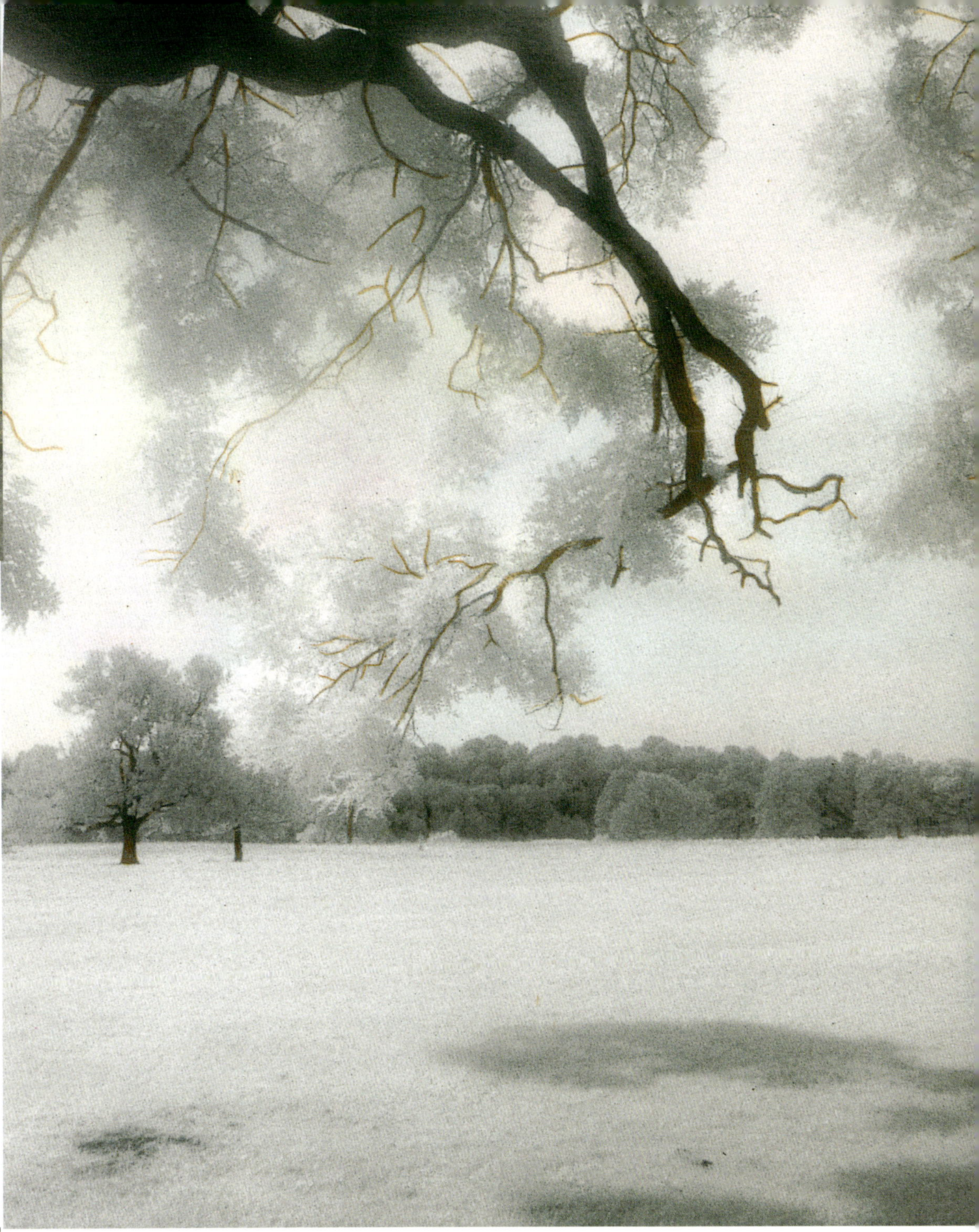

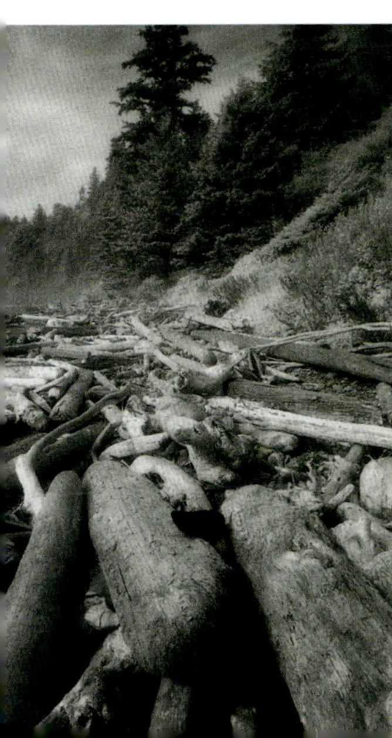

Hand colour to add drama and depth to landscapes.

△ Use a mix of warm and cool colours to create a three-dimensional look.

Working with Photographs of Places

Many painters take a colour photograph of a scene and then use it as a reference when painting. There's a lesson to be learned here. To hand colour a photograph realistically, take two photographs of the same scene—one in black and white (to hand colour) and one in colour (as a reference).

When hand colouring with coloured pencils, experiment to determine a palette that works well for you. Use a mix of warm and cool colours to create a three-dimensional look. Try hand colouring only select areas of the print for emphasis. Achieve a surreal effect by using colours in unexpected ways: Colour the grass purple or add stars or even spaceships in the sky—it's up to your imagination!

▷ Although this picture was taken on a foggy day, which might have resulted in a dark print, the ice-covered pine needles came out pale enough to hand colour because they reflected the available light.

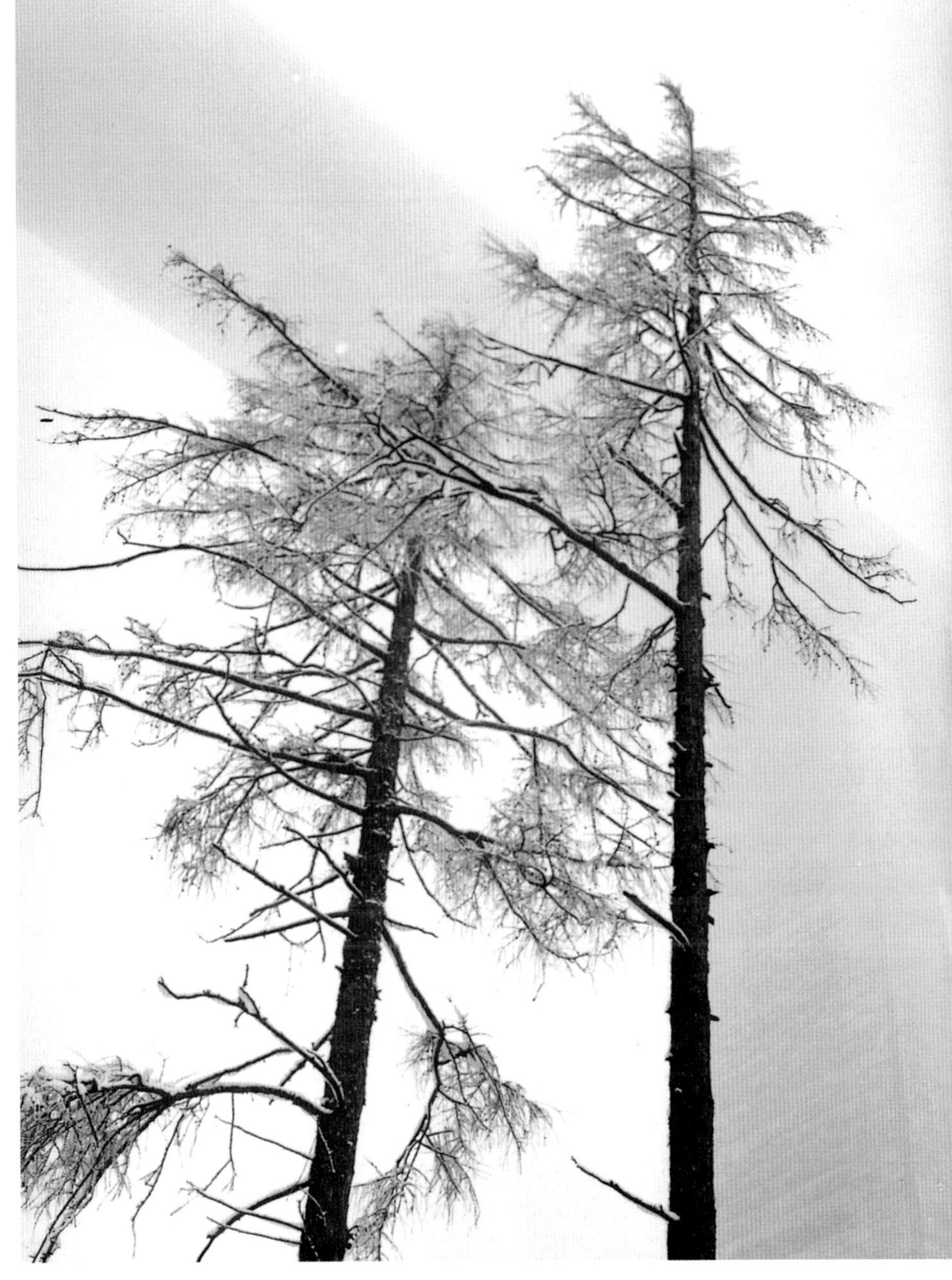

There are several things to look out for when photographing nature. Something that in person looks like the perfect subject for hand colouring may not be so ideal in a black-and-white photograph. Pine trees, for example, often appear too dark to hand colour. Wait until the sun is shining directly on them before taking the photograph and the trees will appear lighter in the print. The same goes for buildings that are in shadow: They will appear darker in black and white.

As for hand colouring nature shots, since so much in nature is green, try using a palette with more than one type of green. Use yellow-green and blue-green, and create your own green by adding pink, orange, or lavender to an existing green hue.

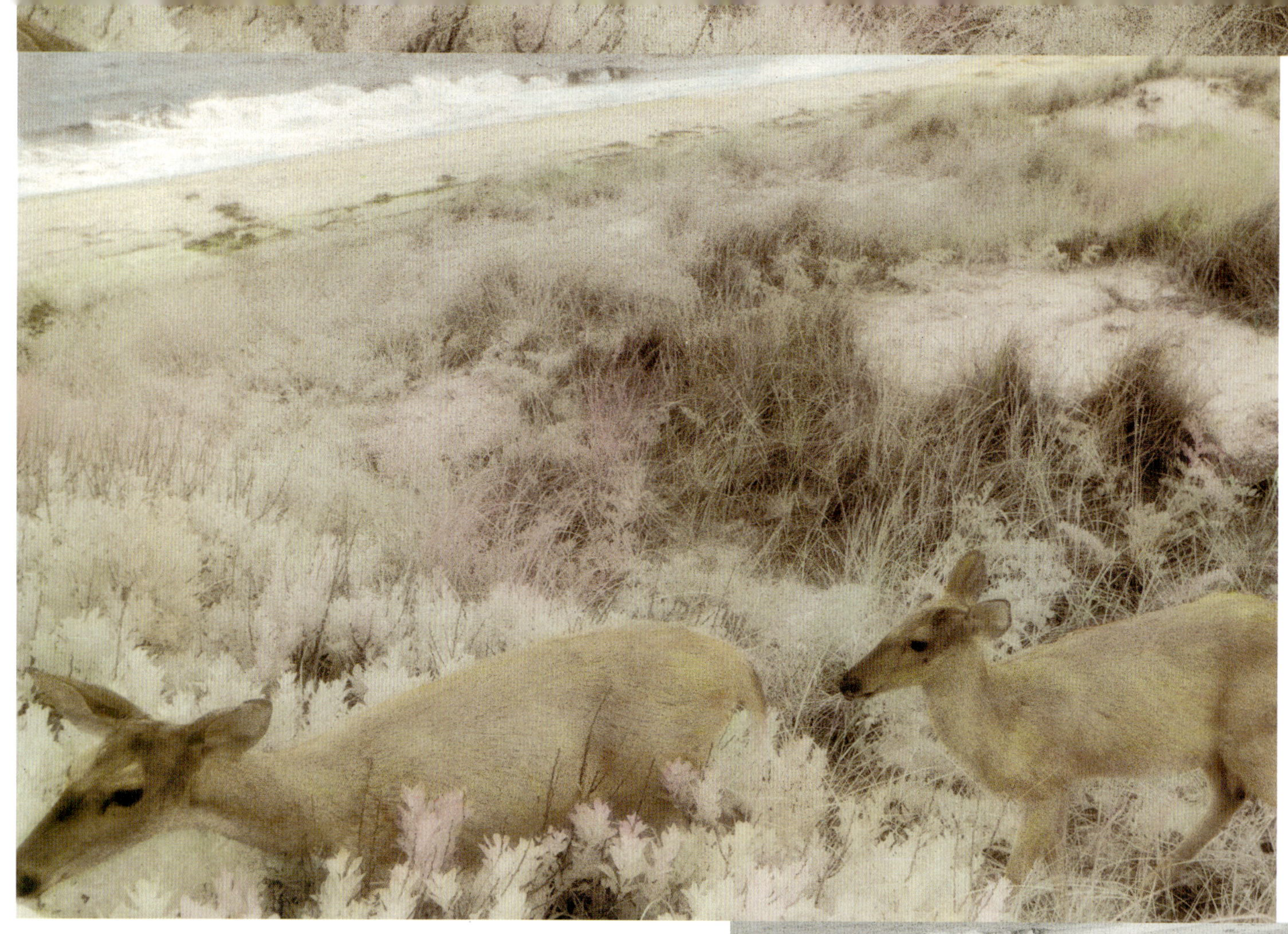

△ The depth of the scene, the different textures in the grass, and the deer make this photograph a good candidate for hand colouring. An image with a distinct foreground, middle ground, and background offers the opportunity to enhance the illusion of depth.

Hand Colouring an Animal in a Landscape

GETTING STARTED

Photographs of animals are wonderful to hand colour because of all the different textures in fur and feathers. For the best results, choose an image of an animal that is light to medium in colour. This image has been sepia-toned (see "Advanced Techniques") to restore the warmth of the animals' coats as well as that of the landscape. Many different colours have been used to bring out the details in this photograph. Compare the photograph that was not hand coloured to the finished one to observe the difference in depth. In the hand-coloured photo, the ocean appears even farther away because of the cool blue used on it; the colours in the middle ground gradually increase in saturation toward the foreground of the scene to add dimension.

MATERIALS

- black-and-white print on matte-surface paper
- coloured pencils: dark brown, terracotta, lemon yellow, sienna brown, lime peel, pale peach, deco peach, salmon, light violet, deco blue, rosy beige, sky blue, warm grey 20%, clay rose, olive green, dark green, pink, purple, orange
- cotton balls
- toothpicks
- cotton swabs
- turpentine-and-oil solution
- sepia toner

DARK BROWN

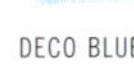
DECO BLUE

TERRACOTTA

ROSY BEIGE

LEMON YELLOW

SKY BLUE

SIENNA BROWN

WARM GREY 20%

LIME PEEL

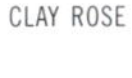
CLAY ROSE

PALE PEACH

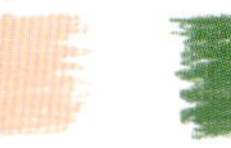
OLIVE GREEN

DECO PEACH

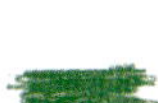
DARK GREEN

SALMON

PINK

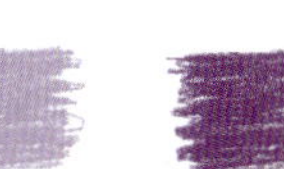
LIGHT VIOLET

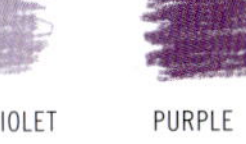
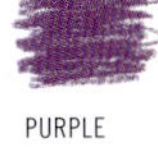
PURPLE

ORANGE

▷ **1**

Sepia-tone the print, then use dark brown to colour the deer. The dark-brown pencil is relatively soft, so solution is not needed. After applying colour to both deer, use a cotton swab to gently rub the pigment in.

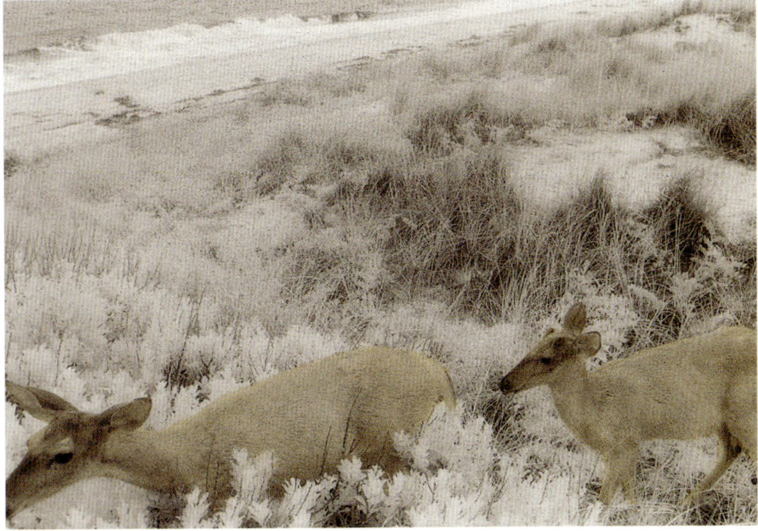

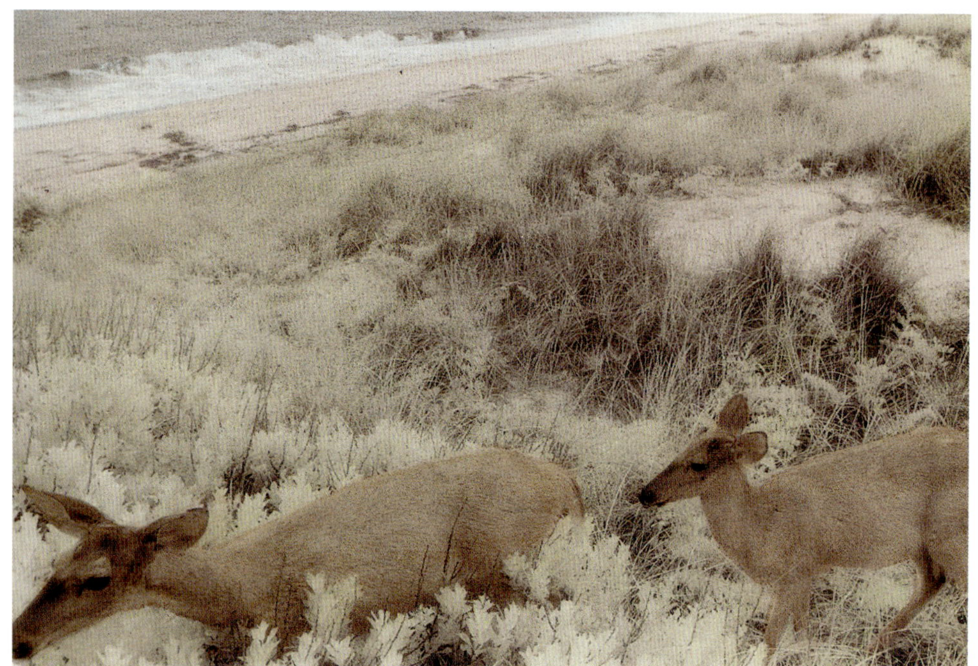

TIP

- Moisten a cotton swab with water and wipe the foam areas of the ocean to pull off some of the blue and brighten the look of the water.

△ 2

Use the sky blue pencil to fill in the water. Smooth the colour in gently with a small amount of solution. Use the grey and clay-rose pencils for the beach and sand dunes. (See "Colour Mixing.") Use olive green to fill in the grass, and smooth the colour in with a cotton swab. Blend the entire area with a cotton ball, but use a cotton swab at the border where the colours meet.

▷ 3

Add details and texture to the deer's coats with lemon-yellow, sienna brown, and terracotta pencils. Use the lemon yellow to add highlights, and use the two browns for the darker areas in the coat and around the deer's face.

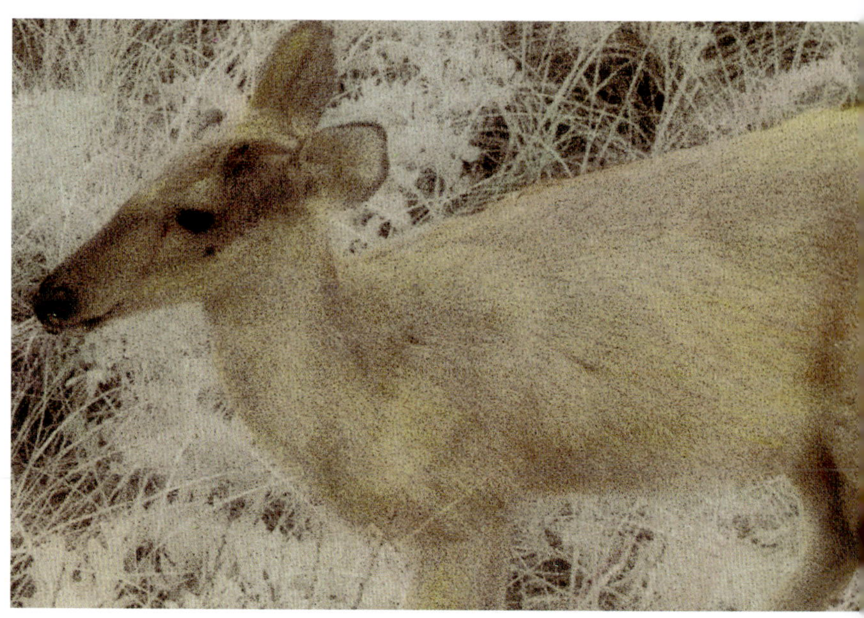

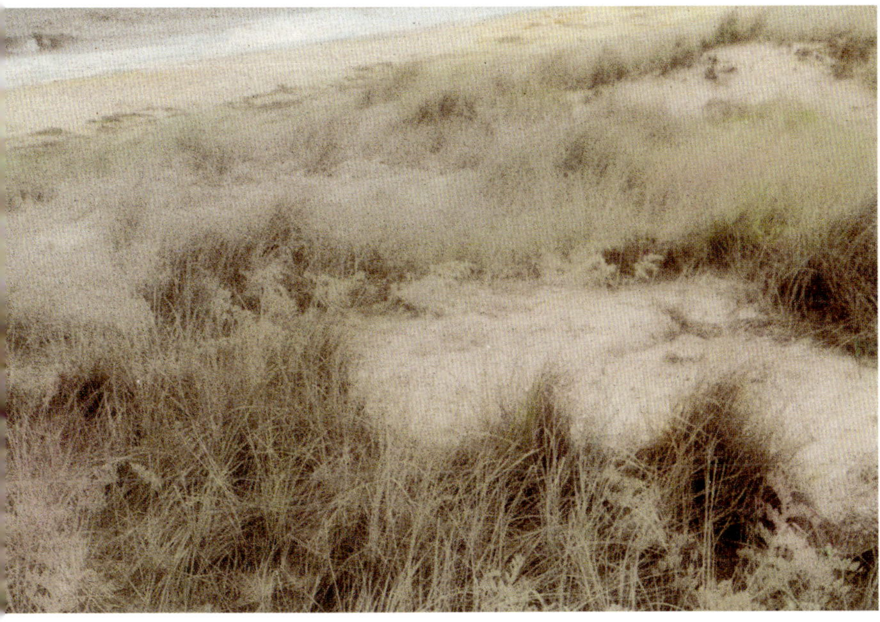

 4

Using a single colour for an entire area tends to flatten the image. To avoid this in the grass area, add other colours either in sections, on individual blades of grass, or on random leaves. To add visual interest, use colours like pink, purple, and orange in the grass. It is important to work each colour throughout the composition to help balance and unify the image as a whole.

VARIATION

Colour everything but the focal point to emphasize its importance.

1. For the grass, first apply lime peel pencil and then use pale peach and deco peach for accents.
2. Colour the ocean with sky blue, and use deco blue on the dark parts of the waves.
3. Use a blend of the rosy beige and grey pencils on the beach and the dunes.
4. Leave the deer uncoloured.

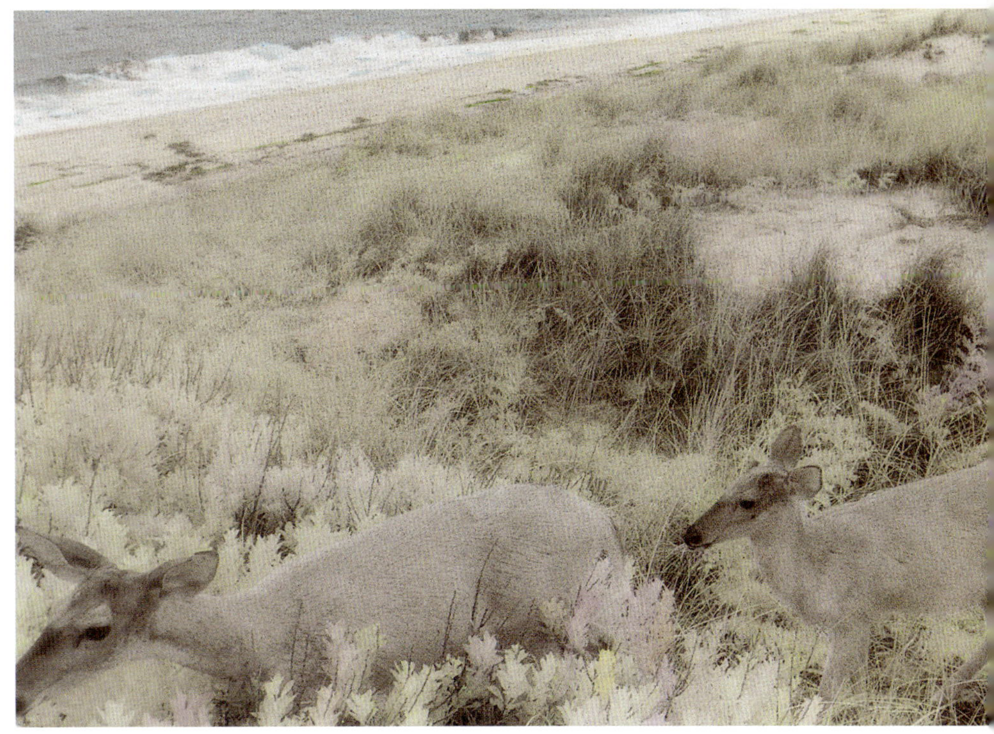

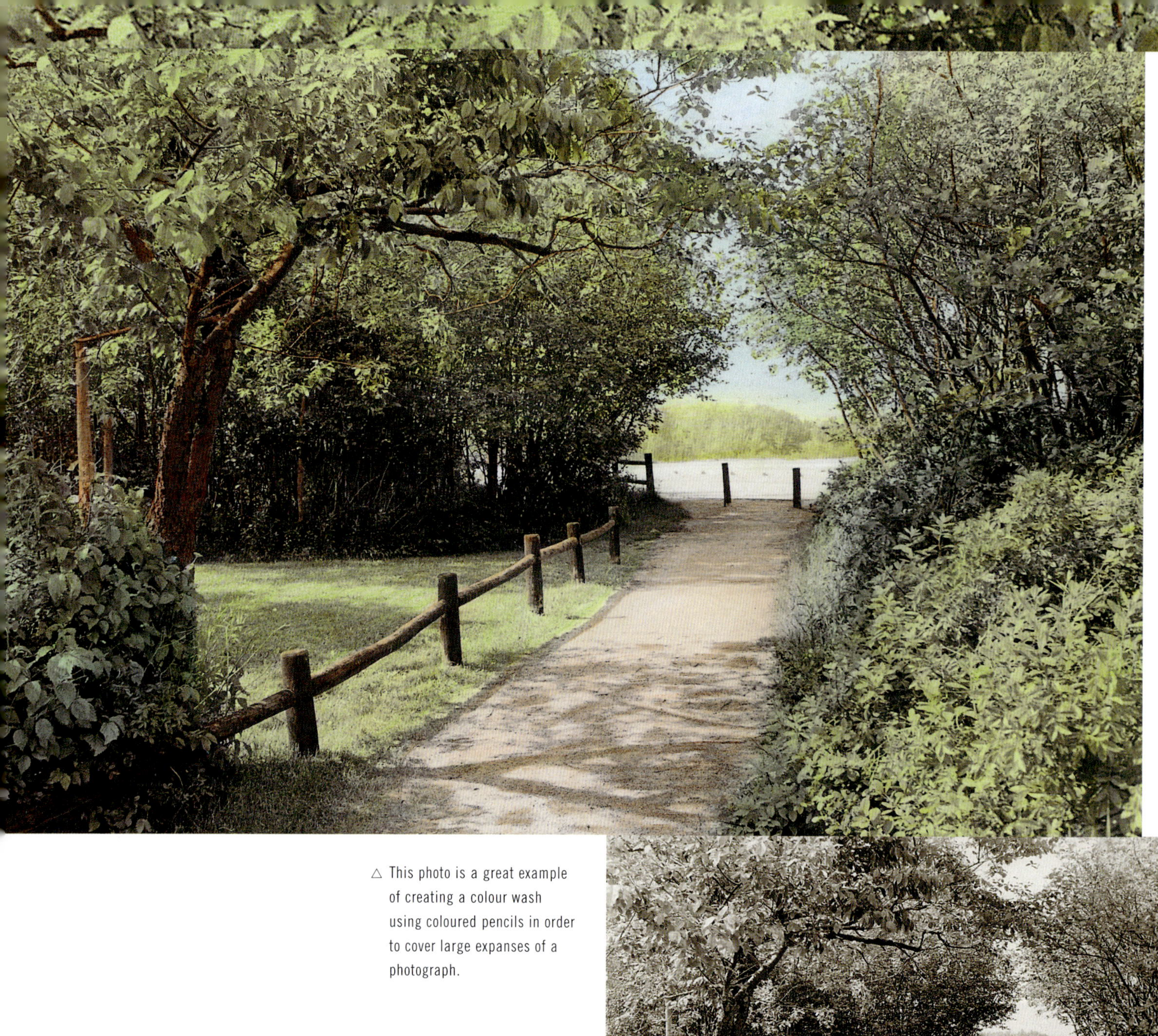

△ This photo is a great example of creating a colour wash using coloured pencils in order to cover large expanses of a photograph.

▷ This image already has many textures. Hand colouring, however, gives it a lot of depth, too.

Hand Colouring Nature

GETTING STARTED

Colouring each individual leaf in the foliage area of a picture such as this one would be very time-consuming. Instead, colour was added and the turpentine-and-oil solution was used to create a wash. Other colours were then used on individual leaves to create depth. A mix of dark and bright colours was used in the foreground. The blue in the sky area makes it recede into the distance. In the hilly area beneath the sky, a lighter green was used. The light green in this area produces a hazy quality, which is exactly what you see when viewing hills from a distance.

MATERIALS

- black-and-white print on matte-surface paper
- coloured pencils: rosy beige, raw umber, terracotta, chartreuse, sky blue, olive green, apple green, green bice, parma violet, peacock blue, dark brown, dark green, true blue
- cotton balls
- toothpicks
- cotton swabs
- turpentine-and-oil solution
- blender

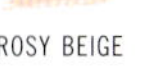

ROSY BEIGE

GREEN BICE

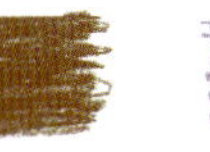

RAW UMBER

PARMA VIOLET

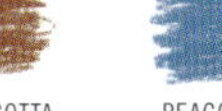

TERRACOTTA

PEACOCK BLUE

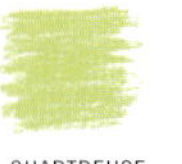

CHARTREUSE

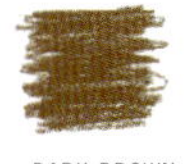

DARK BROWN

SKY BLUE

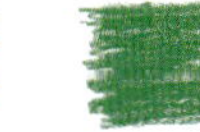

DARK GREEN

OLIVE GREEN

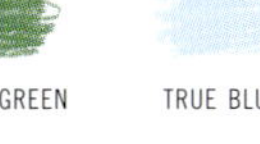

TRUE BLUE

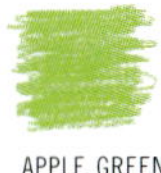

APPLE GREEN

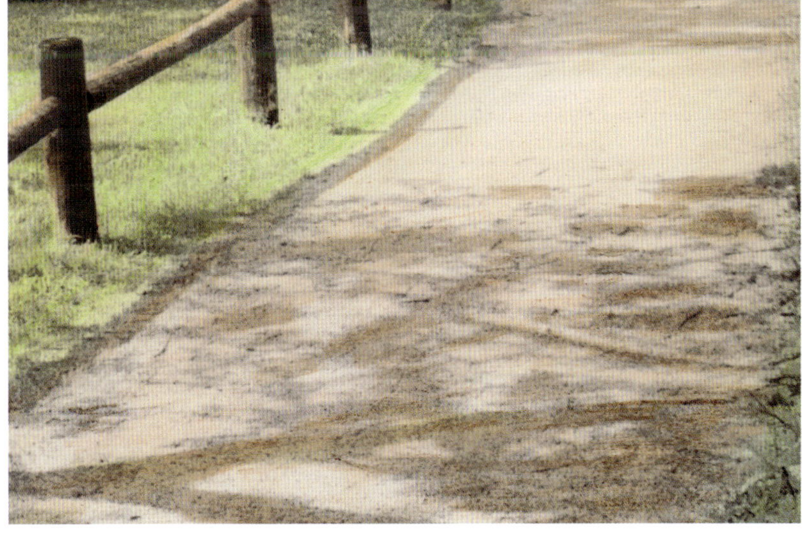

△ **1**

Colour the pathway using the rosy beige pencil. Use a small amount of solution to smooth in the colour, and use a cotton swab to pick up any excess. Use the dark-brown pencil to colour the shadows created by the trees and fence in the pathway. This creates a realistic look of contrast and depth. Using a toothpick wrapped in cotton, smooth in the colour so the pencil strokes are not apparent.

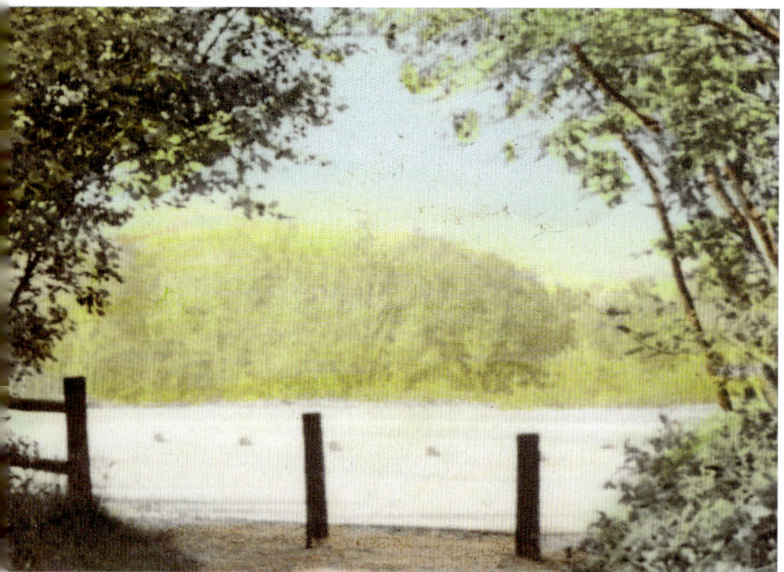

◁ 2

Apply a small amount of solution in the sky area, and then add sky blue. Use a cotton swab to smooth in the colour. (Here, the order of applying colour and then solution was switched. See which way is better for you.) Don't worry if you get some blue in the leaves. Either use the blender to tone down the blue in the leaves or try applying olive green to the leaves. Colour the mountains using the chartreuse pencil. Using a toothpick wrapped in cotton, blend the colour with solution. The colour will be fairly light. There aren't many dark areas in the mountains, but the lighter wash will suggest depth.

TIP

- Where one colour meets another, a third colour will be formed. To make this a smooth transition, use the blender.

▷ 3

Create a colour wash for the foliage instead of colouring each individual leaf. Colour in one area of bushes or trees, and use a small amount of solution on a cotton swab to create an overall smoothness. Green bice was used on the bush in the foreground. The bush behind it was coloured with a mixture of the dark-green and true-blue pencils. More than one layer may be necessary to create saturated, intense colours. (See "Tips for Mixing Colours.") By using the same two-colour mix for the bush on the left (not shown here) a balance is created. A wash of the olive-green pencil was used in the remaining foliage. The chartreuse pencil was used to accentuate a few random leaves to create depth in the bush. The olive-green pencil was used in the remaining foliage.

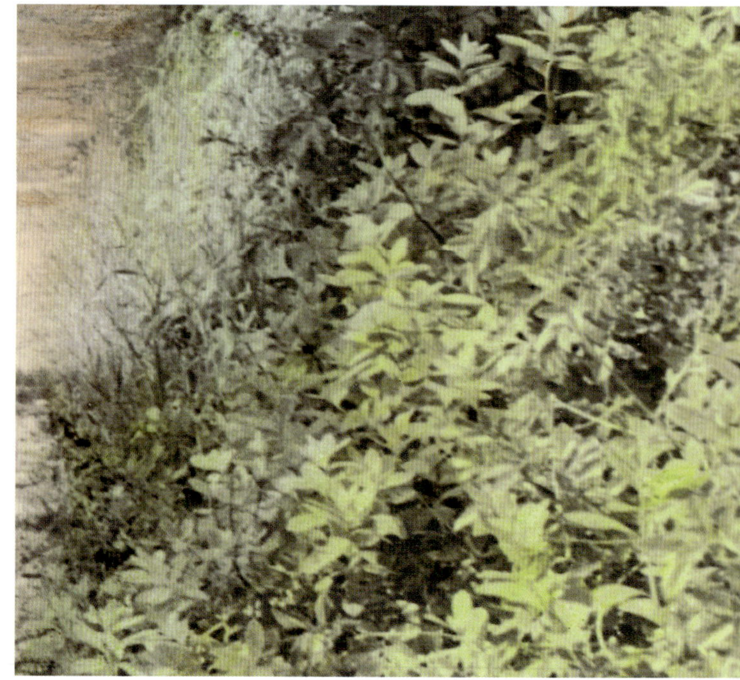

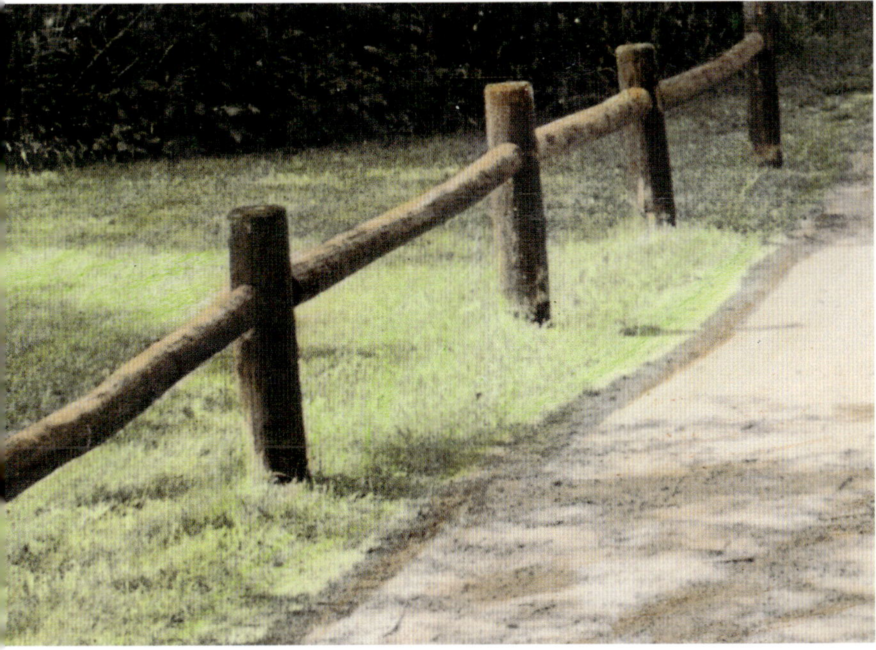

◁ 4

Use the raw umber pencil to colour the railing. To eliminate the pencil strokes, wrap a tiny bit of cotton dipped in a very small amount of solution on a toothpick. You can also choose not to blend it, since pencil strokes add texture. Using the terracotta pencil, colour the trees. Use heavier layering in the tree trunks. Colour the limb areas with the same pencil. There may still be a slight residual of solution on the print, so if blending is necessary, use a cotton swab. Use the apple green pencil for the foreground foliage areas. Use a cotton swab and a small amount of solution to create a wash.

VARIATION

Selective hand colouring adds emphasis to key areas of a photograph.

1. Use the parma violet pencil to colour the pathway, and blend the colour with a small amount of solution.
2. Using the peacock blue pencil, colour the shadows of the trees on the path. Using warm and cool tones in conjunction with dark tones over lighter tones creates contrast and depth.
3. Using the peacock blue, colour the railing. To add texture, let the pencil strokes remain visible.

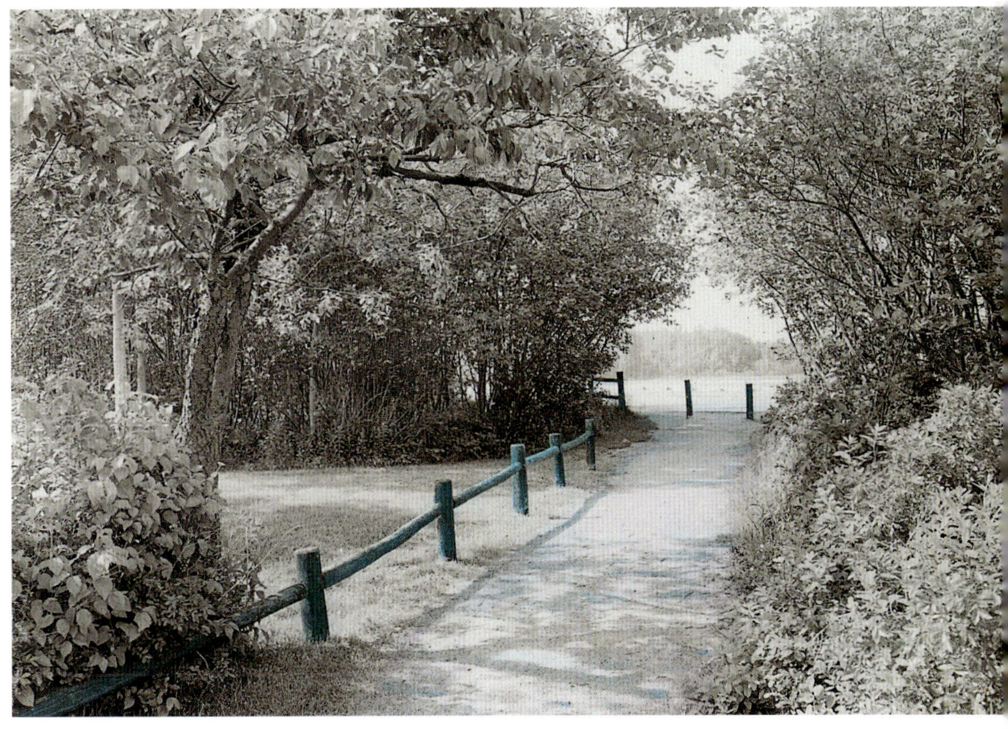

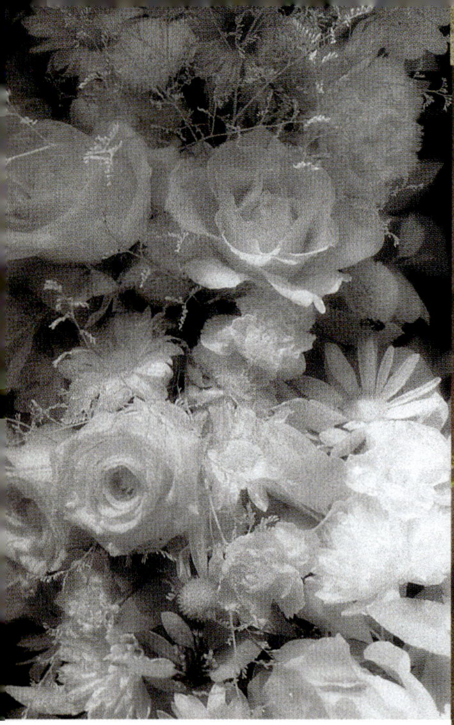

△ This photo was chosen because every area has equal importance.

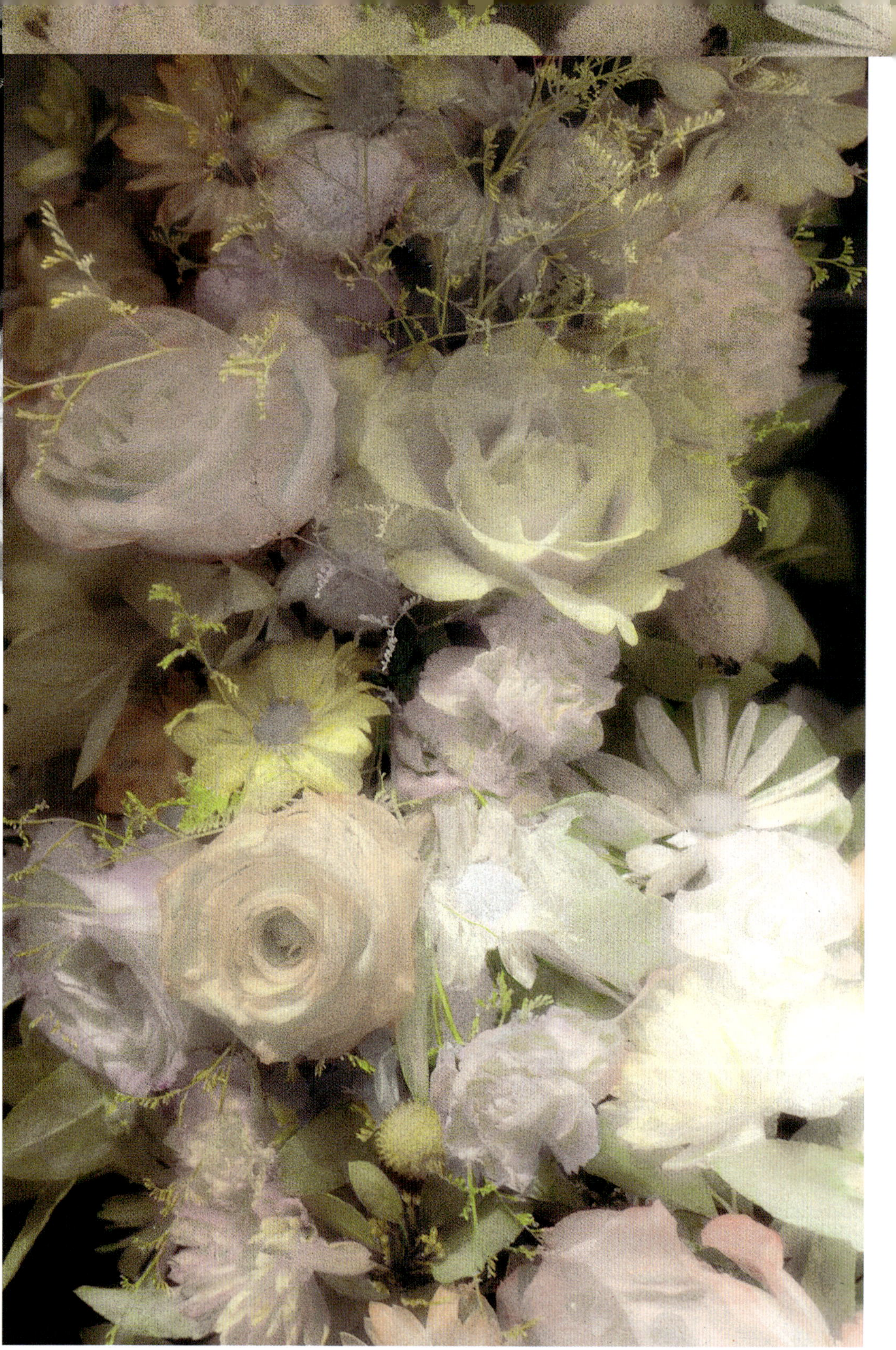

▷ Flowers are one of the best subjects to hand colour. They contain many details, which makes them great for learning and practicing different techniques.

Hand Colouring Flowers

GETTING STARTED

With any photograph, it is natural for the viewer's eye to be drawn to the lightest area of the print. Because the lightest area of this print is right on the edge, the viewer's gaze drifts off the page. To prevent this from happening and to create a tighter composition, add colour to any edges that appear to be too light. Use the turpentine-and-oil solution as little as possible so the colour does not become too thin. Layer the colours to make them appear more saturated and bolder.

MATERIALS

- black-and-white print on matte-surface paper
- coloured pencils: salmon pink, scarlet lake, light violet, Spanish orange, pink, grape, vermilion red, magenta, lemon yellow, deco peach, warm grey 20%, metallic maroon, olive green, green bice, rosy beige
- cotton balls
- toothpicks
- cotton swabs
- turpentine-and-oil solution
- sepia toner

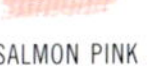
SALMON PINK

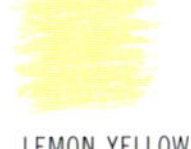
LEMON YELLOW

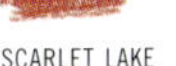
SCARLET LAKE

DECO PEACH

LIGHT VIOLET

WARM GREY 20%

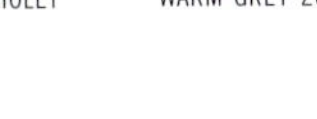

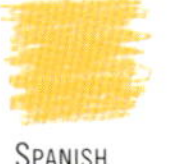
SPANISH ORANGE

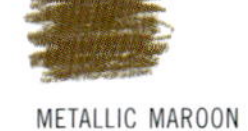
METALLIC MAROON

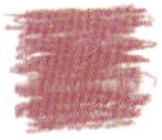
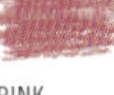
PINK

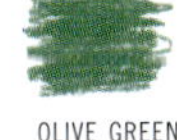
OLIVE GREEN

GRAPE

GREEN BICE

VERMILION RED

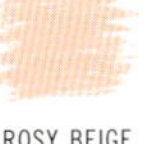
ROSY BEIGE

MAGENTA

▷ **1**

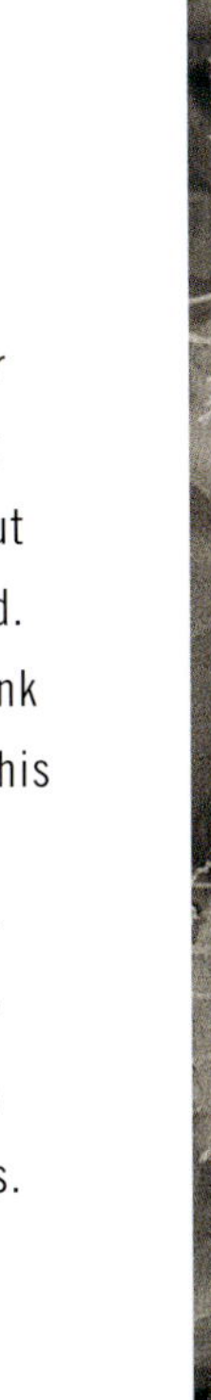

First, sepia-tone the photo. (See "Advanced Techniques.") Then, choose which flower to hand colour first, and use salmon pink to fill it in. Notice how the flower stands out against the uncoloured background. Keep in mind that since salmon pink was used in such a large area of this print, it needs to be repeated in another area to balance the colour composition. Watch how the colour balance shifts as different colours are added to the remaining flowers.

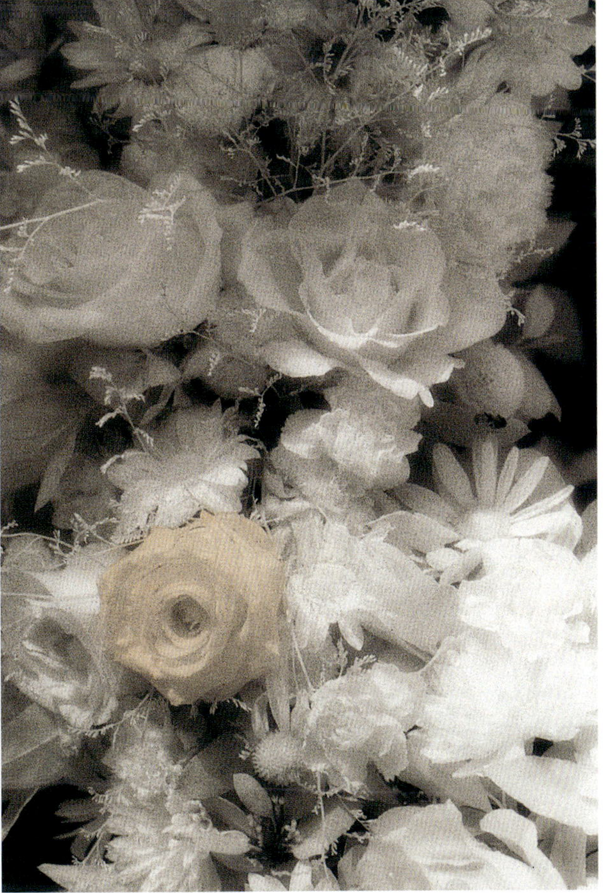

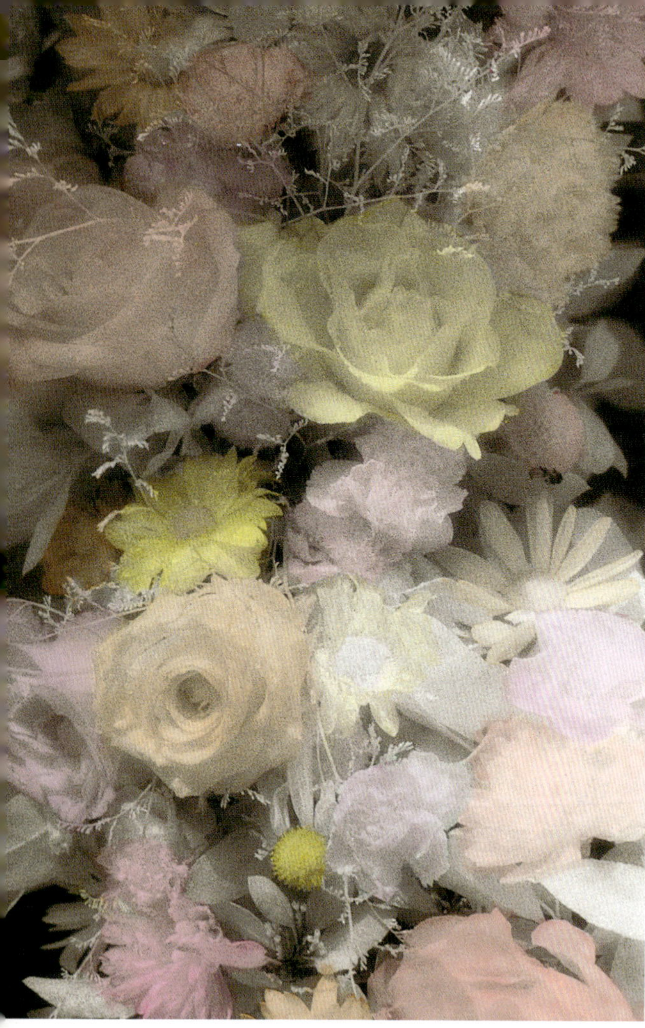

◁ 2

Colour each flower with a base colour. The palette used for this image consists mainly of pinks, peaches, and yellows. This gives it a warm, harmonious look. (See the section on choosing a palette in "The Basics.")

TIP

- Select a palette in advance to ensure the final image appears unified in colour.

▷ 3

After filling in the flower with the grey-coloured pencil, use magenta in the darker areas of the flower to add depth and to tie in the colours in adjacent flowers.

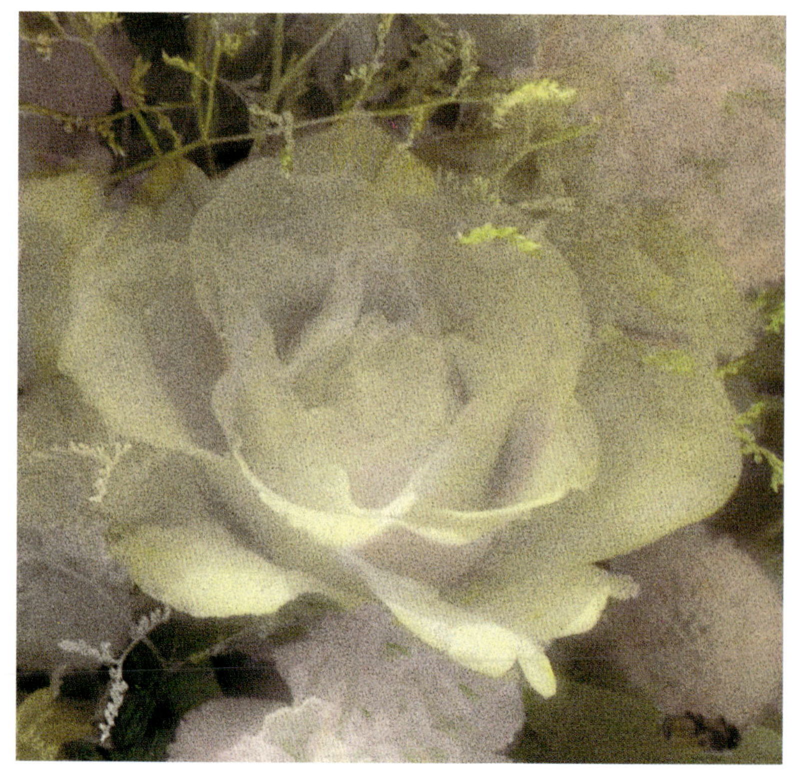

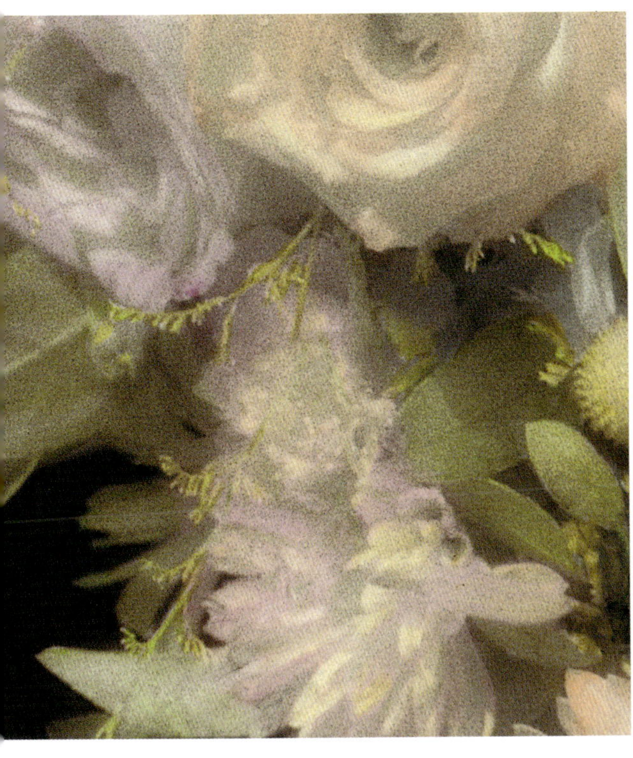

◁ 4

Using the olive-green pencil, colour all the leaves. Then, use the green bice for the sprigs in front of various flowers.

VARIATION

Hand colour selected areas of a toned image for a delicate look.

1. Using a sepia-toned print, colour the rose with scarlet lake. Blend the colour with a small amount of turpentine-and-oil solution.
2. Use olive green in the shadow areas of the rose for depth.
3. Use canary yellow in the highlight areas of the rose to add contour.
4. Colour the sprigs, alternating canary yellow and green bice.
5. Colour the bee with canary yellow to distinguish it from the flower.

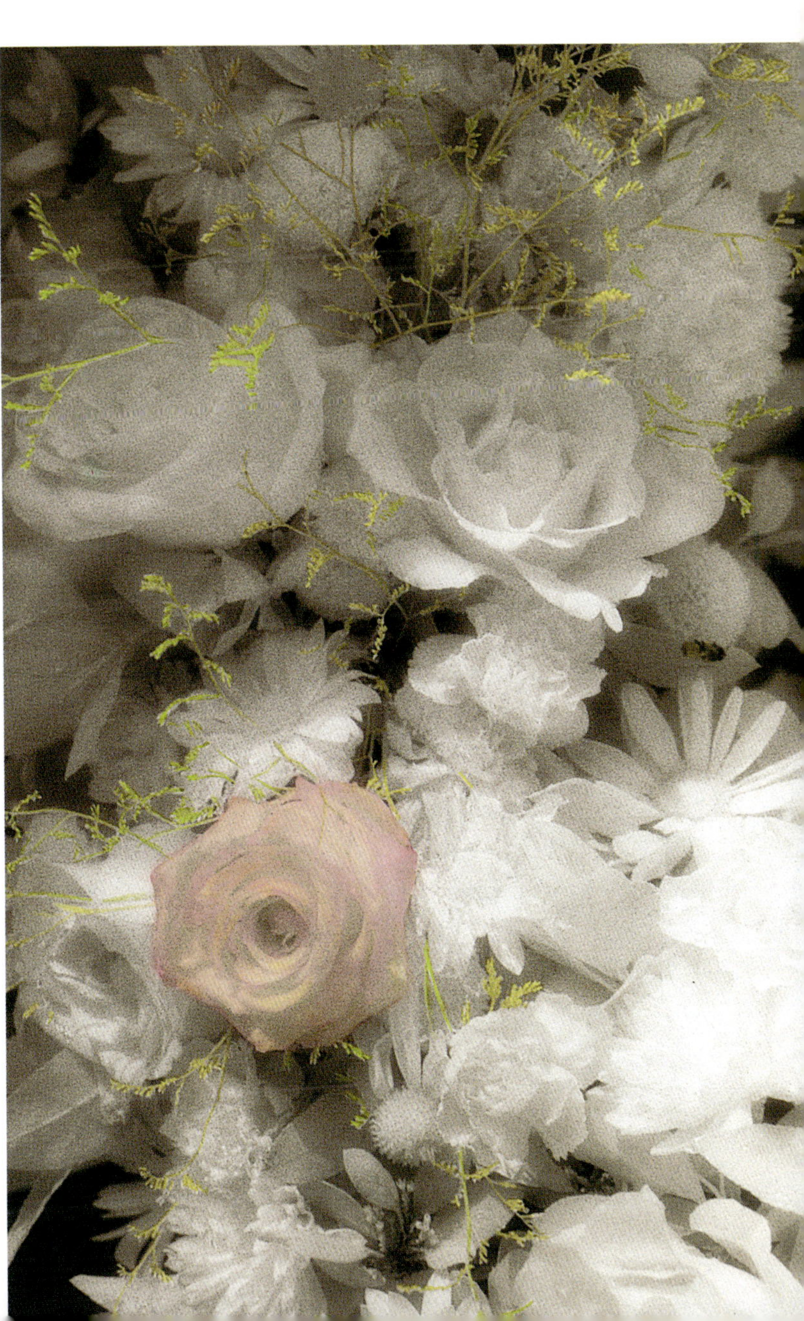

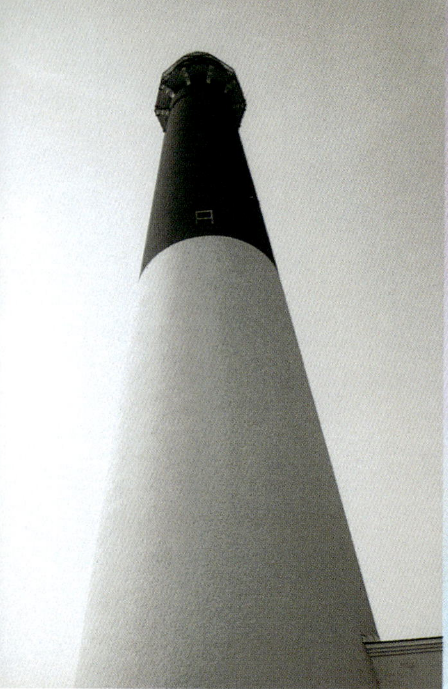

△ The simplicity of this photograph makes it excellent for hand colouring.

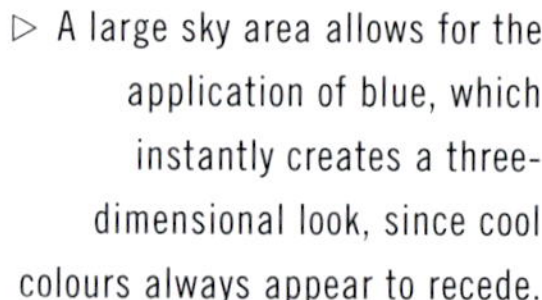

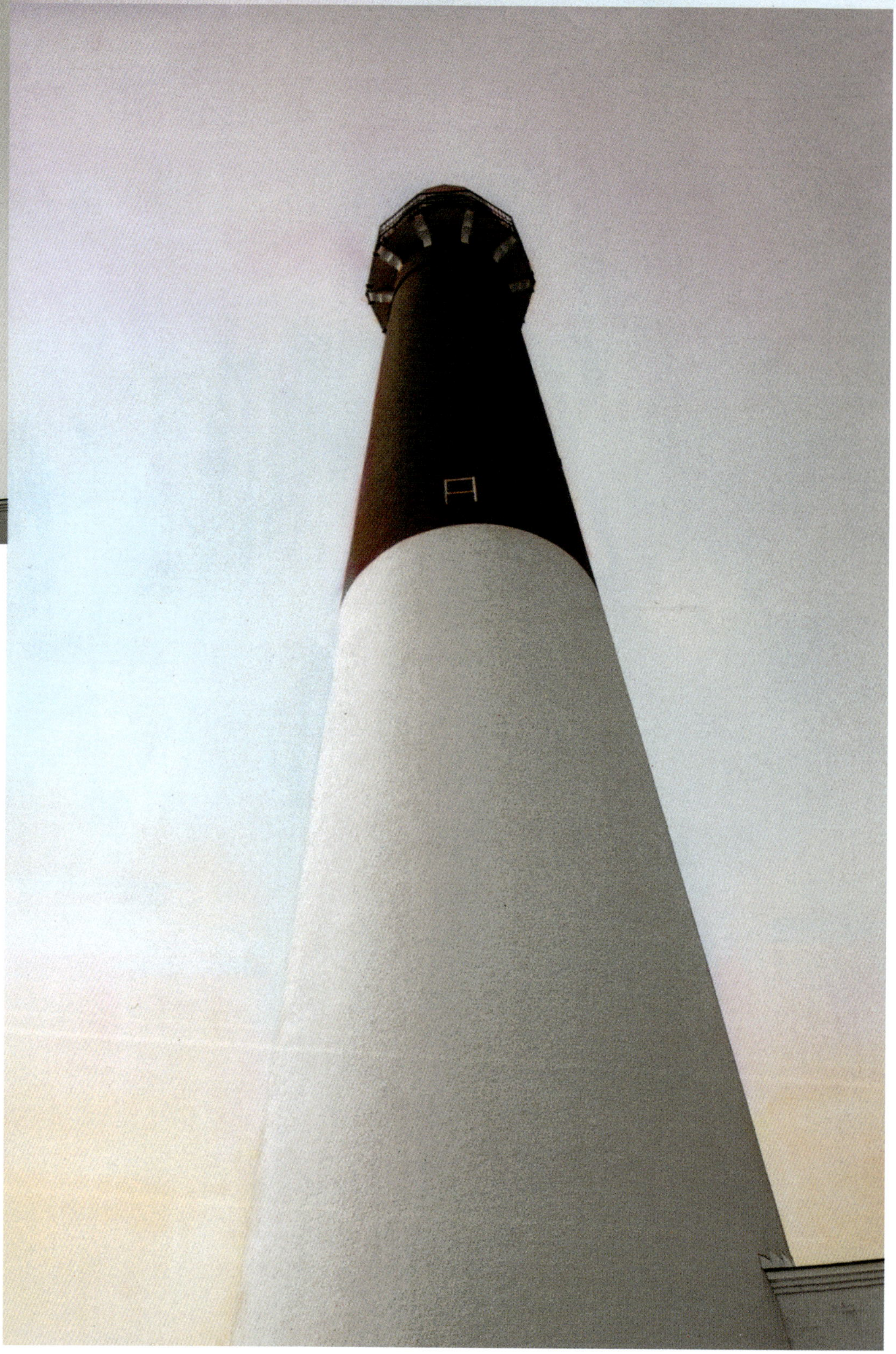

▷ A large sky area allows for the application of blue, which instantly creates a three-dimensional look, since cool colours always appear to recede.

Hand Colouring Architecture

GETTING STARTED

Photographing architecture of all kinds can be great fun. You can create a personal postcard, for example, using a photo of your home, boat, or car to send to friends or family. Just have a 4 x 6 or 5 x 7 black-and-white print made on matte paper from the negative, and then add some colour. On the reverse side, create the look of a store-bought postcard by adding a dividing line down the middle and lines for the address with a fine-point permanent marker. Alternatively, you can buy a premade stamp at a craft store. Keep in mind that after the photograph goes through the mail, it will have been stamped by the post office and will probably look a little worn. These nuances are part of the beauty of postcard art.

MATERIALS

- black-and-white print on matte-surface paper
- coloured pencils: true blue, vermilion red, magenta, grape, aqua marine, terracotta, light violet, dahlia purple, warm grey 20%, Tuscan red
- cotton balls
- toothpicks
- cotton swabs
- turpentine-and-oil solution
- fine-point permanent marker (optional)
- transparent tape (optional)

TRUE BLUE

TERRACOTTA

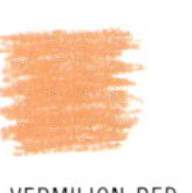

VERMILION RED

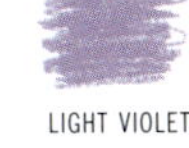

LIGHT VIOLET

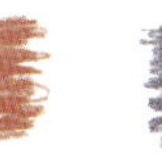

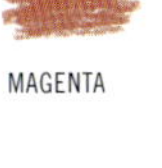

MAGENTA

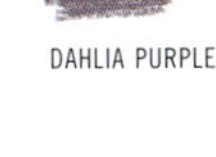

DAHLIA PURPLE

GRAPE

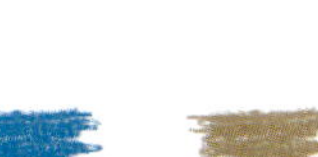

WARM GREY 20%

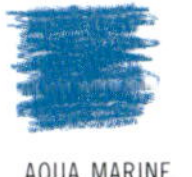

AQUA MARINE

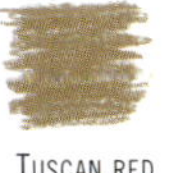

TUSCAN RED

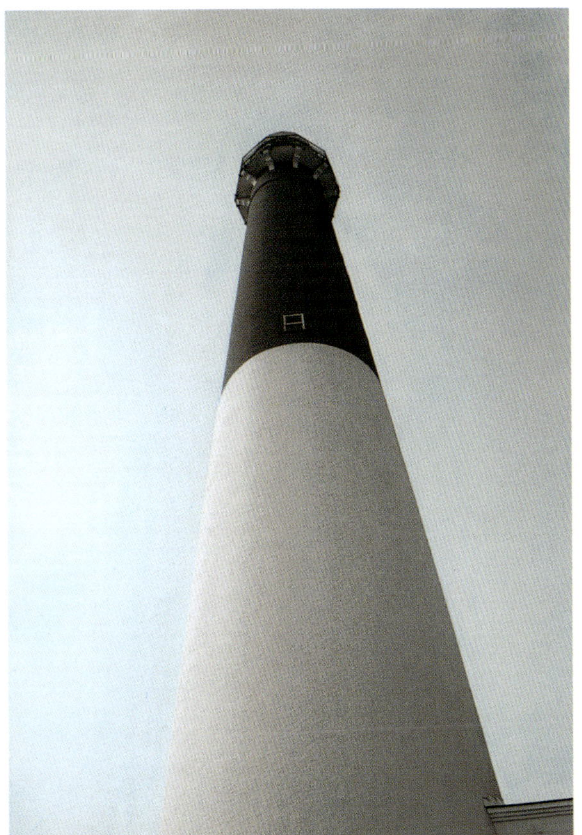

▷ 1

Begin with the sky, using the true blue pencil.

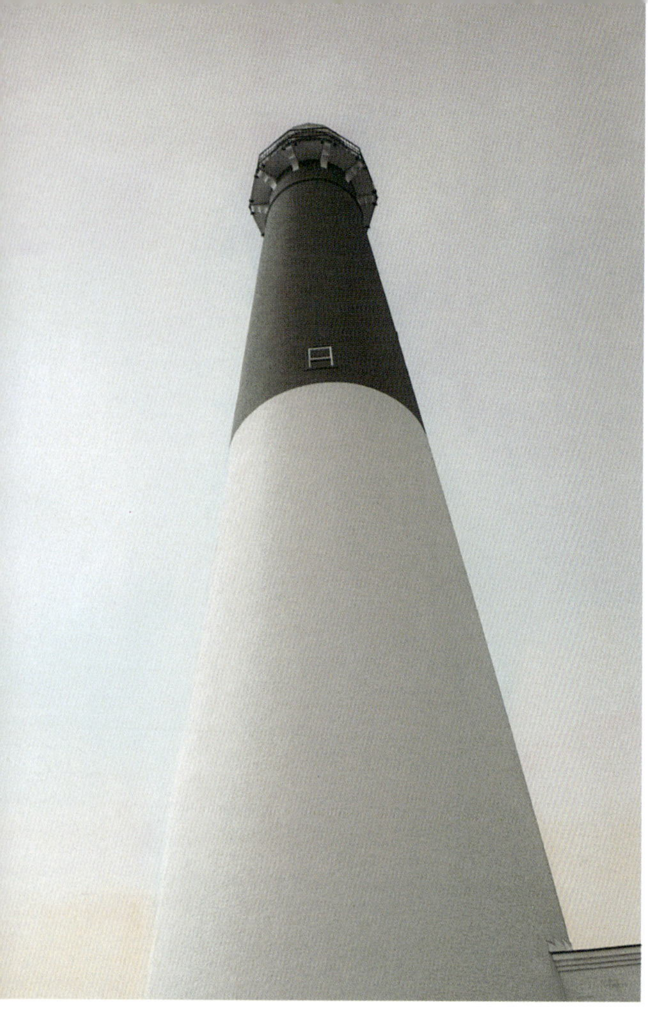

TIPS

- If colour bleeds from one area into another, use the tip of a toothpick wrapped tightly in cotton and dampened with water to erase it or to clean up edges.
- Try applying the turpentine-and-oil solution before applying the colour. Experiment and see which order works best for you.
- Use the solution on a cotton swab to blend in the colour, and remove the pencil strokes with a cotton ball.
- To prevent the blue sky colour from bleeding into other areas, mask these areas with transparent tape and remove the tape after the colour has been smoothed in.

△ 2

Enhance the mood of an image by adding different colours to the sky area. Apply vermilion red to the horizon area and magenta directly above that. Feather the two colours together so it's not apparent where one begins and the other ends.

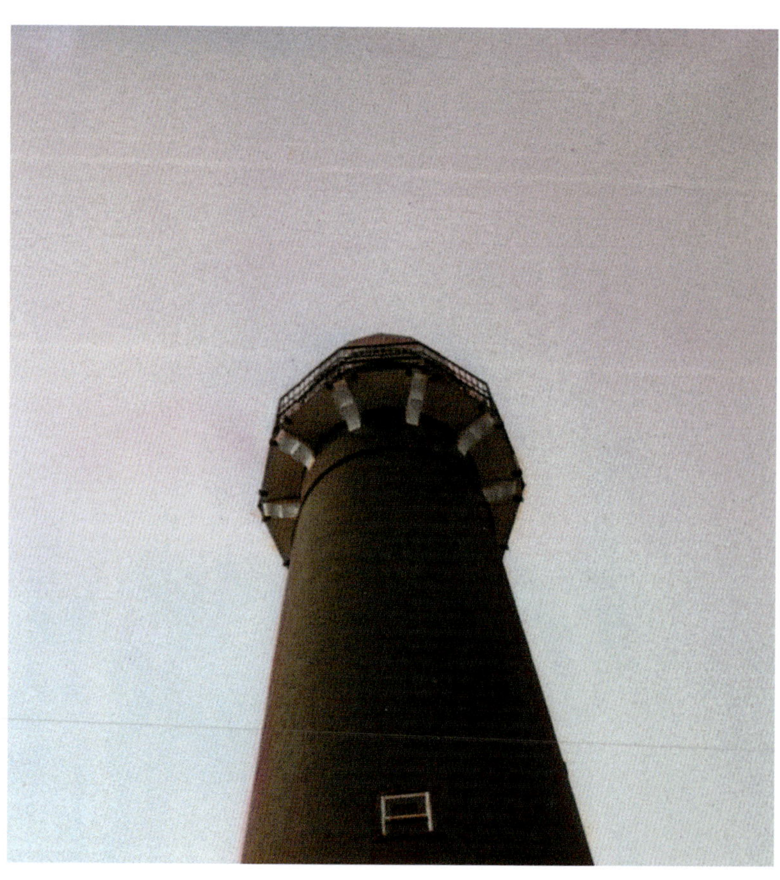

▷ 3

Above the magenta, use the grape pencil to darken the top of the sky. This creates the illusion of depth, since it separates the top of the lighthouse from the receding sky. To enhance this effect, add aqua marine along the top of the print.

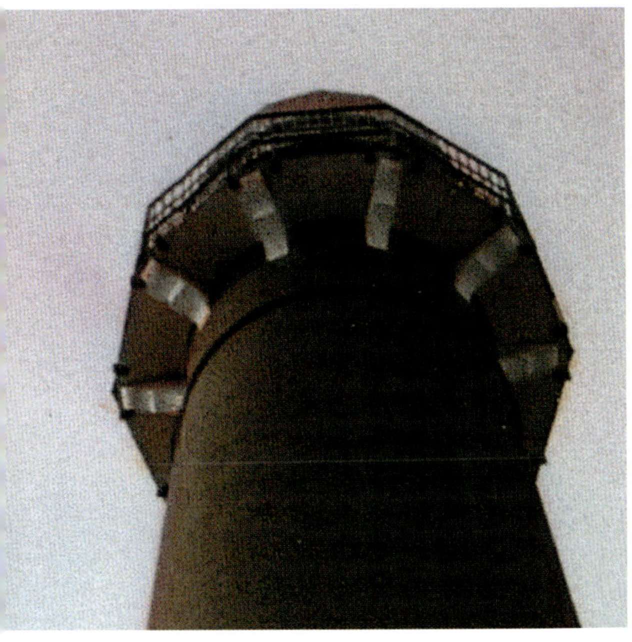

◁ 4

Use terracotta for the top of the lighthouse. Notice how colour applied in dark areas of a print has a subtle appearance.

VARIATION

Use varied colours for a dramatic sky.

1. Mask the lighthouse with tape.
2. Start at the bottom of the sky, using the grey-coloured pencil.
3. Use the pink pencil above the area coloured with grey, and blend the two colours where they meet with a little solution.
4. Use the light violet pencil above the pink.
5. Finish the sky area with the dahlia purple pencil.
6. Use the grey-coloured pencil in the sky around the lighthouse to make it look like it's glowing.
7. Use a cotton ball to blend the whole sky area after all the colours have been applied.
8. Remove the tape from the lighthouse. Use Tuscan red for the upper section, leaving the very top uncoloured, and remove any colour from the window. Colour the bottom section of the lighthouse canary yellow.

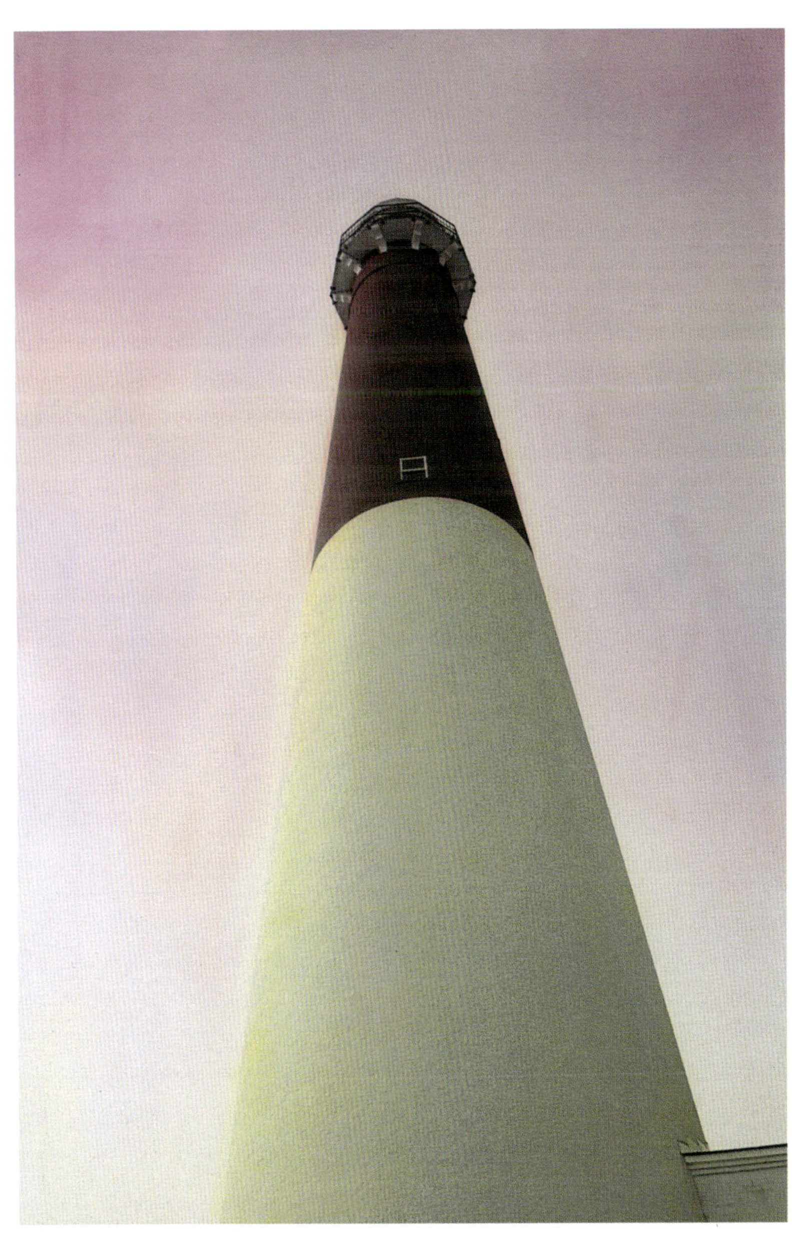

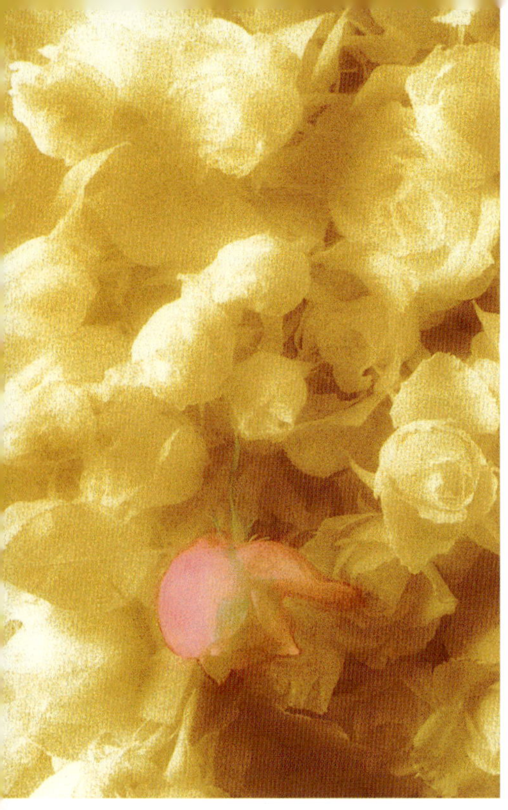

ADVANCED TECHNIQUES

With time, you'll get a feel for hand colouring and the effects it can produce. Then, consider trying another method to colour black-and-white prints. Experiment with a variety of materials, such as oil paints, watercolours, or markers, to name a few. Make collages using your prints and other supplies from around the house. Some of these mediums will yield a heavier colour treatment as well as texture (brush-strokes, finger marks, etc.).

Change the overall colour of a print with household products such as grape juice, fabric dyes, coffee, tea, and food colouring. Anything that stains will work. Toners and nonorganic dyes are also an option. By making multiple prints of one image and trying different techniques on them, you can gain a better understanding of what effects each method produces. Keep records of what you do in case you want to re-create the result.

In this section, we'll look at toning, staining, dyeing, and painting with oils. Mix and match the different processes for different effects. By the time the artwork is finished, you may not even recognize it as having originated as a photograph!

▷ This photo was hand coloured with both oils and coloured pencils.

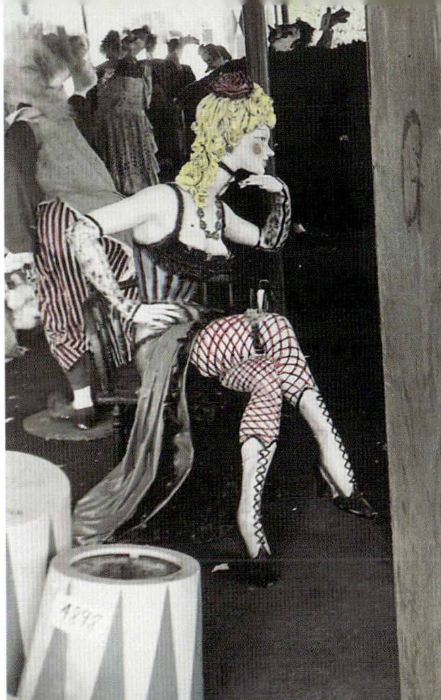

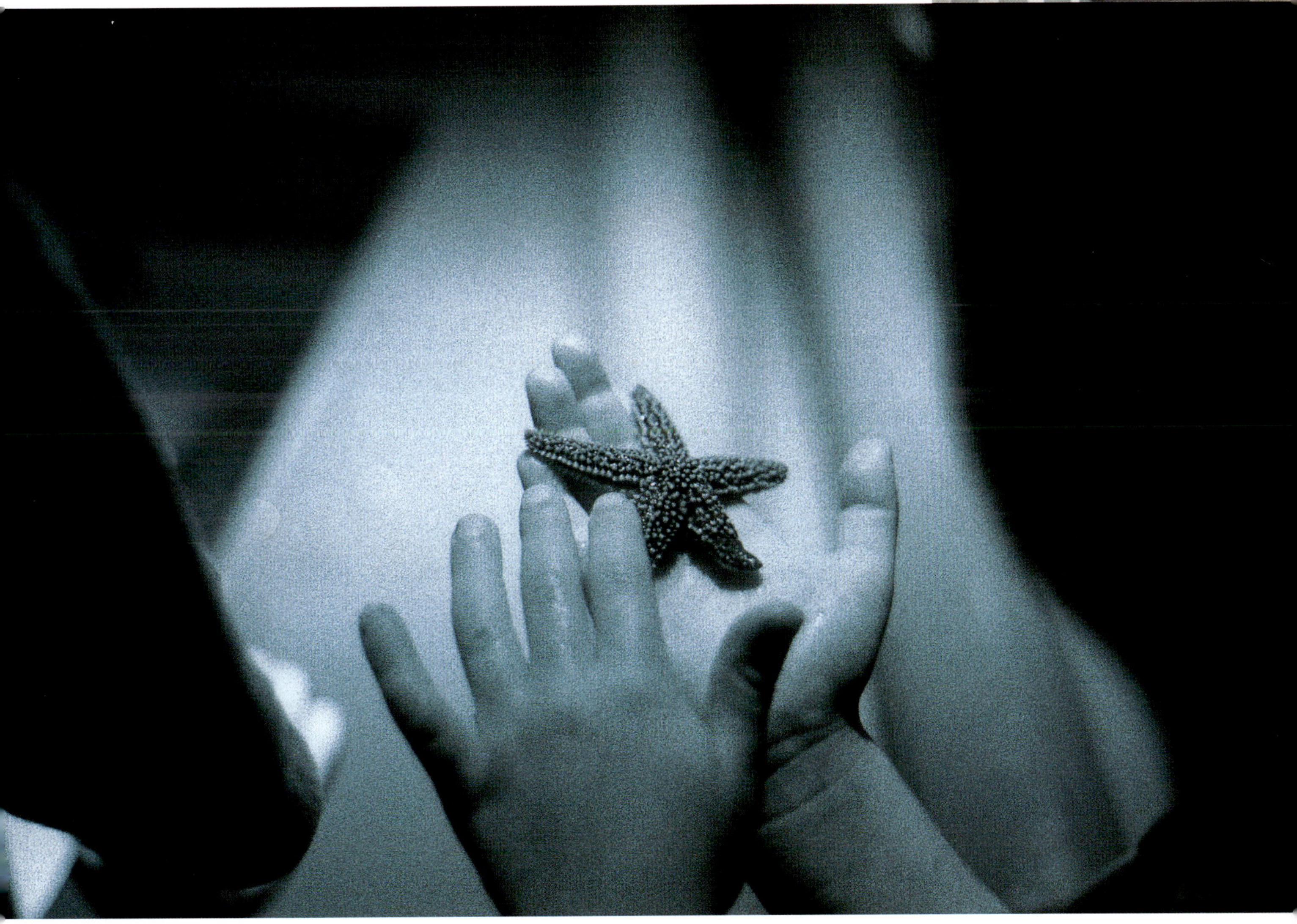

△ Blue toner was used to change the overall colour of this image.

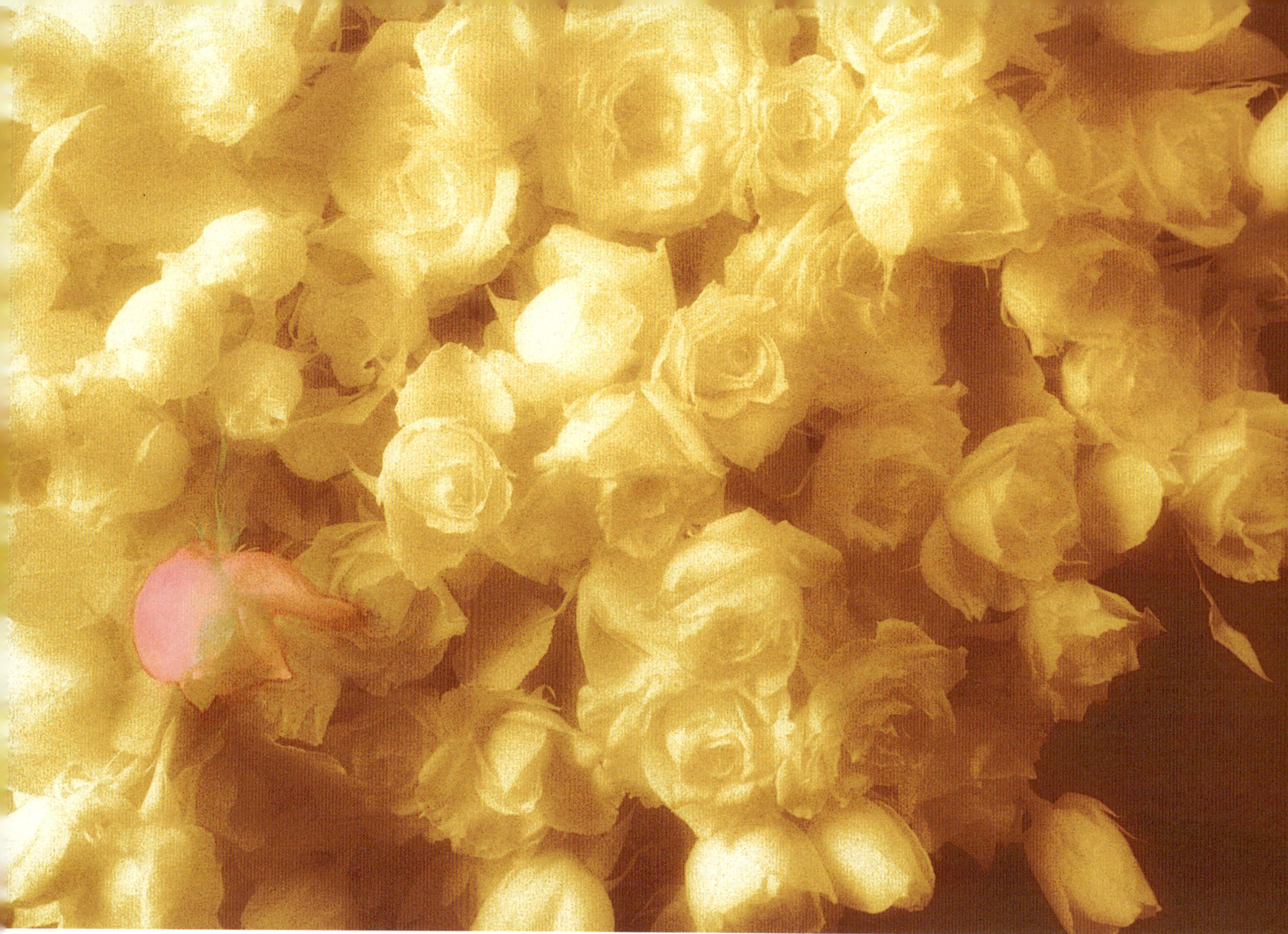

△ This photograph was toned and hand coloured.

Working with Other Mediums

Choose a medium based on the desired effect. To change the overall colour of the print, use toner, stains, or dyes, or create a wash using pencils or oils. For a textured look, try crayons or acrylics. To obscure the image, use an opaque medium such as air brushing, spray paint, acrylics, or oil pastels. You may want to mix mediums, adding bold, graphic lines of intense colour with markers or metallic pens, or colouring with oil paints and using coloured pencils for fine details. Try extending the image into the white borders of the print with pen and ink. Experiment with watercolours. Liquid or tube watercolours are more vibrant and work best on fibre-based paper, but mistakes are harder to remove, and the colours fade more rapidly.

▷ Coloured pencils and oils added life to this photo.

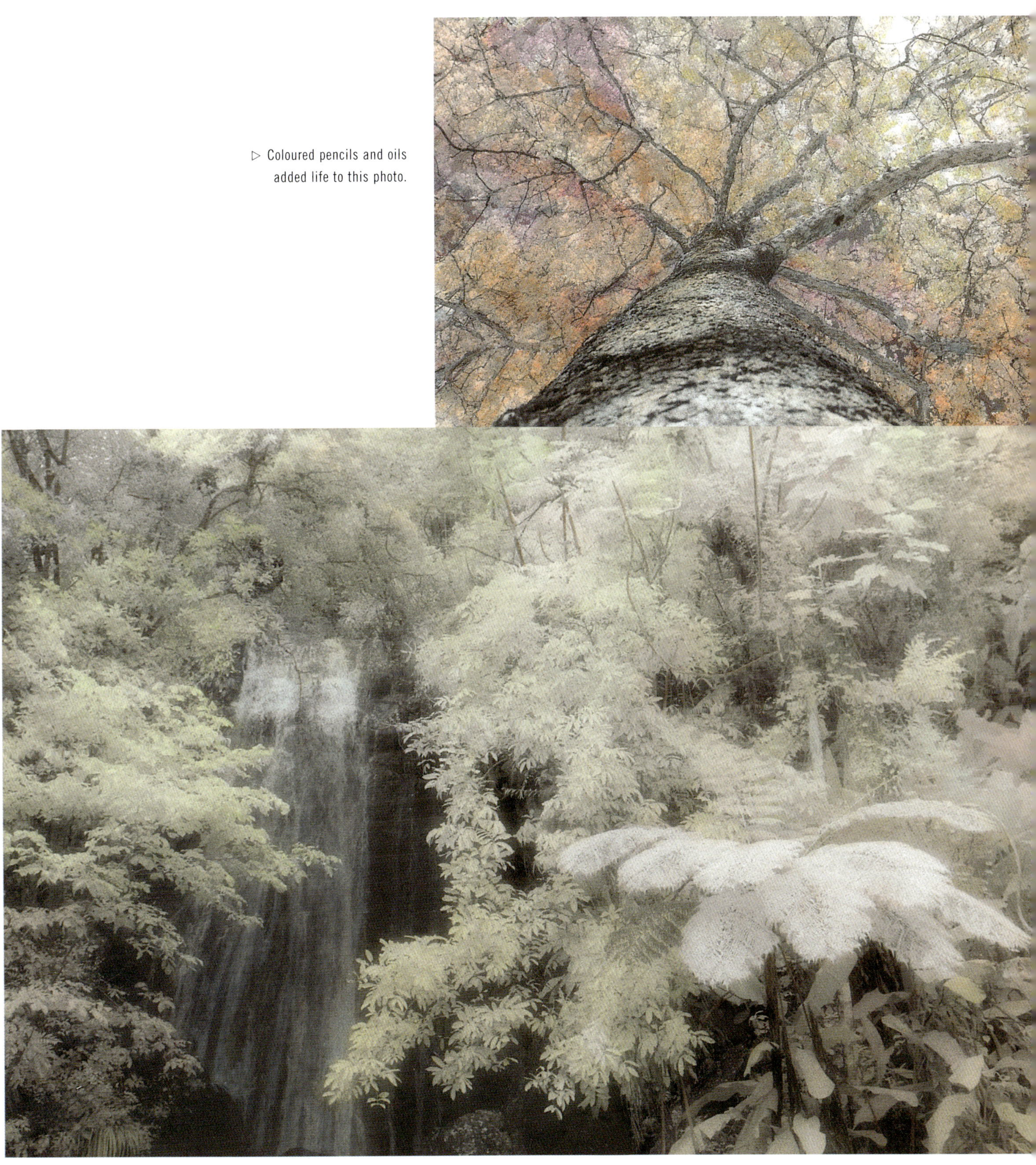

△ Oils create a dreamy effect

▽ This photograph was toned brown and hand coloured.

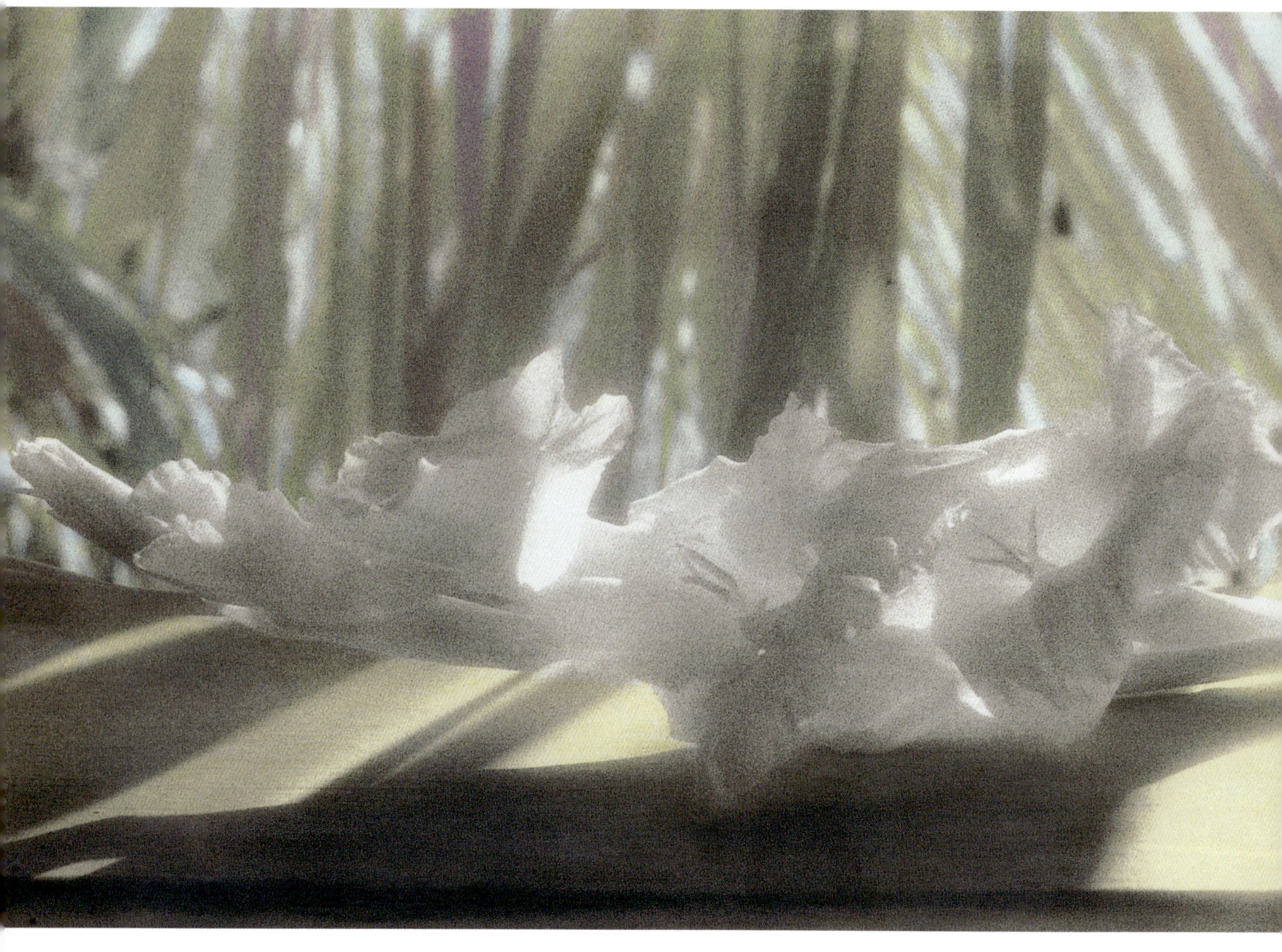

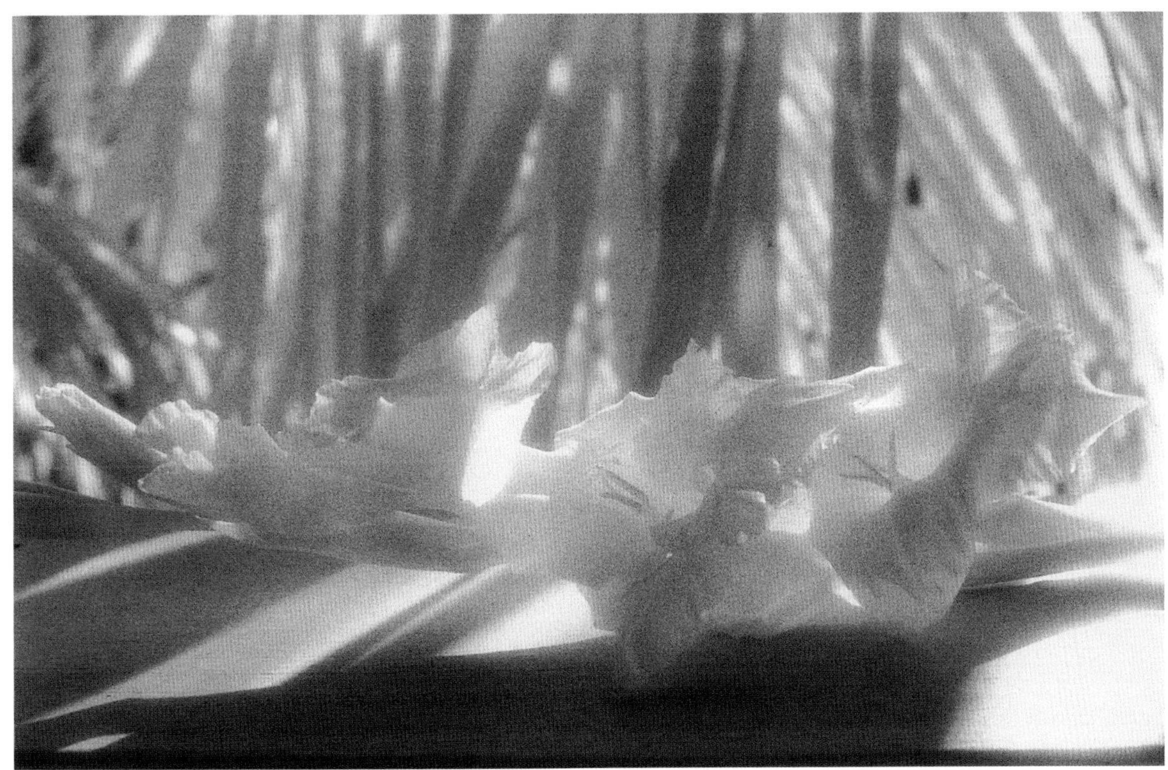

◁ This photograph was simply toned.

Toners

What images tone best? Most toners are very vibrant in colour, so strong, bold images work well. The most popular toner is sepia toner, which gives the image a timeless, antique look. Get a feel for the image first, and then you'll have a better idea of whether or not to tone the print and which toner to use.

Toner will affect different parts of a photo differently. White and highlight areas in the print will take on the exact colour of the toner, but the colour will look darker in mid-tone and shadow areas. It's a good idea to keep an extra, untoned print handy as a reference to gauge how heavily to tone the image. The effects of the toner also depend on the kind and brand of paper the photograph was printed on, whether the print is matte or semimatte, the toner type, how diluted the toner is, and how long the image is toned.

If you're interested in hand colouring part of the print after toning it, use rubber cement to mask that part of the print before toning. The colour will be more vibrant that way. As a rule, when combining hand colouring and toning, always do the hand colouring last.

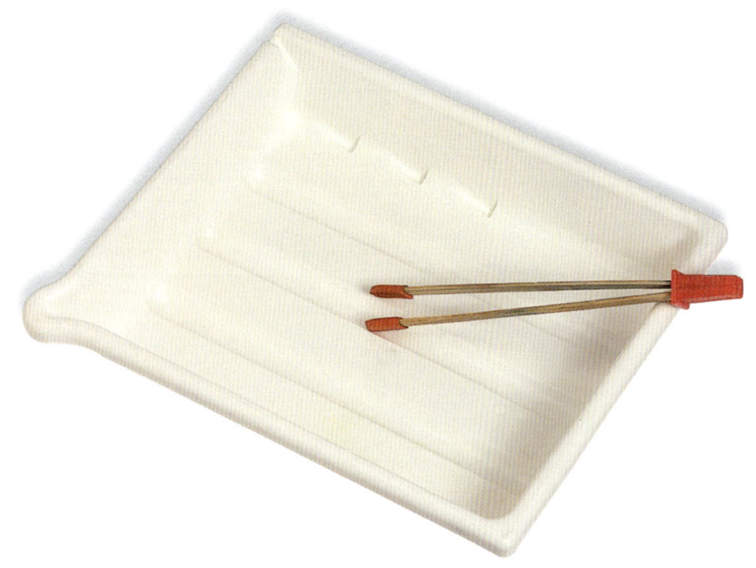

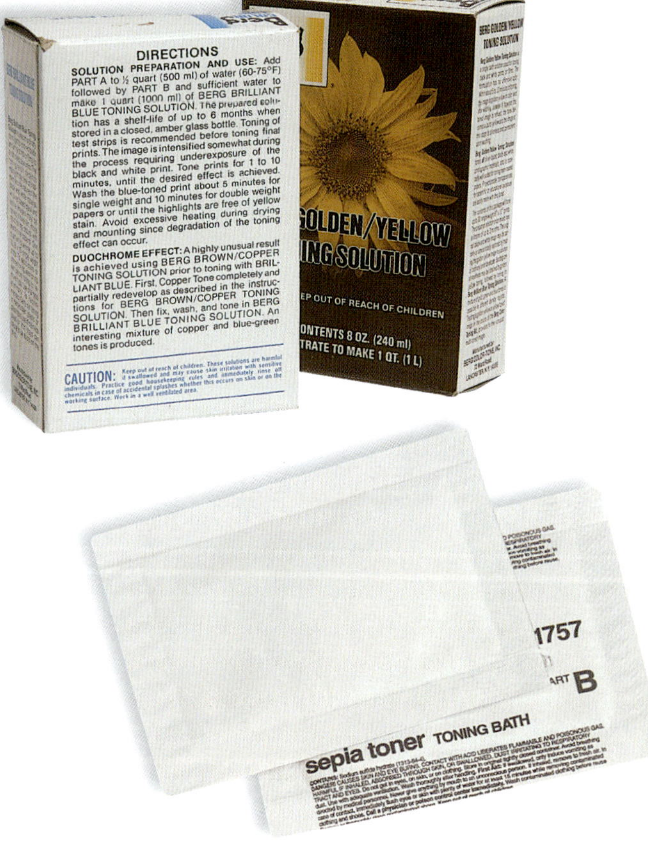

There are many different types and brands of toners on the market today, and photographic supply stores are the best place to find them. Some are in liquid form, some come as a powder. Some have one or two steps, some require many steps. Some toners are odourless, while others are not. Some are safe to use in the kitchen and around children, but the majority are not.

Toners can be reused if they are stored properly. Never use metal trays when working with toners, since these materials interact chemically. Use photographic trays because they are made of a heavy plastic and are meant solely for this purpose (unlike food trays).

Many toning processes include a bleach step. With these, make sure your images are 10–15% darker than they'd normally be printed. If you've never toned an image before, keep it simple: One toner per print. And remember: Always read the directions.

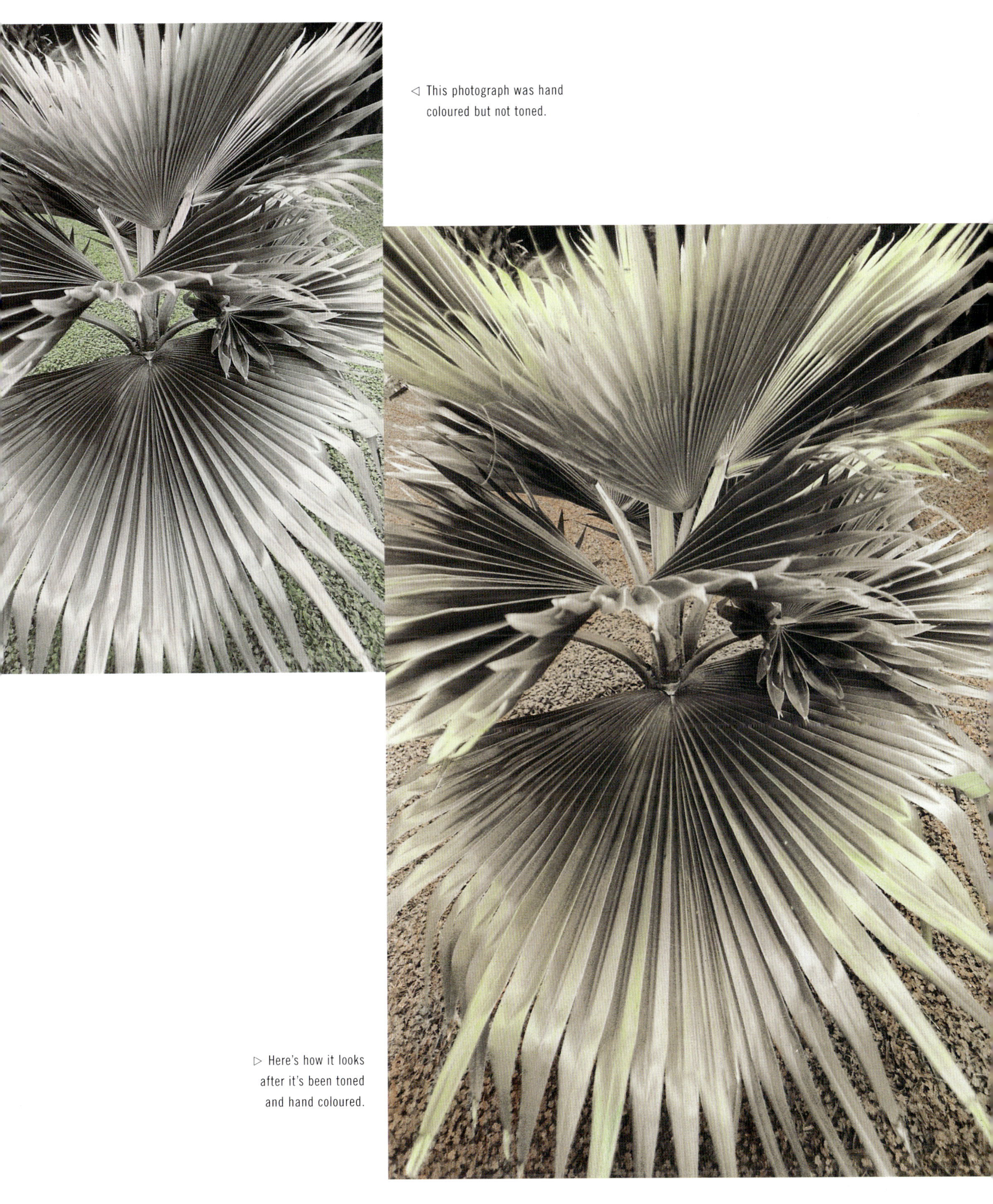

◁ This photograph was hand coloured but not toned.

▷ Here's how it looks after it's been toned and hand coloured.

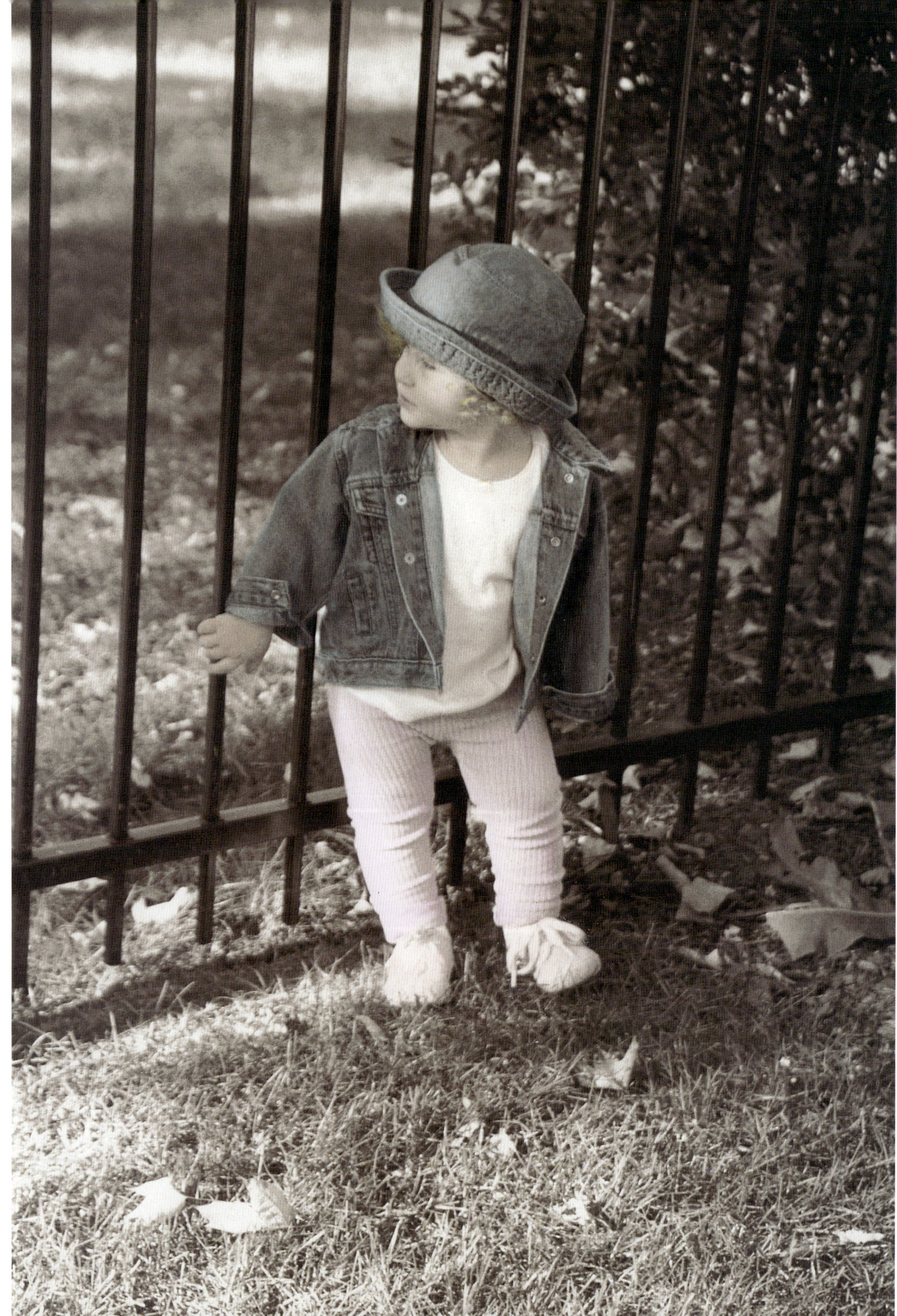

Sepia Toning

GETTING STARTED

This photograph was chosen for sepia toning because the toner's brown colour would lend the image warmth. It also would make the image appear timeless, giving a sense that this photograph could have been taken years ago. Toning and then hand colouring a print such as this one gives it a totally different feel, especially if it's hand coloured with warm colours.

MATERIALS

- black-and-white print on matte-surface paper, printed slightly darker than normal
- coloured pencils: sky blue, apple green, hot pink, light violet, orange
- rubber cement
- five trays
- two pairs of tongs (wooden or plastic)
- measuring cup
- sepia toner
- two dark plastic quart-size jugs for storing toner, one labelled "A," the other labelled "B"
- rubber gloves (optional)
- cotton swabs
- turpentine-and-oil solution

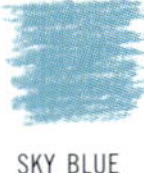
SKY BLUE

APPLE GREEN

HOT PINK

LIGHT VIOLET

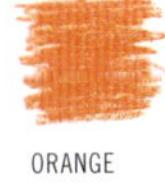
ORANGE

 1

Follow the instructions on the package for mixing, storing, and toning the toner in a well-ventilated area away from young children. (None of this, however, needs to be done in a darkroom or under subdued light.) The toner used in this example is a two-part toner, which can be mixed in advance and stored in dark jugs. Set up five trays next to each other. The first will be a pre-wash and holding tray for prints to be toned. In the second tray, pour enough of part "A" solution, which is the bleach step. Put one set of tongs in solution "A." Use only one set of tongs for each part—don't interchange them. The third tray is for washing the print in running water in between the chemical steps. In the fourth tray, pour solution "B," the brown toner, and add a pair of tongs. The last tray will be for rinsing the print in running water when you've finished toning.

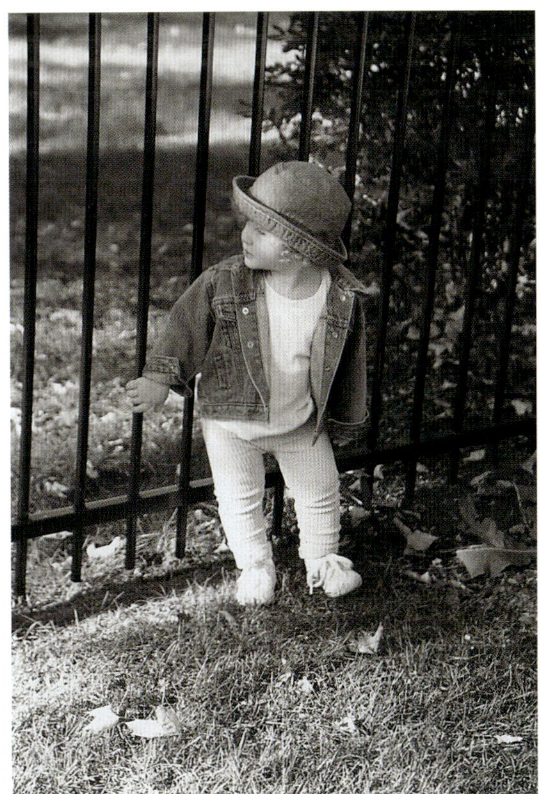

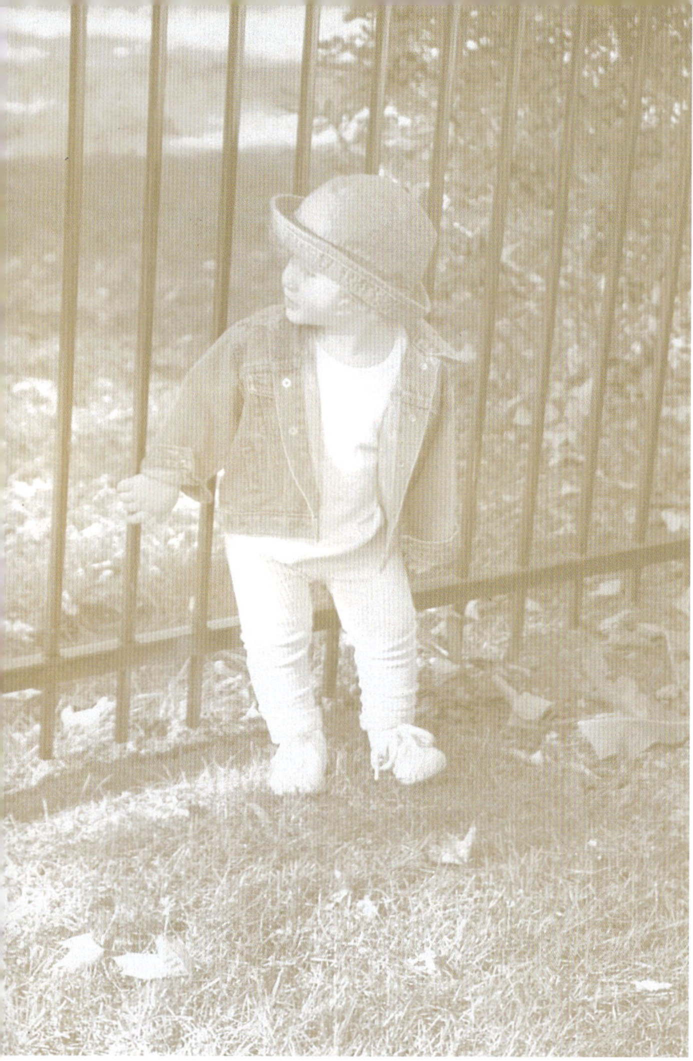

△ 2

Bleach until the shadows start to disappear. This print has been bleached for the full amount of time. The print will have a yellowish cast after being bleached.

▽ 3

The browns from the toners will fill in the bleached areas, creating the sepia tones.

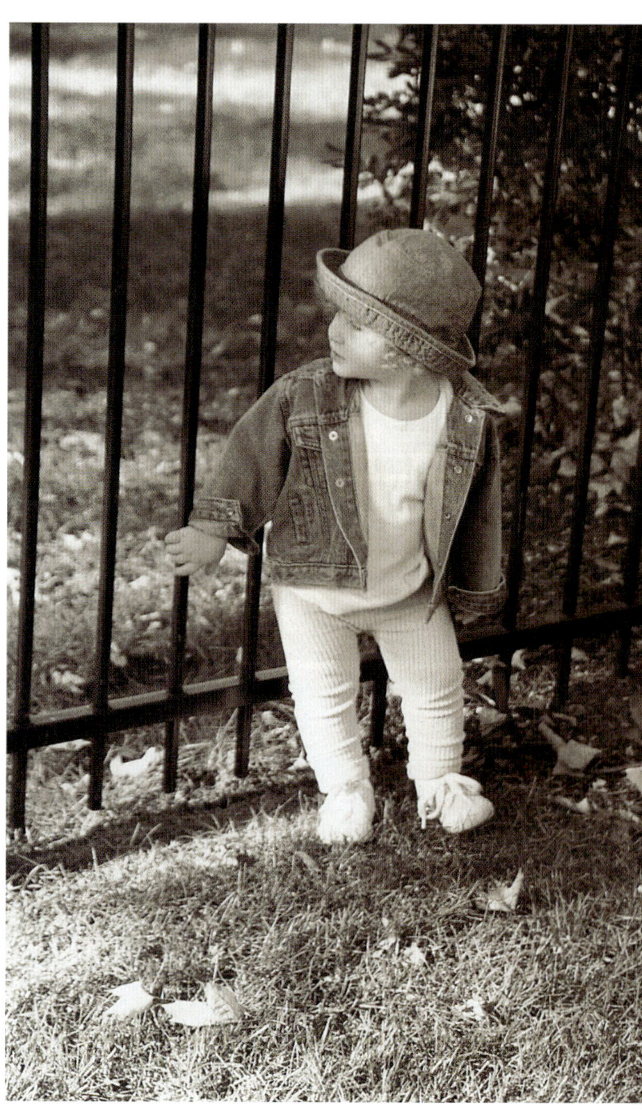

TIP

- When bleaching a photograph, don't worry about losing the image; the image must bleach out. Bleaching is necessary so the brown tones can exist, which is why prints you plan to sepia tone should be darker than usual.

VARIATION

Use multiple toners to make key areas stand out.

1. Rubber cement was applied to the girl before the print was toned. This prevented bleach or toner from affecting that part of the print. As a result, the masked area has the original tones, which can be coloured later or left as is. To use another toner colour, mask the background with rubber cement, and tone just the girl. Start by using a cotton swab to apply rubber cement to the girl.
2. Tone as per instructions and allow the print to dry.
3. Rub off the rubber cement with your finger, and finish the print by hand colouring or retoning it.

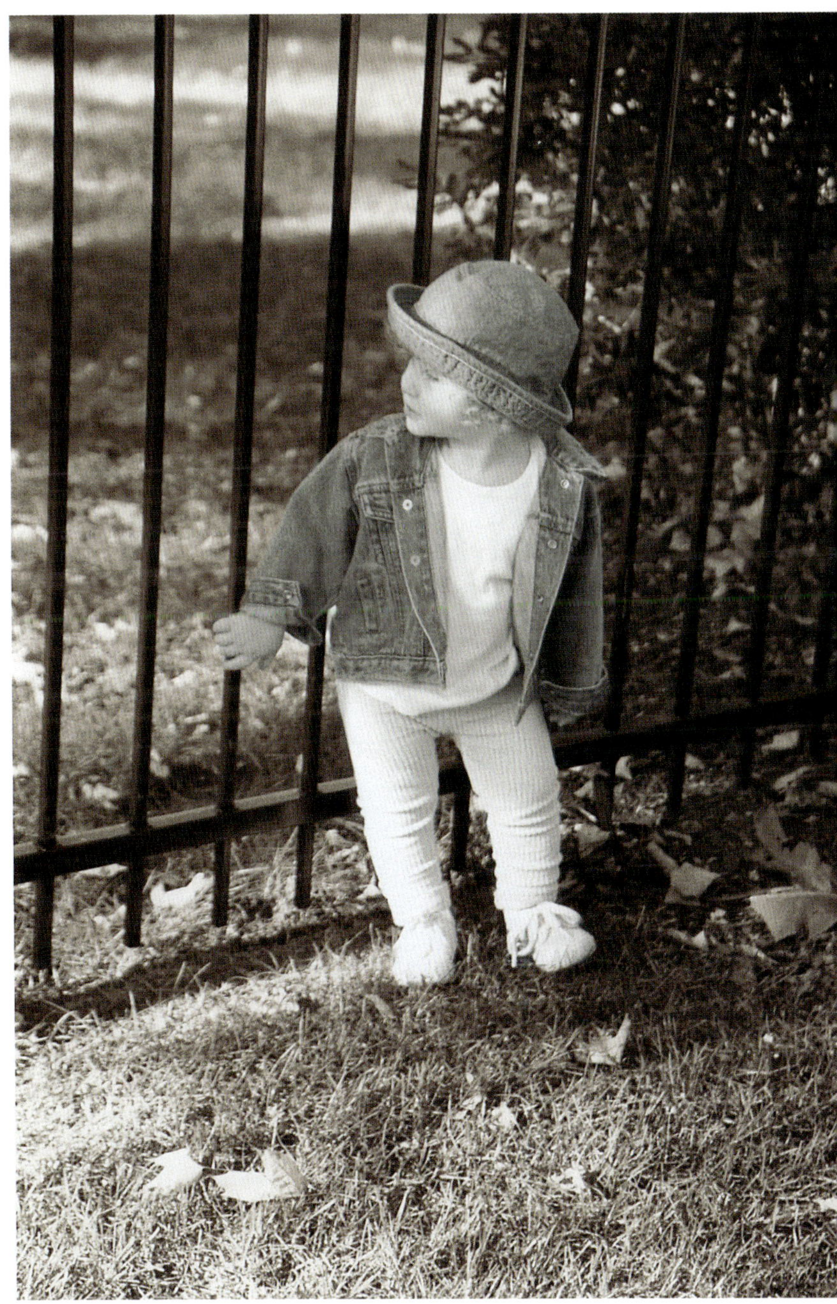

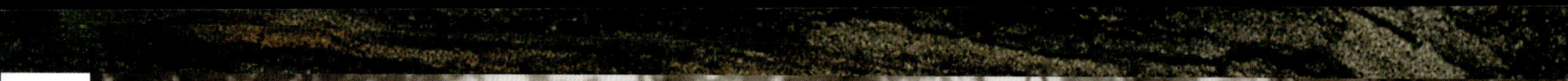

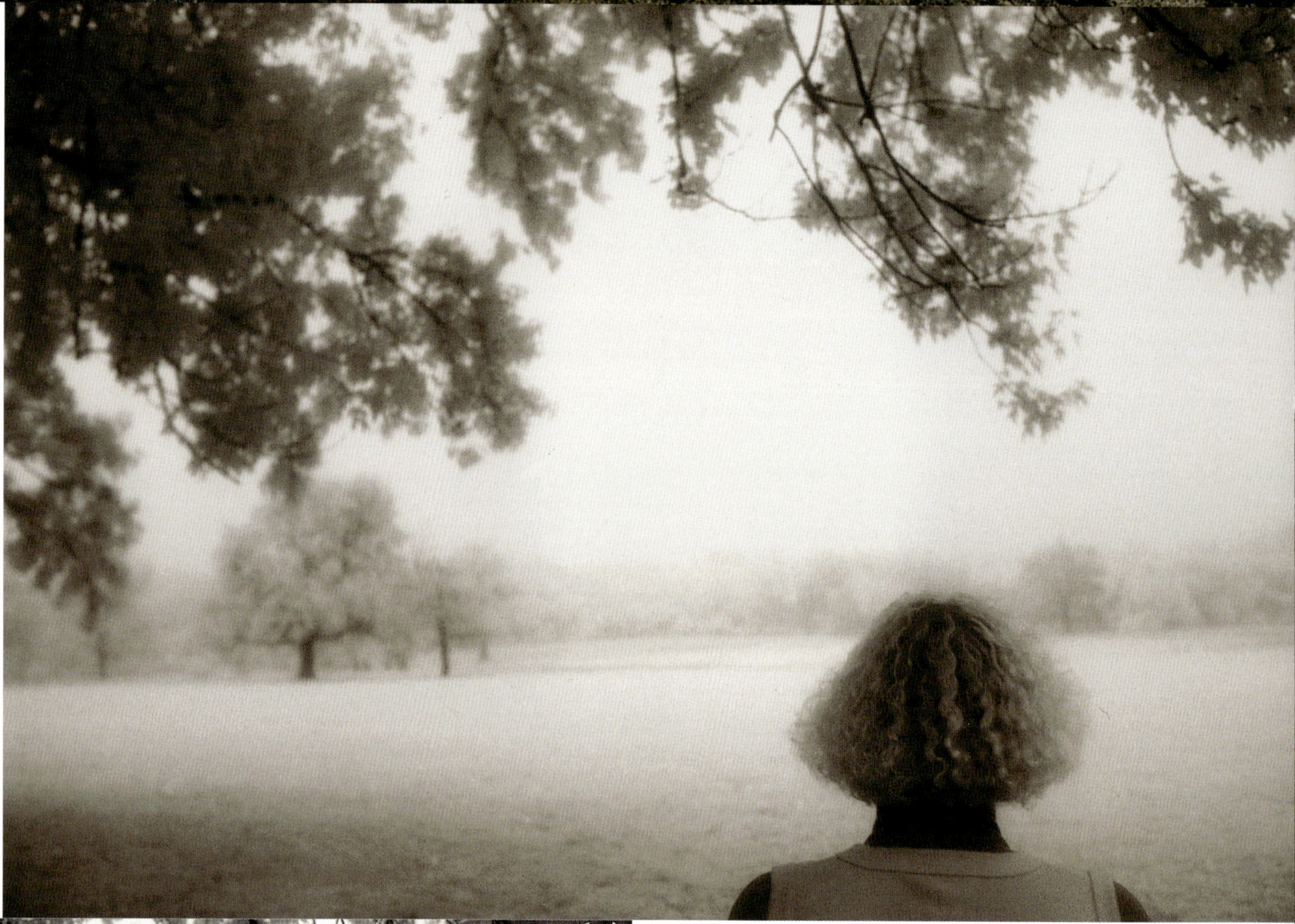

△ This print was toned using copper/red toner, which is a liquid dye. It was left in the toner for only one minute.

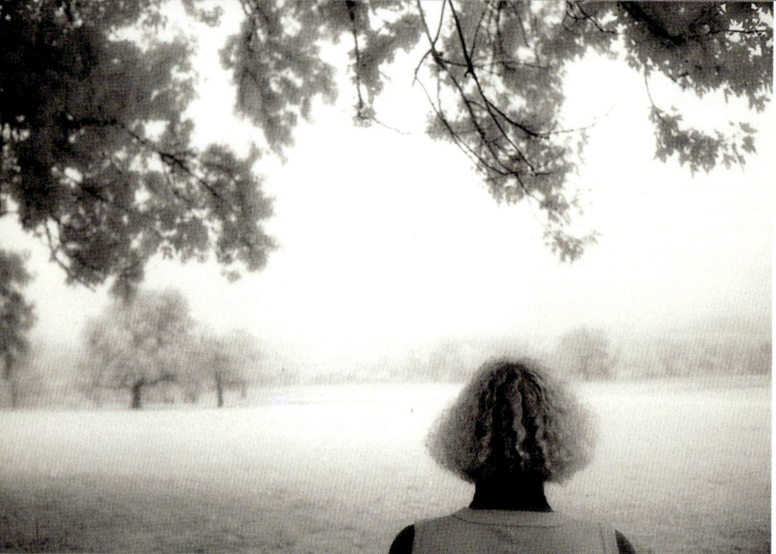

△ This is how the photo looked before it was toned. It is useful to keep one untoned print as a guide. Wet the toned print before comparing it to the one you're working on, because prints are slightly darker when they are wet.

TIP

- The most noticeable effects of toning will be in the shadow areas, but check the whites to see the true colour of the toner.

Toning Photographs

GETTING STARTED

Produce different effects and moods by hand colouring toned and untoned prints. Placing a toned and an untoned print side-by-side is a good way to judge the effects of these experiments. When getting started in hand colouring and toning, make more than one print and compare the results.

MATERIALS

- black-and-white print on matte-surface paper
- measuring cup
- 3–4 trays
- 1–2 pairs of tongs (wooden or plastic)
- 2–4 prints of the same image to experiment with
- blue toner
- red toner
- yellow toner

▽ This print was toned for ten minutes.

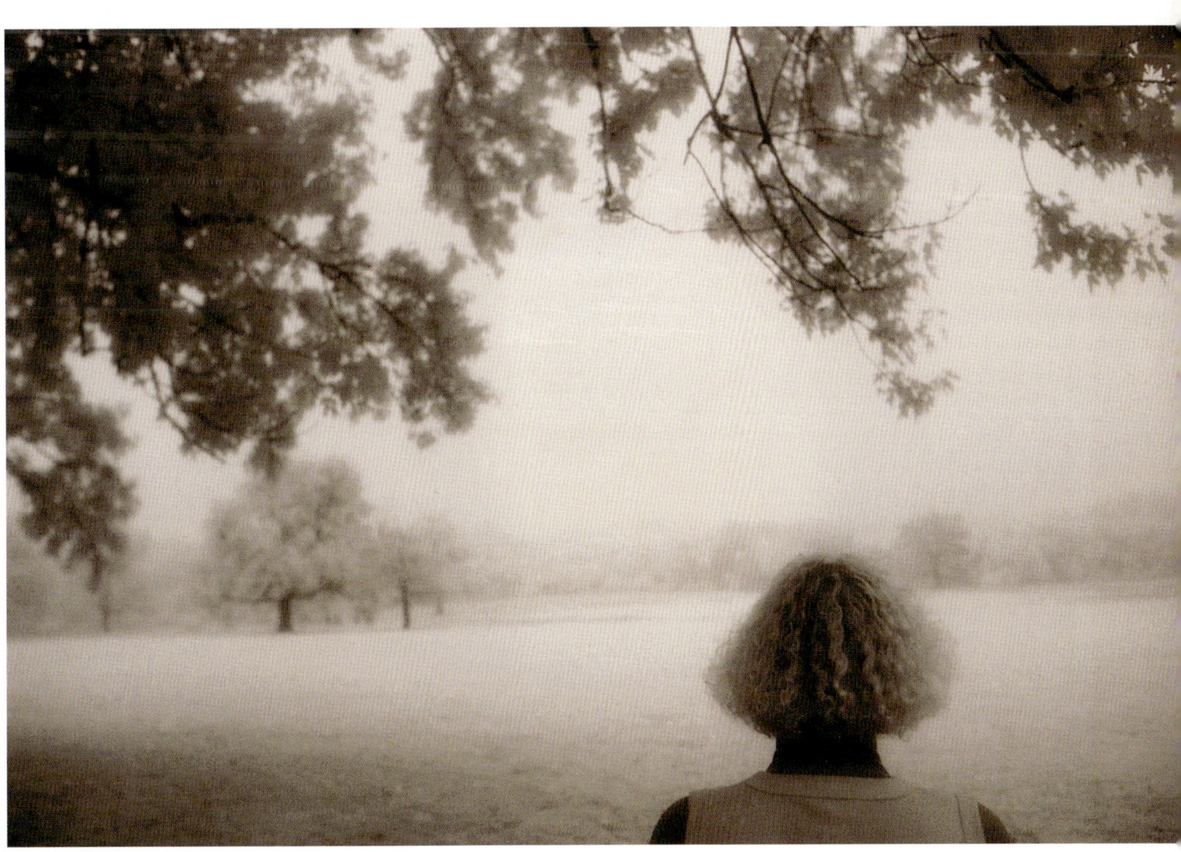

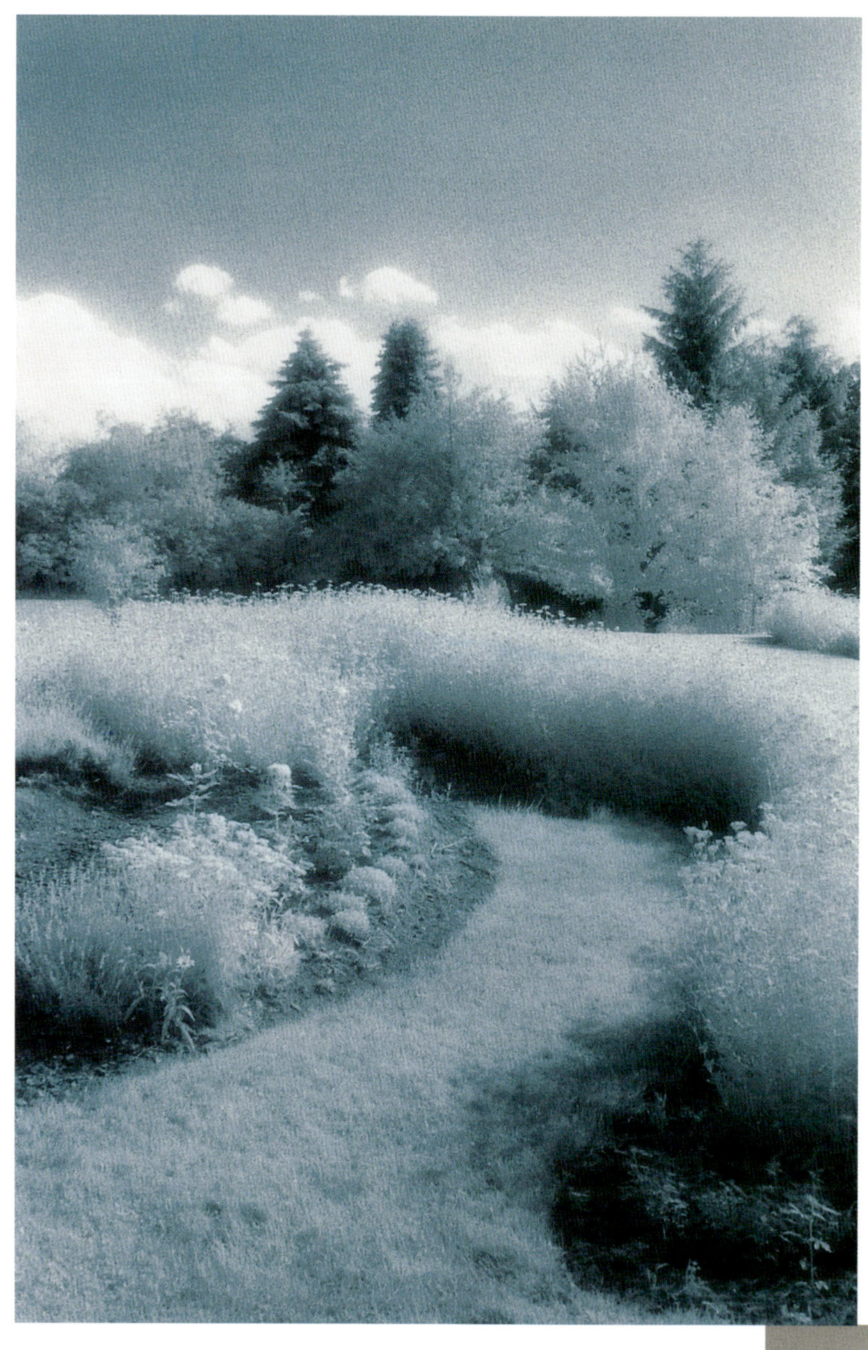

△ This print was toned with blue toner for ten minutes.

▷ This is how the photo looked before it was toned.

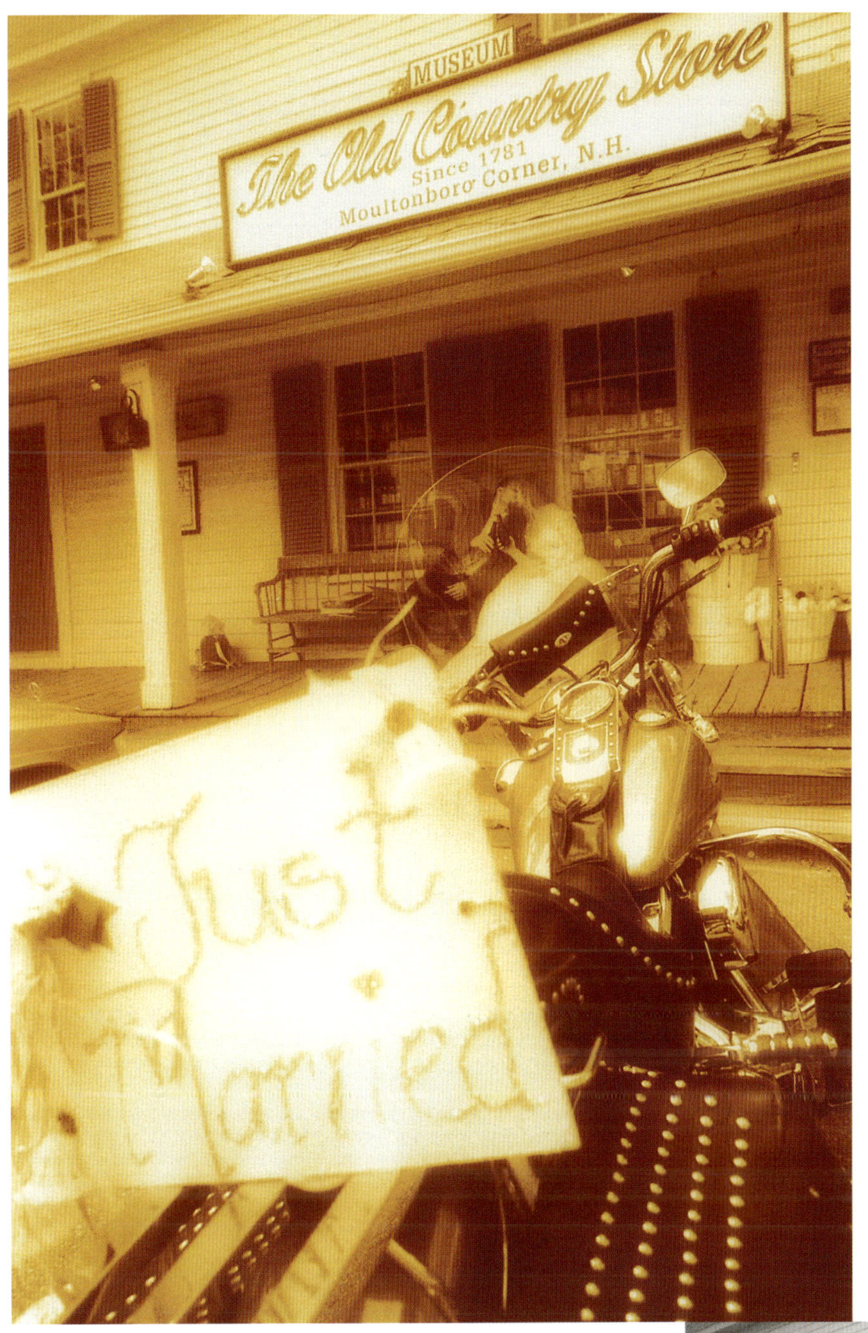

△ This print was toned with yellow toner for ten minutes.

▷ This is how the photo looked before it was toned.

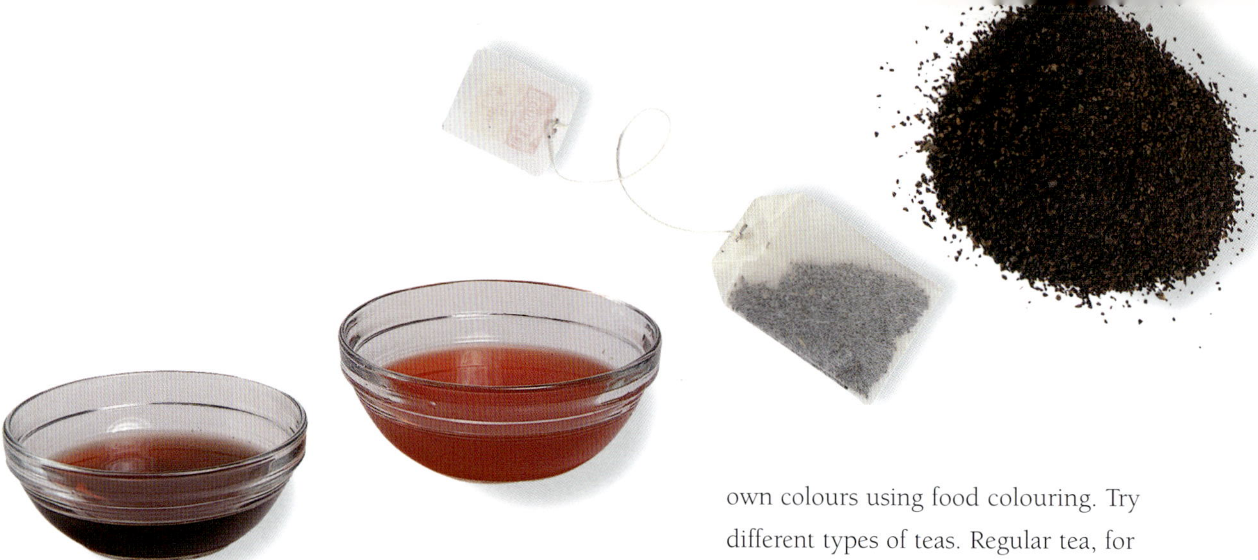

Stains

The following pages contain staining demonstrations that are wonderful projects to do with children. The products used are readily available in many households. In fact, they're typically food items, like fruit punch and coffee, that are non-toxic and can be found in the kitchen. A few stains are mixed with hot water and need to be cooled to room temperature before using (hot liquid can ruin a print).

Since stains are usually less vibrant in colour than toners and dyes, select images that are more subtle. The intensity of the colours can be altered, though, by varying the concentration of the stain and the length of time the print is stained. Keep records of the dilutions used in order to create the same results with a new batch of prints. (Note the dilutions on the back of the print with a waterproof marker.) Experiment with different household foods and see which results you like the best. Try different coloured fruit punches, or create your own colours using food colouring. Try different types of teas. Regular tea, for example, creates a much deeper colour stain than coffee does. Stains can be used over again. Store them in a labeled container in a cool place so they don't become moldy.

Set up a tray with water and soak the print for a minute before staining. This way, the emulsion is already saturated and will take the colour as soon as it goes into the stain bath. After staining it, rinse the print in another tray of running water. (Change the water in this tray frequently.) Wash the print with room-temperature water for approximately five minutes. Take care when drying the print because stain can collect on the back or edges if dried improperly and can drip onto the image, resulting in uneven staining. Always hand colour *after* dyeing or staining the prints.

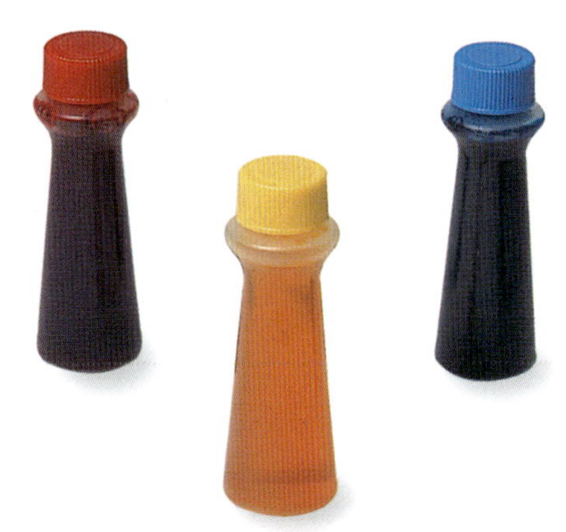

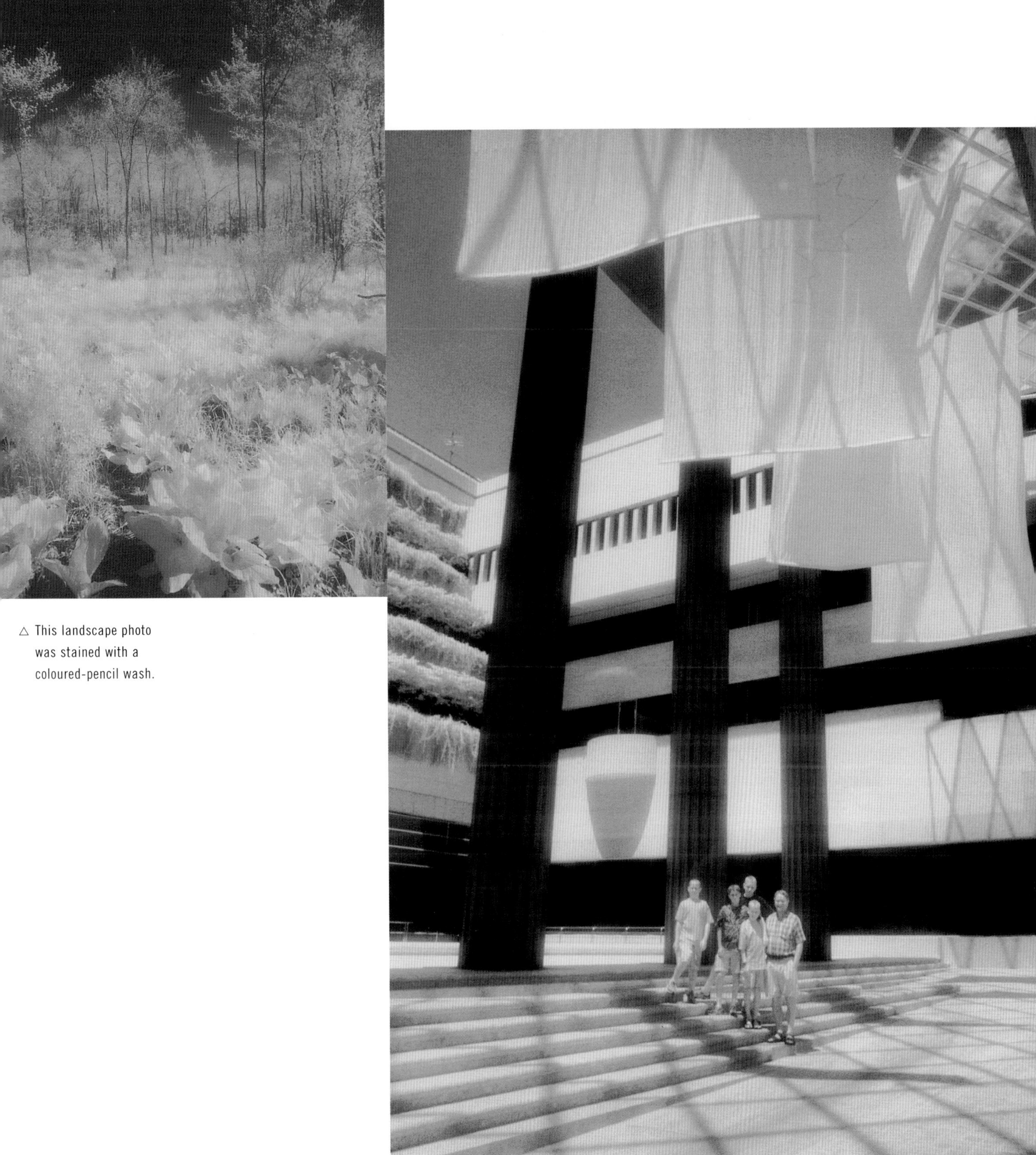

△ This landscape photo was stained with a coloured-pencil wash.

△ This photograph was stained in wine for ten minutes.

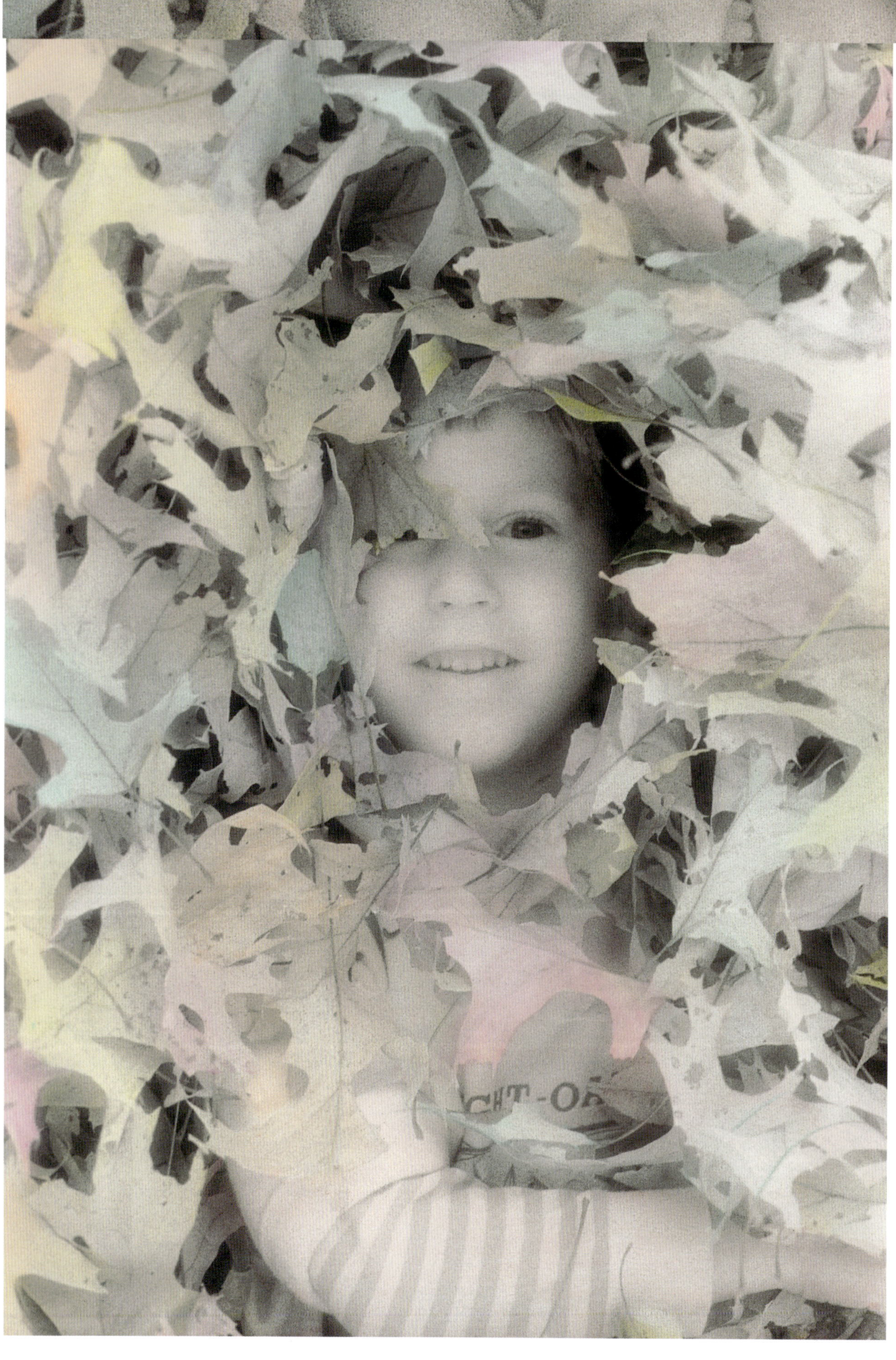

Staining Photographs

GETTING STARTED

Stains are usually less vibrant than toners and dyes. Select an image that contains a lot of highlights (lighter sections) and is subtle, like this photo of a boy looking out from a mass of leaves. This photo was stained with red wine at room temperature and then hand coloured when it was completely dry. Some stains are made with hot water and therefore must be prepared in advance so they have time to cool to room temperature. When staining photos with food colouring or actual food or drinks (such as tea), it's okay to use kitchen trays or pans. Set up two trays: one with water, the other with stain. Use wooden or plastic tongs to keep from staining your hands.

MATERIALS

- black-and-white print on matte-surface paper
- coloured pencils: crimson red, violet, scarlet lake, purple, chartreuse, hot pink, apple green, salmon pink, true green, bright purple, light violet, orange
- red wine
- blue food colouring
- red punch
- coffee
- tea
- measuring cup
- glass or plastic trays large enough to accommodate prints
- cotton swabs
- turpentine-and-oil solution
- tongs (wooden or plastic)

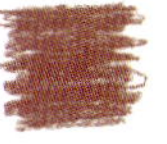
CRIMSON RED

APPLE GREEN

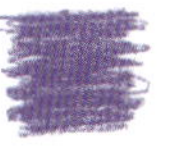
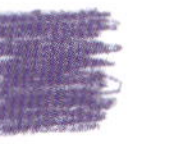
VIOLET

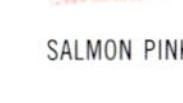
SALMON PINK

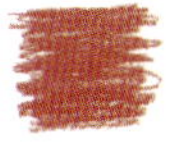
SCARLET LAKE

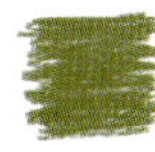
TRUE GREEN

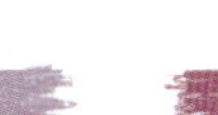
PURPLE

BRIGHT PURPLE

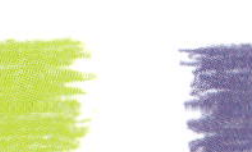
CHARTREUSE

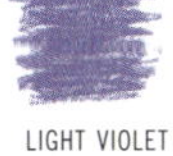
LIGHT VIOLET

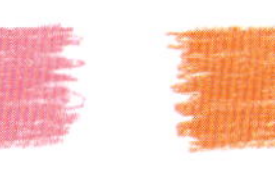
HOT PINK

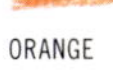
ORANGE

▷ 1

First, prepare the surface. Immerse the print in a tray filled with water. Leave it in for one minute. Remove it from the water and put it in a tray filled with staining bath. Use your judgment as to how long to keep it in the stain. Keep a record of the amount of time you soak the print in the stain as well as of the concentration of the stain. This way, you can keep track of how you obtained your favourite results.

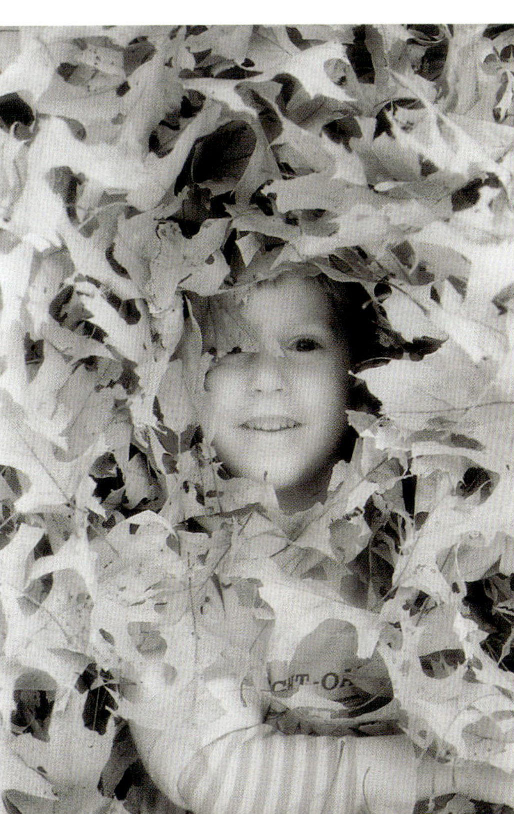

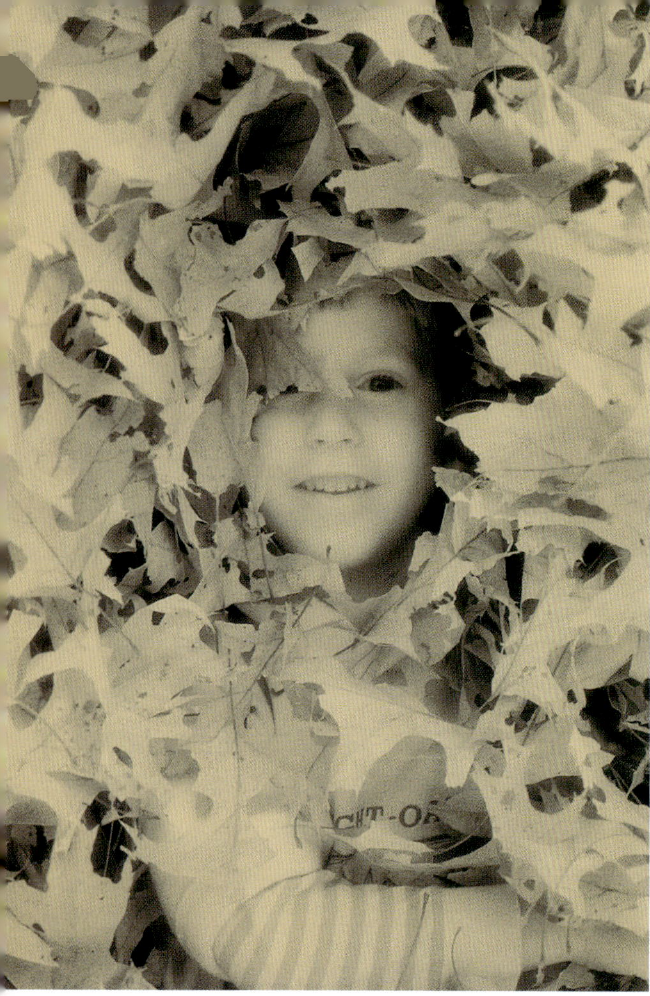

◁ 2

Boil four tea bags in approximately 20 ounces (600 ml) of water, then let the tea steep until it cools to room temperature. This print was stained for ten minutes. Rinse the print for five minutes when done to remove excess tea.

▽ 3

Brew approximately 20 ounces (600 ml) of coffee. Let it cool to room temperature. This print was stained for ten minutes. Rinse the print for five minutes when done to remove excess coffee.

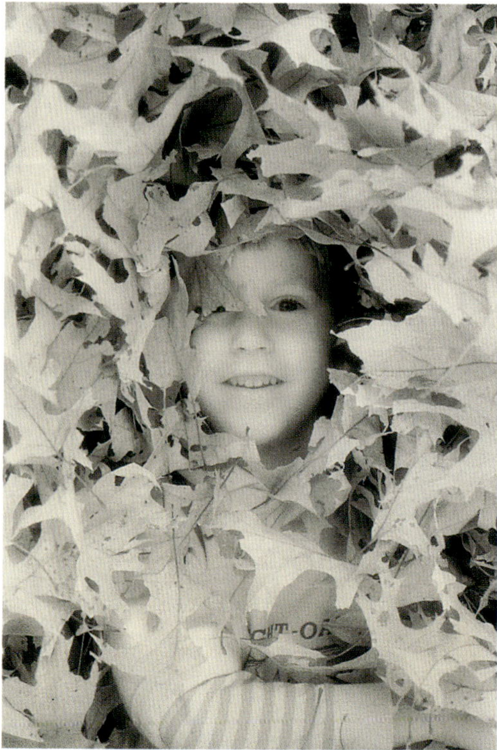

TIP

- To dry prints, use a hair dryer at a low setting or hang the prints by a corner with a clothespin. Don't lay them flat to dry because excess colour and water will collect and stain parts of the print darker than the rest.

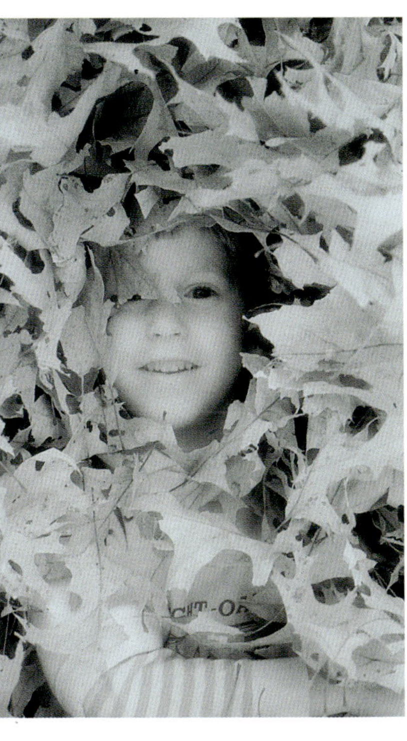

◁ 4

Mix 10 drops of blue food colouring with 20 ounces (600 ml) of room-temperature water. Allow the picture to soak for ten minutes. Rinse the print when done to remove excess food colouring.

VARIATION

Fruit punch produces an appealingly vibrant stain.

1. Immerse the print in water in the first tray.
2. Stain the print for ten minutes in fruit punch.
3. Rinse the print and hang it to dry.

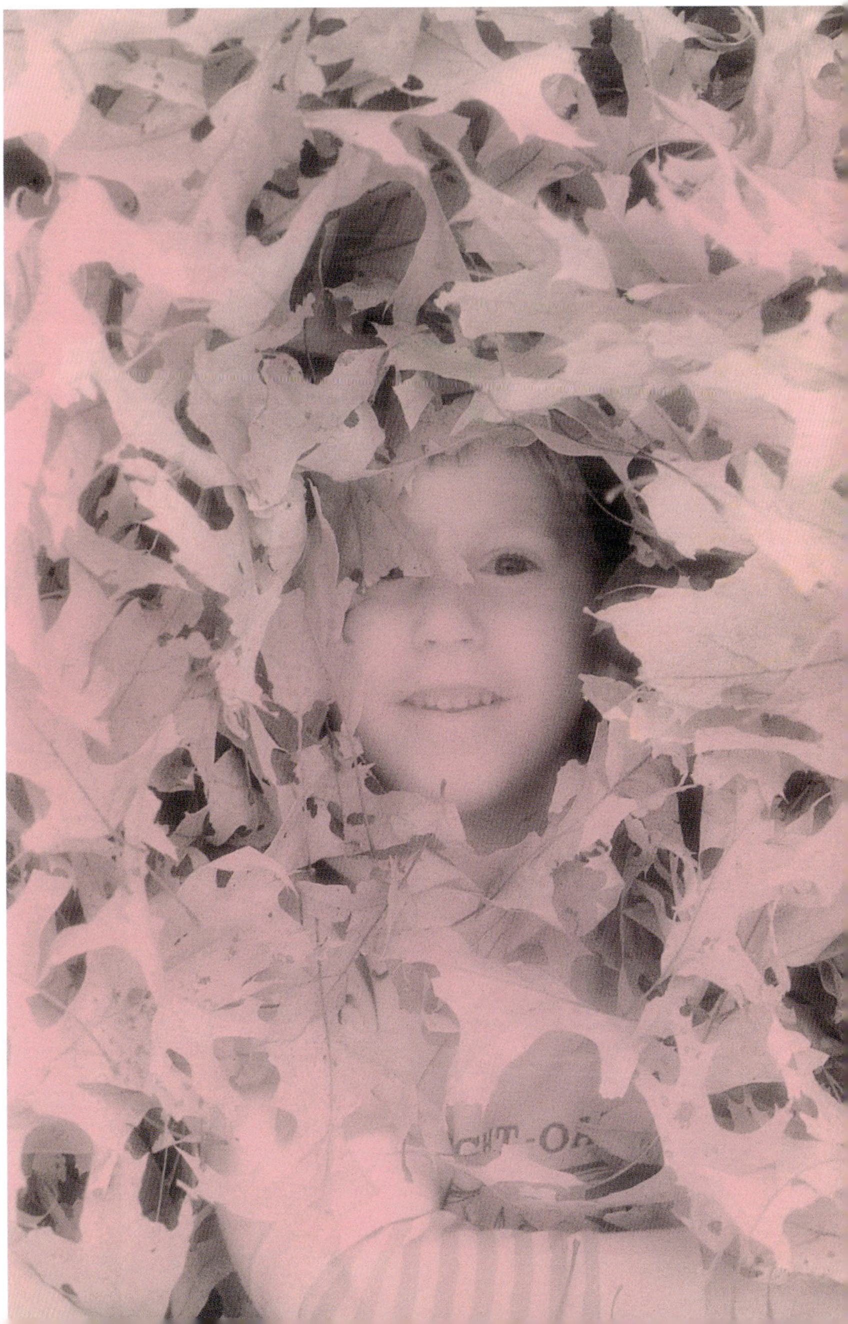

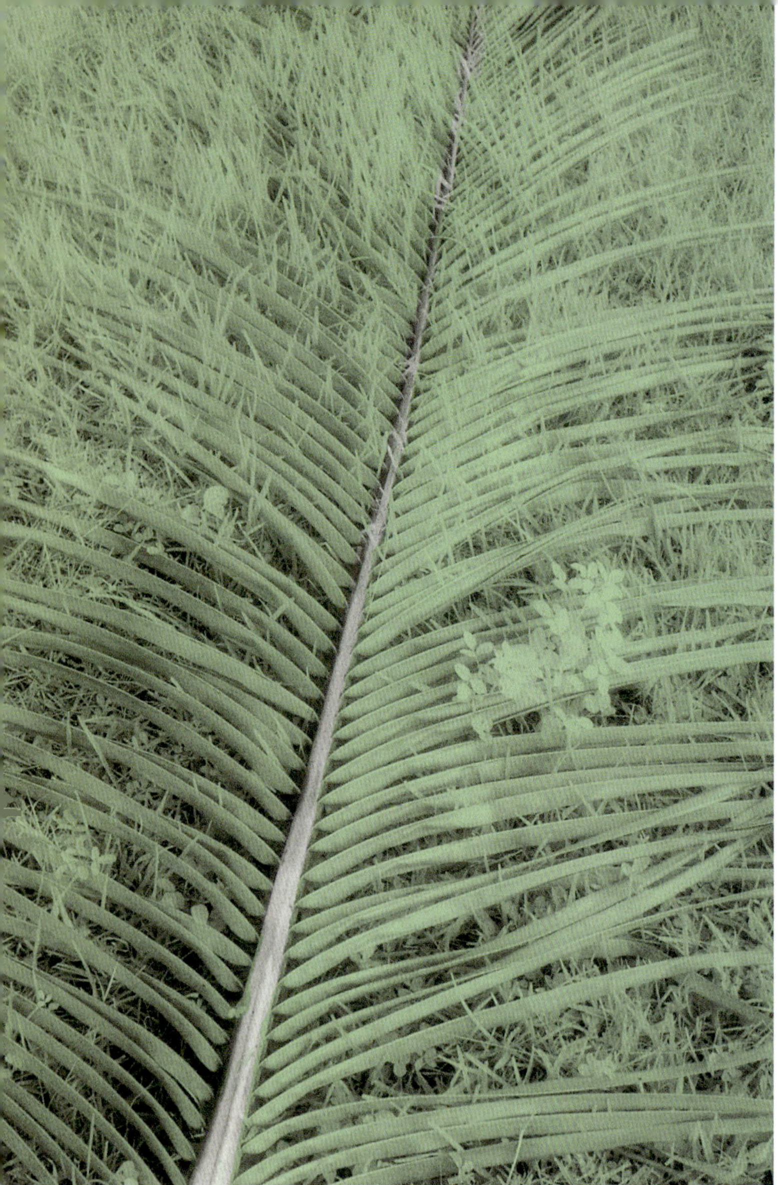

◁ Rubber cement was applied to the stem of the branch before this print was dyed green for ten minutes.

Dyes

Dyes do not chemically react with a print; instead, they dye the base colour of the print. Because of this, dyes are not as permanent as toners. If a print that has been dyed is exposed to strong sunlight for any length of time, it is likely to fade. Still, dyes are sometimes desirable because they often produce more brilliant colours than stains. Photographic or liquid dyes are available at art-supply and craft stores or at photo-supply stores.

Since most dyes are vibrant, choose a photograph that is compositionally strong and graphic—one with strong lines or shapes. Also look for action shots in which someone or something is moving, which you can capture by using a fast shutter speed (or use a slow shutter speed to blur the image). Combine colours to create a hue that suits the subject matter.

Dyeing a print is fairly simple. Combine the dye with water to create a dye bath. Immerse the print in the bath. You don't need to work in a darkroom, but it is still a good idea to keep dyes out of the kitchen area and to supervise young children. Be sure to read the directions since different manufacturer's dyes are handled differently.

Remember to keep records of your experiments with dyes so you can re-create results you like. Also, the general rule of thumb for hand colouring also applies to dyeing: The print should contain a lot of highlight areas. All hand colouring should be done after dyeing or staining a print.

▽ This photograph was dyed magenta for ten minutes.

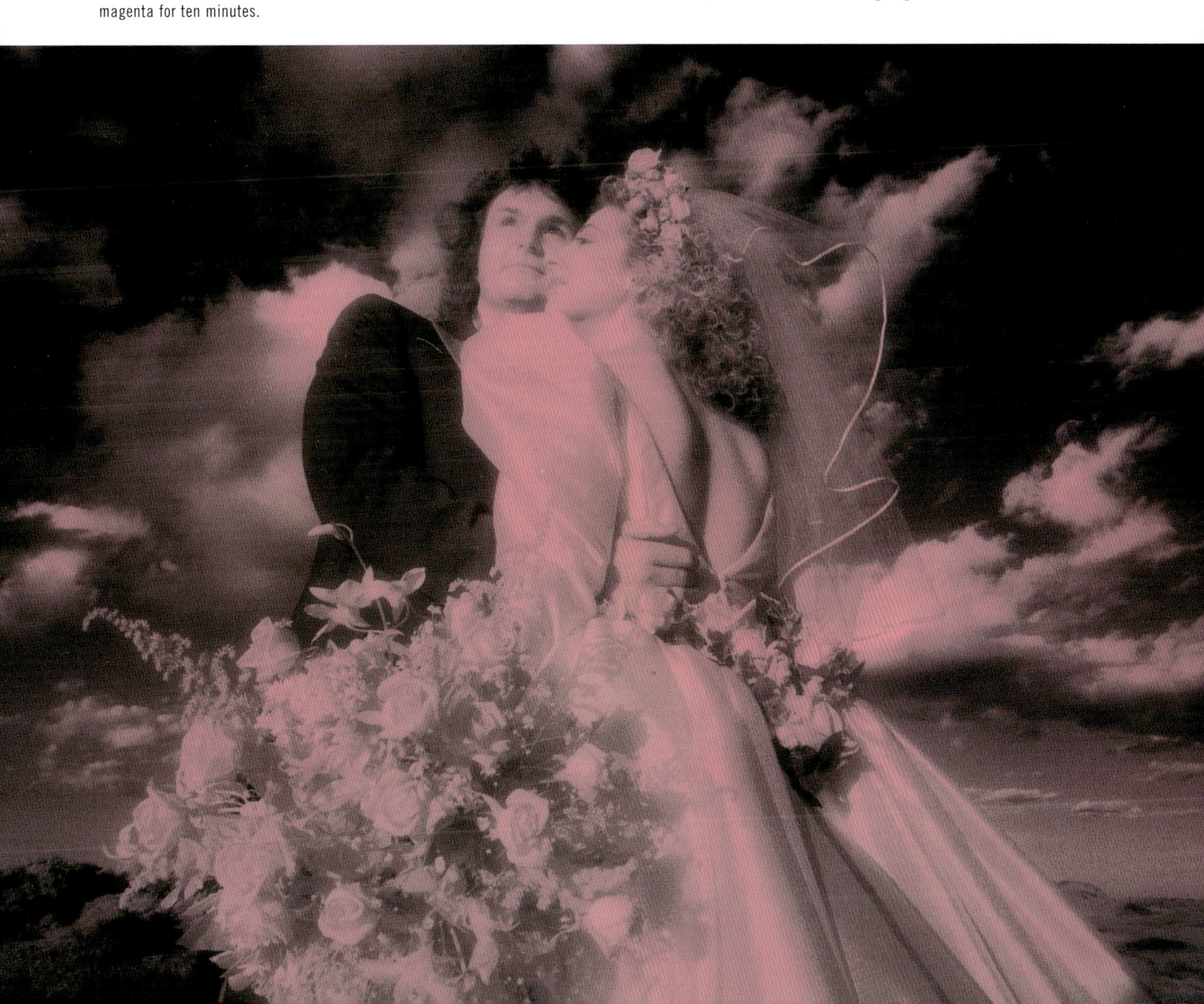

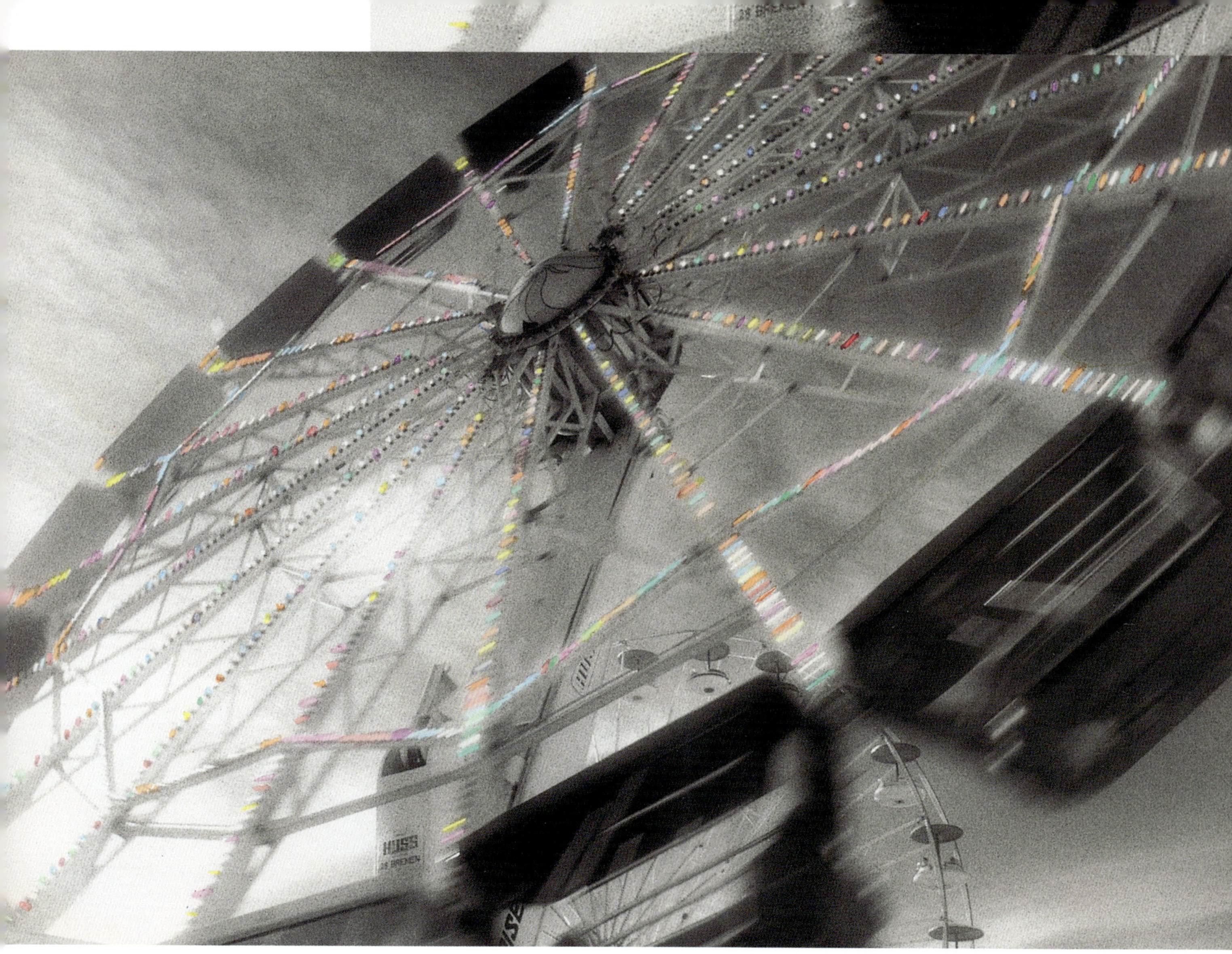

△ Hand colouring with dyes works for this photo because Ferris wheels are associated with bright colours.

Dyeing Photographs

GETTING STARTED

Dyes, which are usually very vibrant, are ideal to use on photographs of brightly coloured subject matter, like a Ferris wheel. To add the illusion of movement in this photo, a slow shutter speed was used when the picture was taken. The photo was hand coloured using a photographic flesh-coloured dye.

MATERIALS

- black-and-white print on matte-surface paper
- lemon-yellow coloured pencil
- plastic tray from a photo store
- tongs (wooden or plastic)
- measuring cup
- photographic dyes: flesh, magenta, magenta mixed with cyan, green, orange
- rubber cement
- small brush

LEMON YELLOW

FLESH

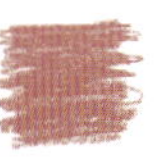

MAGENTA

CYAN

GREEN

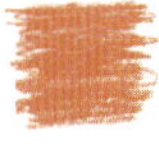

ORANGE

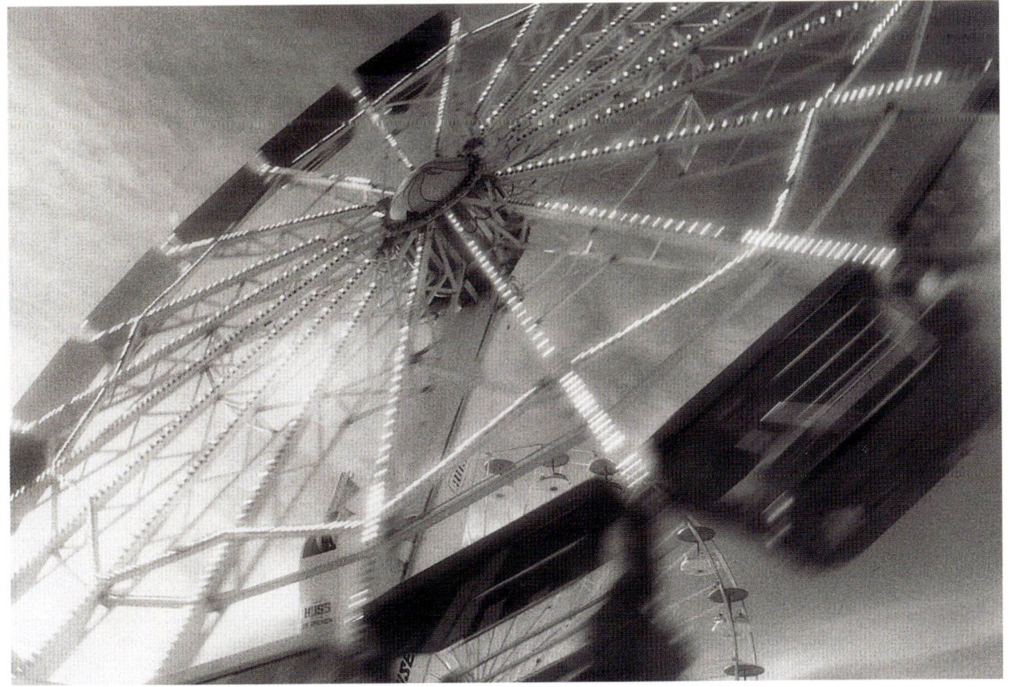

△ 1

Prepare the surface by soaking the photograph in a tray of fresh water for at least one minute.

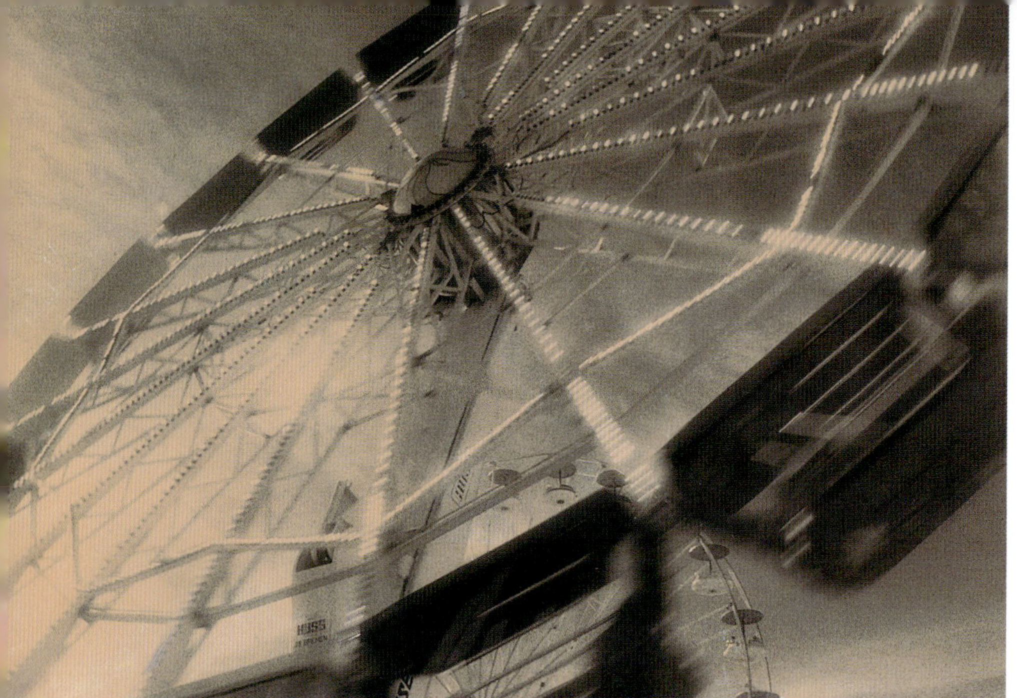

△ 2

Prepare a tray with 20 ounces (600 ml) of room-temperature water. Add 10 drops of dye (in this case, orange) to the water and mix with the tongs. Make sure the colour is evenly dispersed. After dyeing, wash the print in a tray of fresh tap water at room temperature for five minutes. Hang the print to dry or use a blow dryer at a low setting. This print was dyed for eight minutes.

TIP

- Make sure to use fresh water and clean tongs when you go from one coloured dye to the next. Staining or contamination can occur if you're not careful.

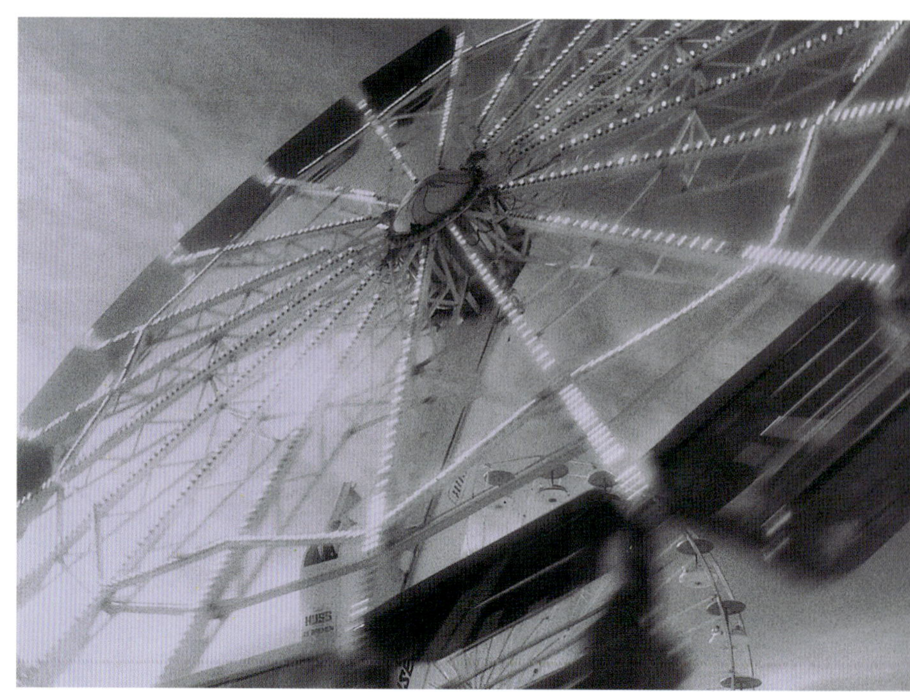

▷ 3

Try combining different colours to create a new one. This colour was created by mixing 5 ounces (150 ml) of magenta with 5 ounces of cyan in 20 ounces (600 ml) of water. The print was dyed for ten minutes.

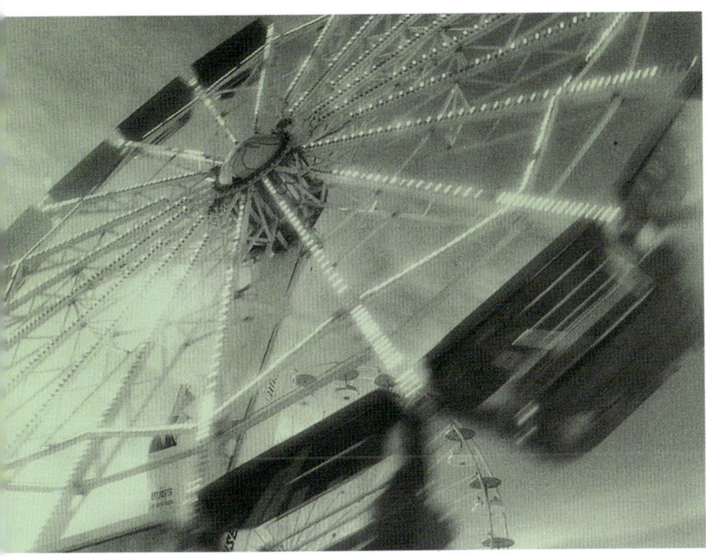

△ 4

Mix 10 drops of green dye into 20 ounces (600 ml) of water. This print was dyed for eight minutes.

VARIATION

Contrasting colours bring out a picture's highlights.

1. Rubber cement was used as a mask to cover the lights on the Ferris wheel so they could be hand coloured separately, adding colour contrast to this image.
2. Pre-wash the print. Then, soak it in dye for eight minutes and allow it to dry.
3. Rub off the rubber cement with your finger, and hand colour the lights using the lemon-yellow pencil.

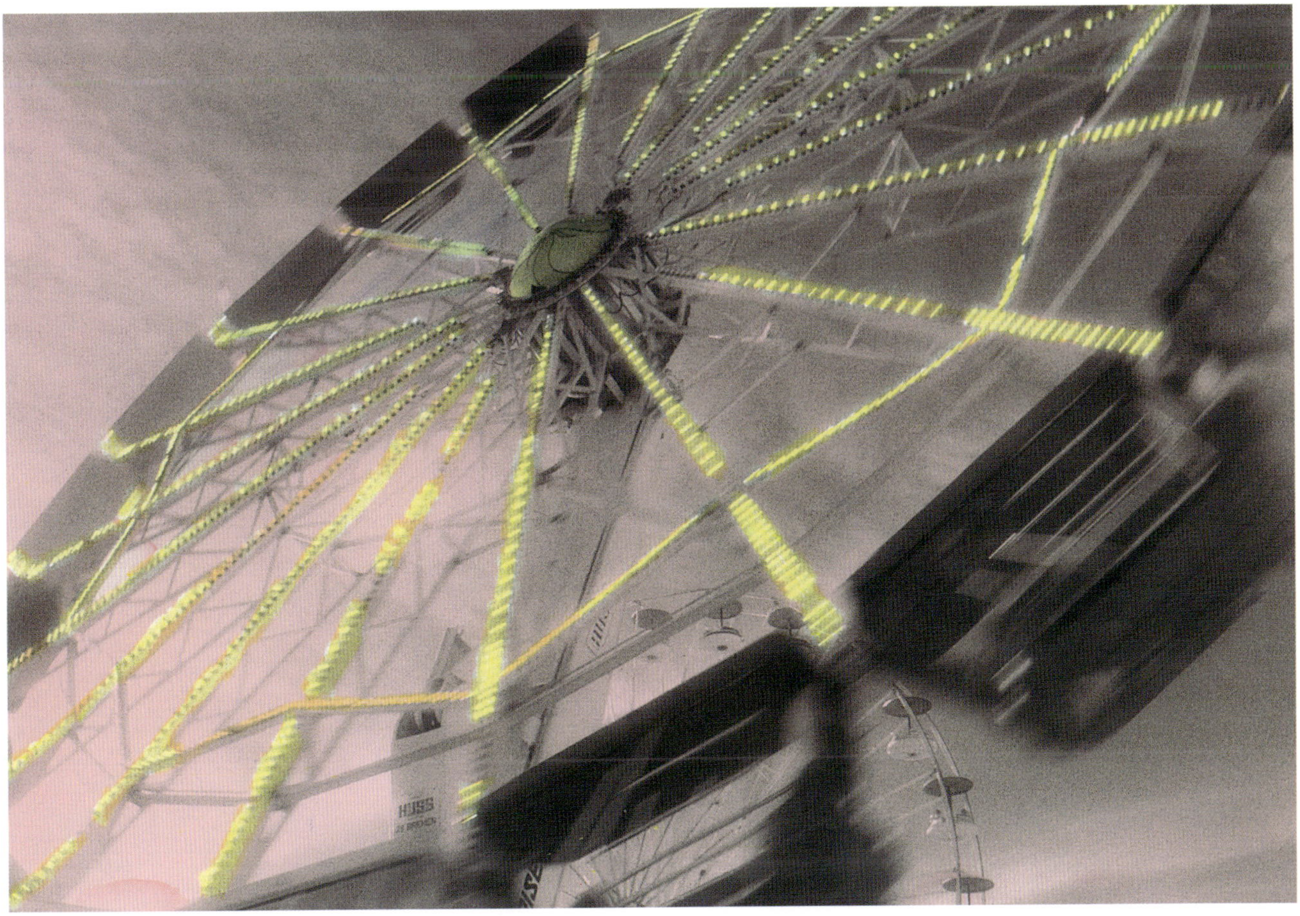

▷ Some black-and-white postcards are perfect for hand colouring with oils.

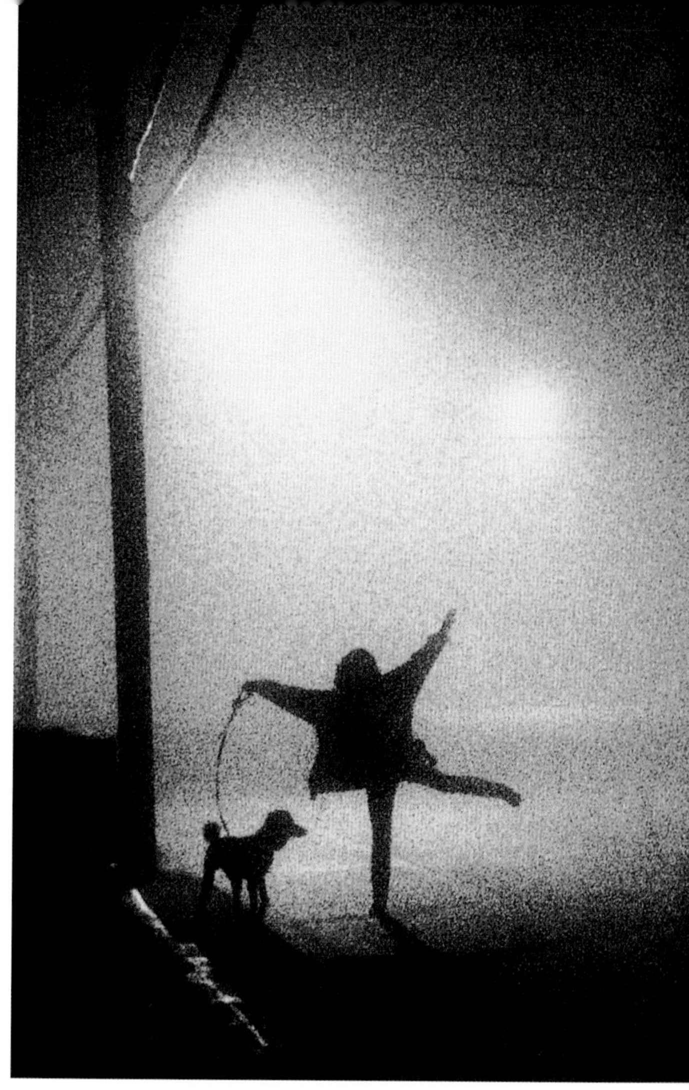

Oils

Hand colouring with oils can produce a much different effect than using coloured pencils. For starters, oil colours are slightly more intense and vibrant. Also, oils are noted for their permanence.

There are many different types of oil paints. Photographic oils are designed specifically for hand colouring prints. Oils can be used on a semimatte or matte paper, but if you plan to do detail work with coloured pencils afterward, you'll need to work on matte paper. If you use artist's oil paints, try thinning the oils with transparentizing gel before using them. This will make them more transparent without affecting the intensity of the colours. Another option is to use extender, which can be added to oil paint to reduce colour intensity.

Like pencils, oils are, for the most part, easy to remove (although some of the more vibrant colours do not come off so easily). Gently rub mistakes away with a cotton swab or cotton ball, or use the turpentine-and-oil solution or mineral spirits. If the print has white borders, protect them with transparent tape. This is also a fingerprint-free means of holding the photo down while you work on it.

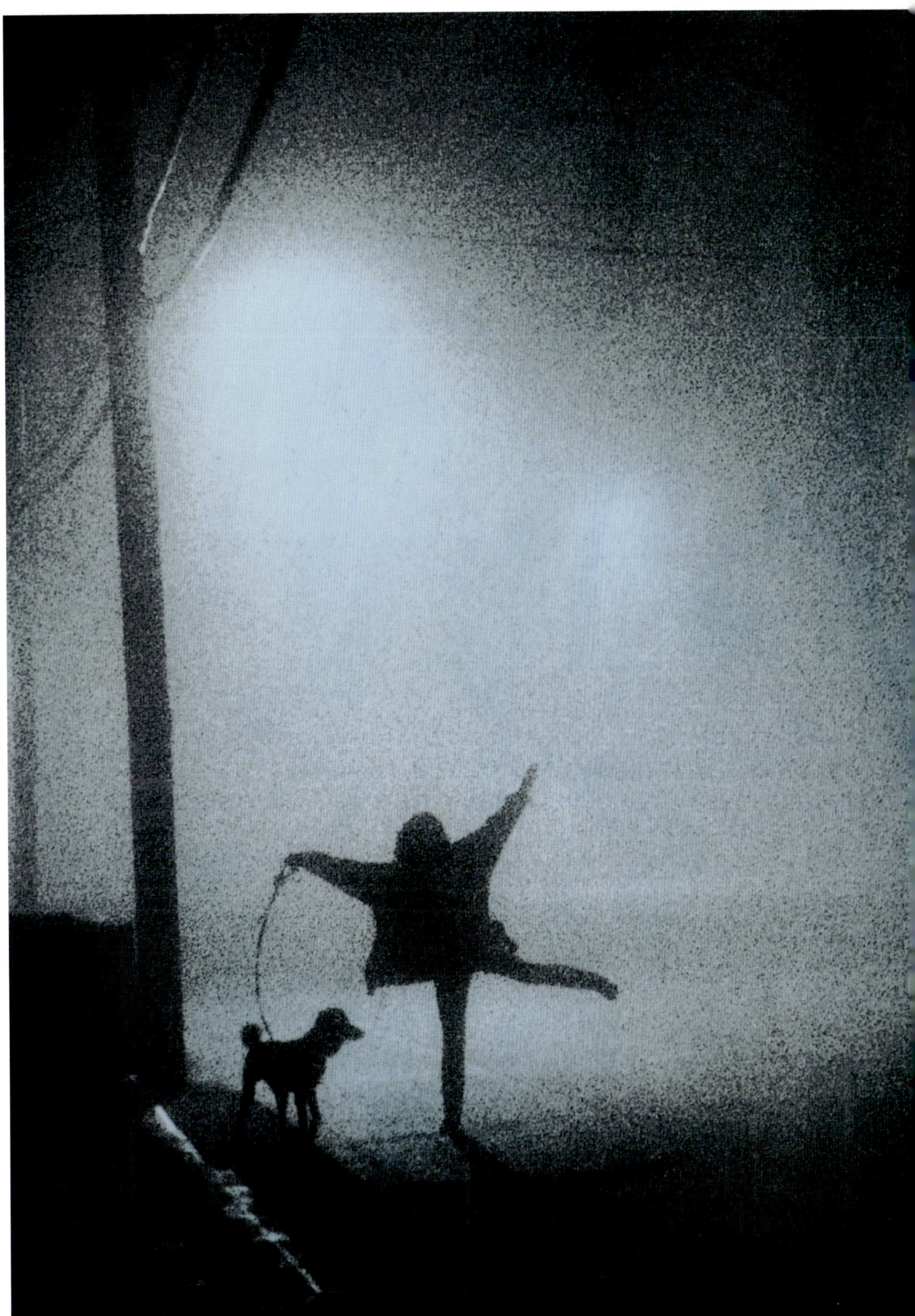

▷ This postcard was coloured blue with a wash of oil paint.

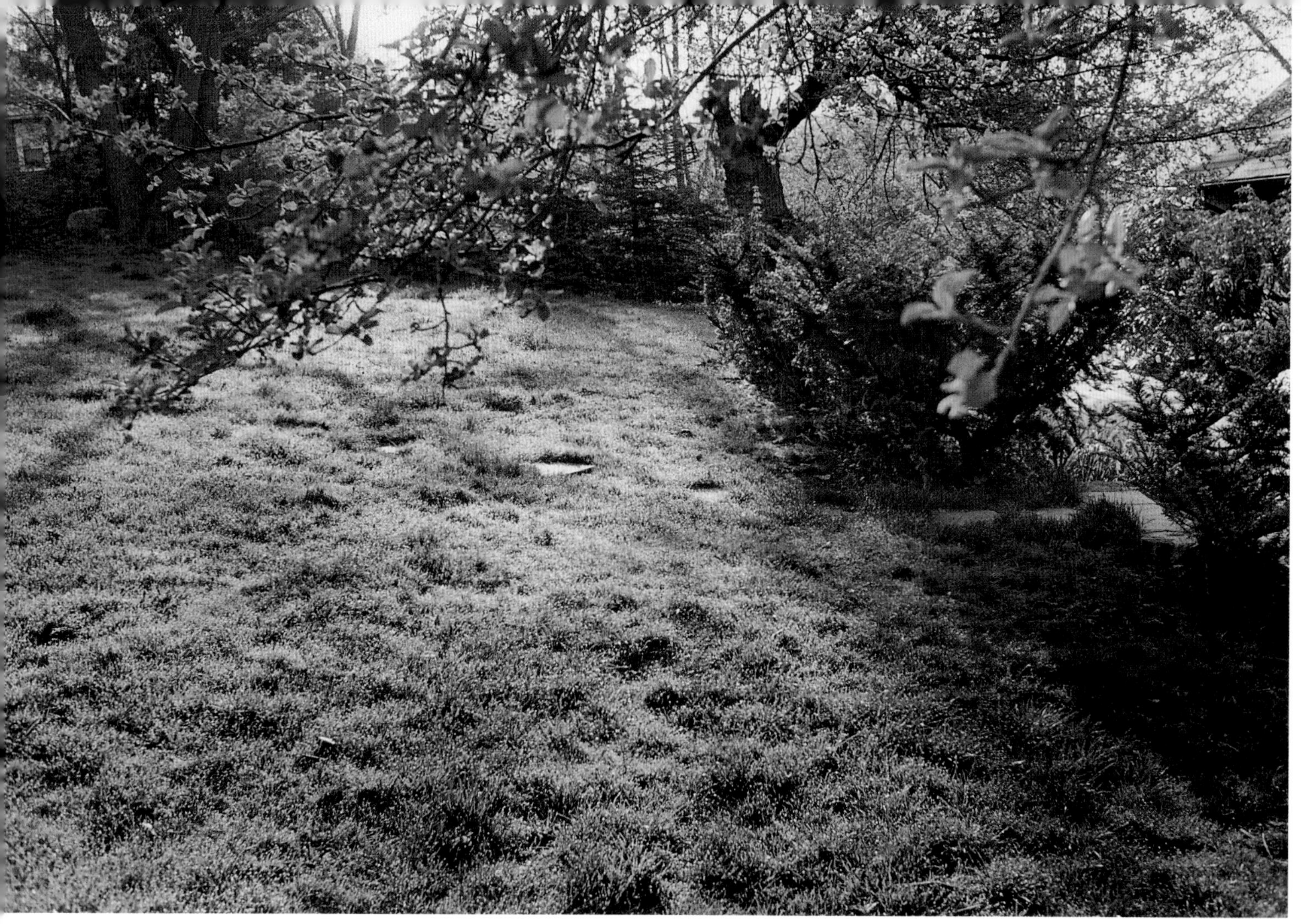

△ A good candidate for hand colouring, this photograph has strong elements in the foreground (the leaves) and a lot of depth.

First, prepare the print surface; otherwise, the colours may appear too strong. Using a cotton ball, apply a small amount of either mineral spirits or turpentine-and-oil solution directly to the print surface. (Resin-coated paper requires less solution than fibre-based.)

Using a palette, whether it is store-bought or just a plastic plate, is recommended. Place small amounts of oil paint directly on it and mix the colours with a toothpick. It's difficult to exactly re-create a mixed colour, so be sure to mix more than you think you'll need.

Save any left-over colour by putting the palette in a sealable plastic bag. Oils can take hours or days to dry anyway, depending on how thickly they have been applied, but the plastic bag is an extra measure to prevent them from drying. This way, you can come back to your print later to add more colour.

Use cotton swabs to dab colour directly from the palette onto the print surface. For large areas, use a cotton ball to work the colour in. For the smallest areas, use a cotton swab or wrap a toothpick with cotton and use it as a paintbrush. For very fine details, try using the end of a plain toothpick (but don't press down hard with the toothpick—this can scratch the emulsion of the print).

Layering colours will increase their intensity, but allow time for each layer to dry before adding another or the paint might crack.

▽ Oils were used to colour the large areas, such as the grass, and coloured pencils were used to punch up the small details, like the leaves.

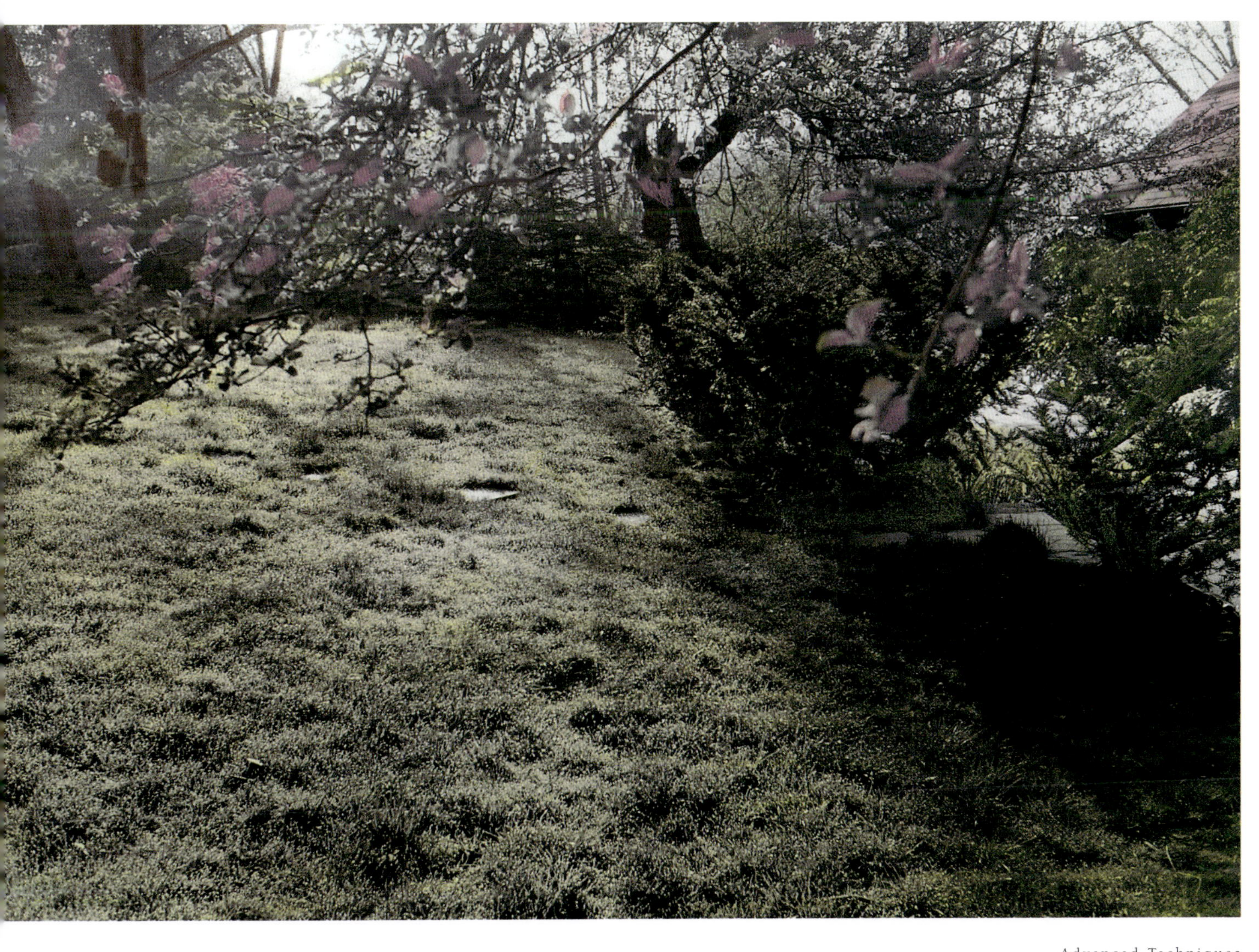

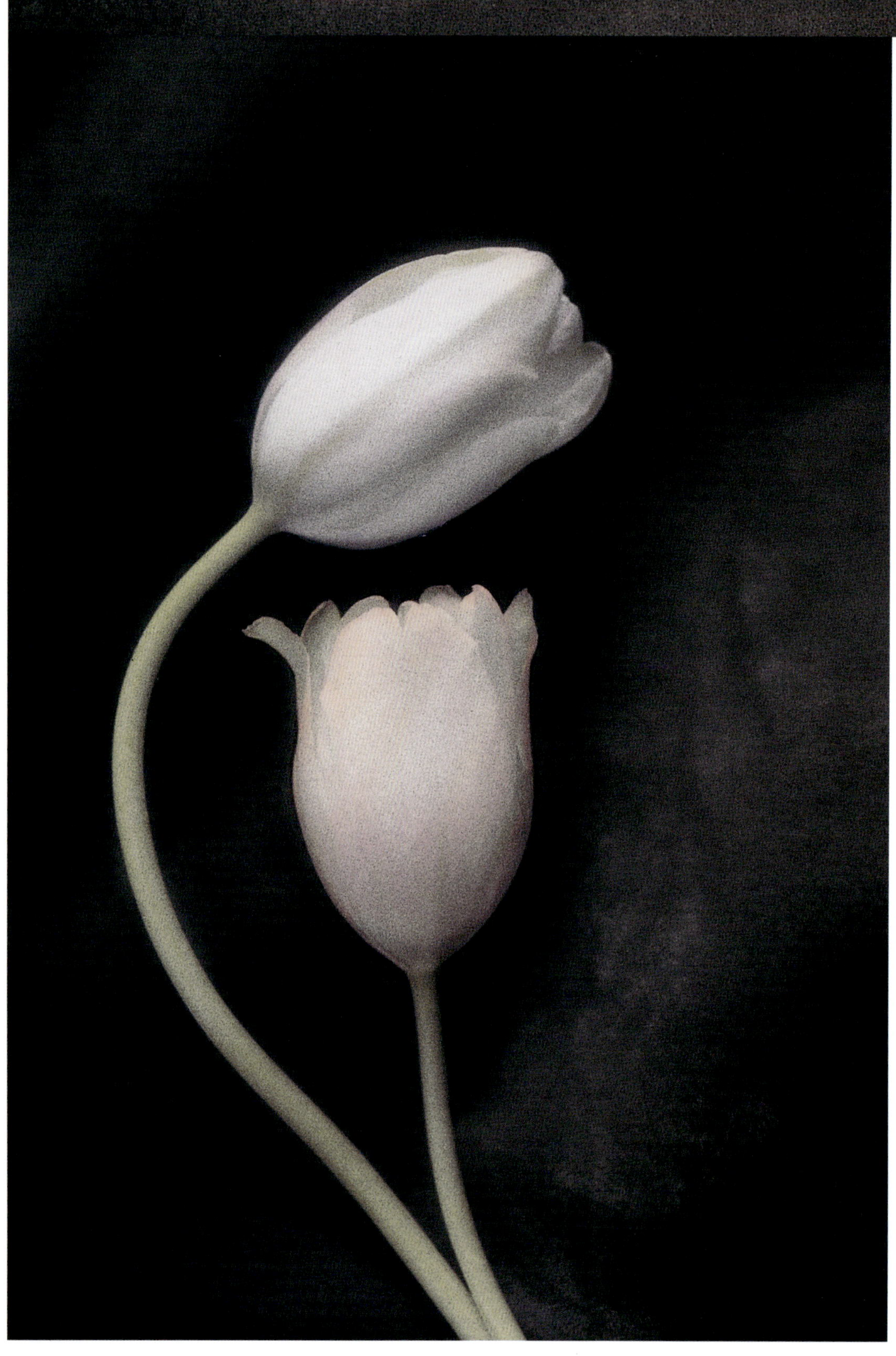

◁ The beauty of hand colouring this image is its simplicity, yet a lot of detail work can be added to the tulips.

Adding Subtle Details with Oils

GETTING STARTED

These tulips were photographed on top of a piece of black velvet to enhance the contrast. When working with large dark areas, like the background in this picture, wear nylon or cotton gloves, or place a piece of soft gauze between your hand and the surface of the print. This will prevent the oils from your hands from leaving marks in the dark sections. Start by adding colour to the large areas of the flowers and end by doing the fine detail work. This is a great picture in which to mix mediums. Colour the flowers and stems with oils, and add details in the flowers with either oils or pencils.

MATERIALS

- black-and-white print on matte-surface paper
- oils: yellow, yellow-green, warm red, cadmium orange, dioxazine purple, chartreuse, imperial violet
- cotton balls
- toothpicks
- cotton swabs
- turpentine-and-oil solution
- palette
- gloves

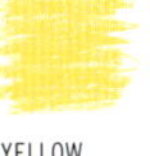
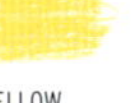
YELLOW

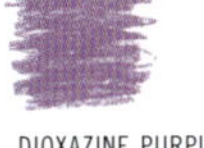
DIOXAZINE PURPLE

YELLOW-GREEN

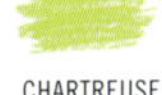
CHARTREUSE

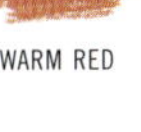
WARM RED

IMPERIAL VIOLET

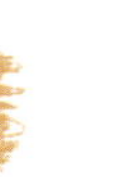
CADMIUM ORANGE

 1

Start with a semimatte or matte print. (Use a flat matte print if you plan to also use pencils.) Select your colours and place a small amount of each on a palette.

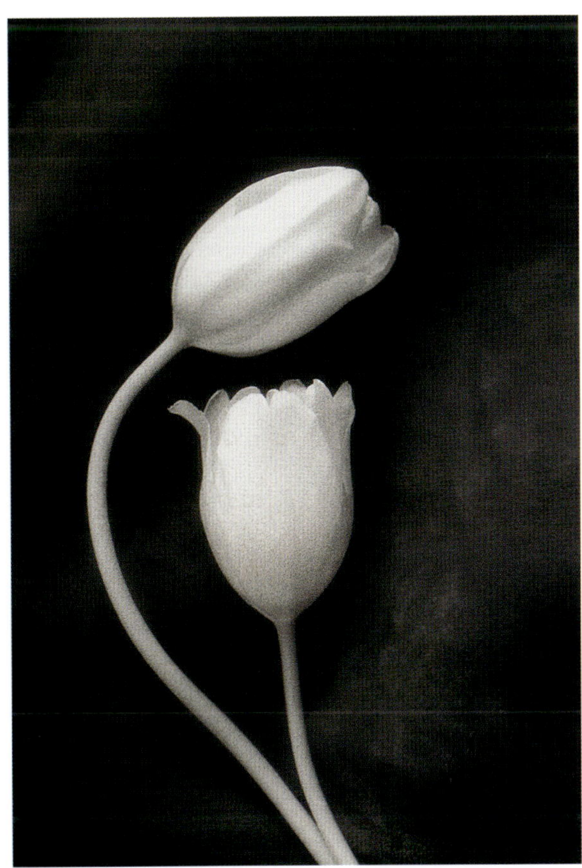

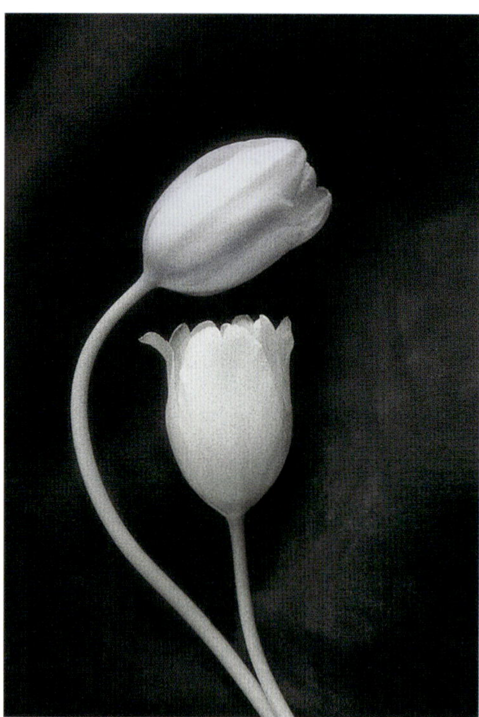

2

Treat the surface of both tulips with solution. Apply imperial violet oil from the palette to the top tulip with a cotton swab. Use a circular motion to work the oil in so that it is smooth.

▷ 3

Apply a small amount of warm red to a second tulip to complement the coolness of the imperial violet tulip, using the same circular motion with a cotton swab. Continue to use clean swabs until all the colour is smoothed in.

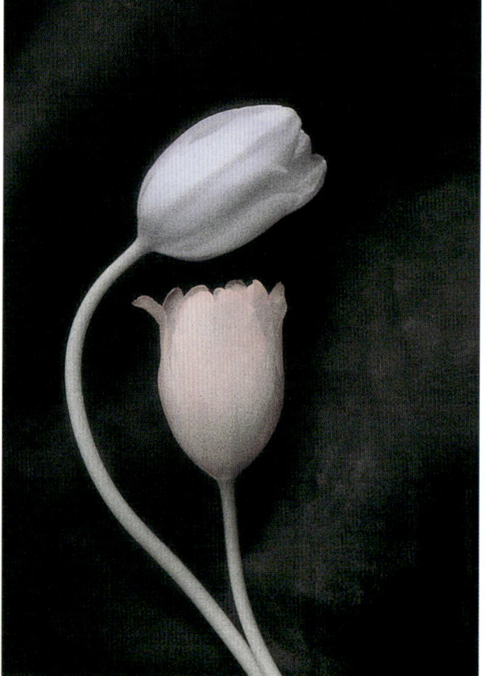

▷ 4

Use a toothpick wrapped tightly with cotton to apply a very small amount of yellow-green from the palette to the stems of the tulips. (It is not necessary to prepare the print surface of the stems for this step.) Have a few more toothpicks with cotton already made. Work back and forth until all the colour is blended. If you accidentally get some of the colour in the background area, erase it with a cotton swab moistened with a very small amount of water.

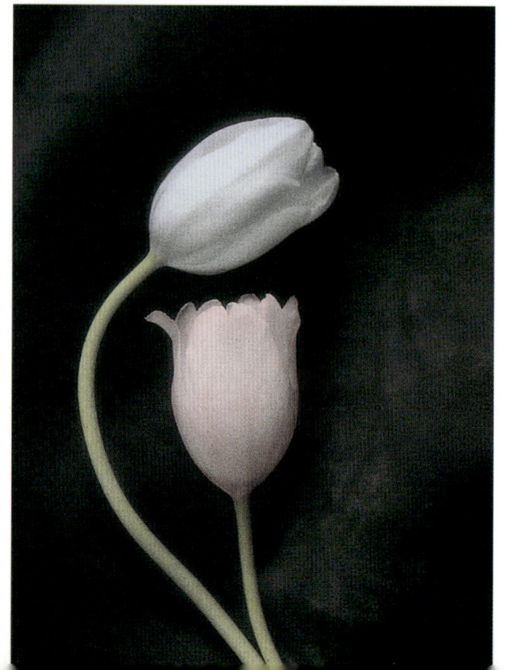

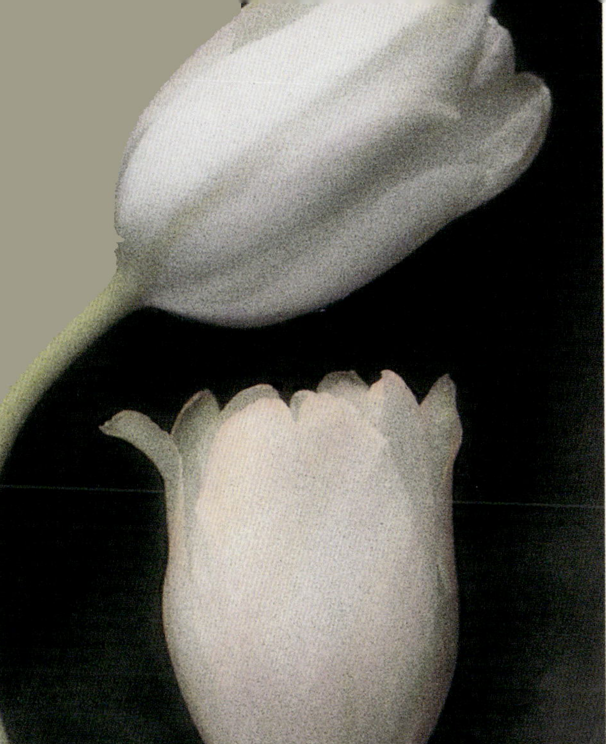

◁ 5

Flowers contain a lot of green. Extend the green from the stem up into the darker (shadow) areas of the flowers. Apply colour with a toothpick wrapped tightly with cotton, following the shading in the flower. A very small amount of warm red (the same colour as the bottom tulip) was used in the highlights of the top tulip, and yellow was used in the bottom tulip in the lighter areas. Using another colour gives the flowers depth.

TIPS

- Keep in mind that the same colour oil paint can differ in appearance from manufacturer to manufacturer.
- Layer colours for a more saturated look. Allow each layer to dry before adding another.

VARIATION

Build up colours for a textured look.

A heavier application of colour was used for this variation. The colour appears to sit on the surface, giving the image a bolder quality. The buildup of colour also adds texture. The print surface was not prepared beforehand, so the colours stayed opaque.

1. Colour the background using red oil applied with a cotton ball (use a cotton swab near the flower areas). Here, cadmium orange was used in the lighter areas of the background.
2. Using a cotton swab, apply dioxazine purple to the bottom tulip. Dab the colour on without smoothing it in.
3. Apply cadmium orange to the top tulip with a cotton swab, and smooth it in a bit. Dab all over with a cotton ball, getting some of the colour to go outside the lines of the flower. The feathering of orange in the background of this picture was created by the fibres from the cotton ball.
4. Use green to colour in the stem, using the same technique as on the other stems.

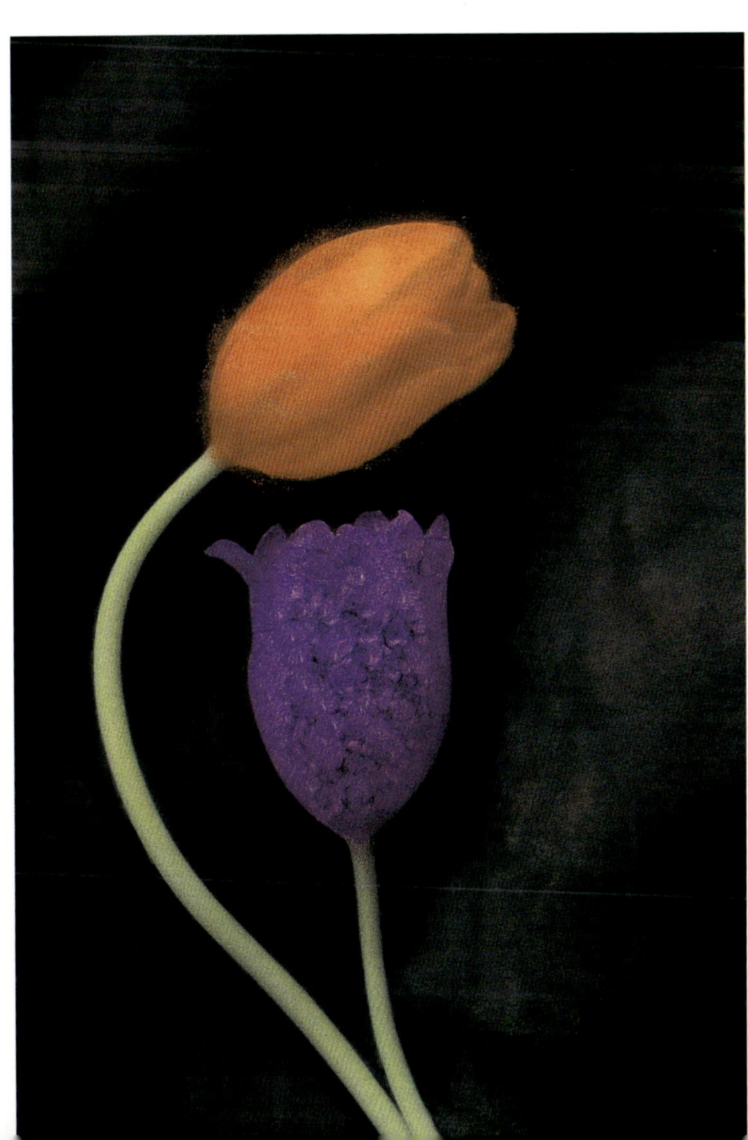

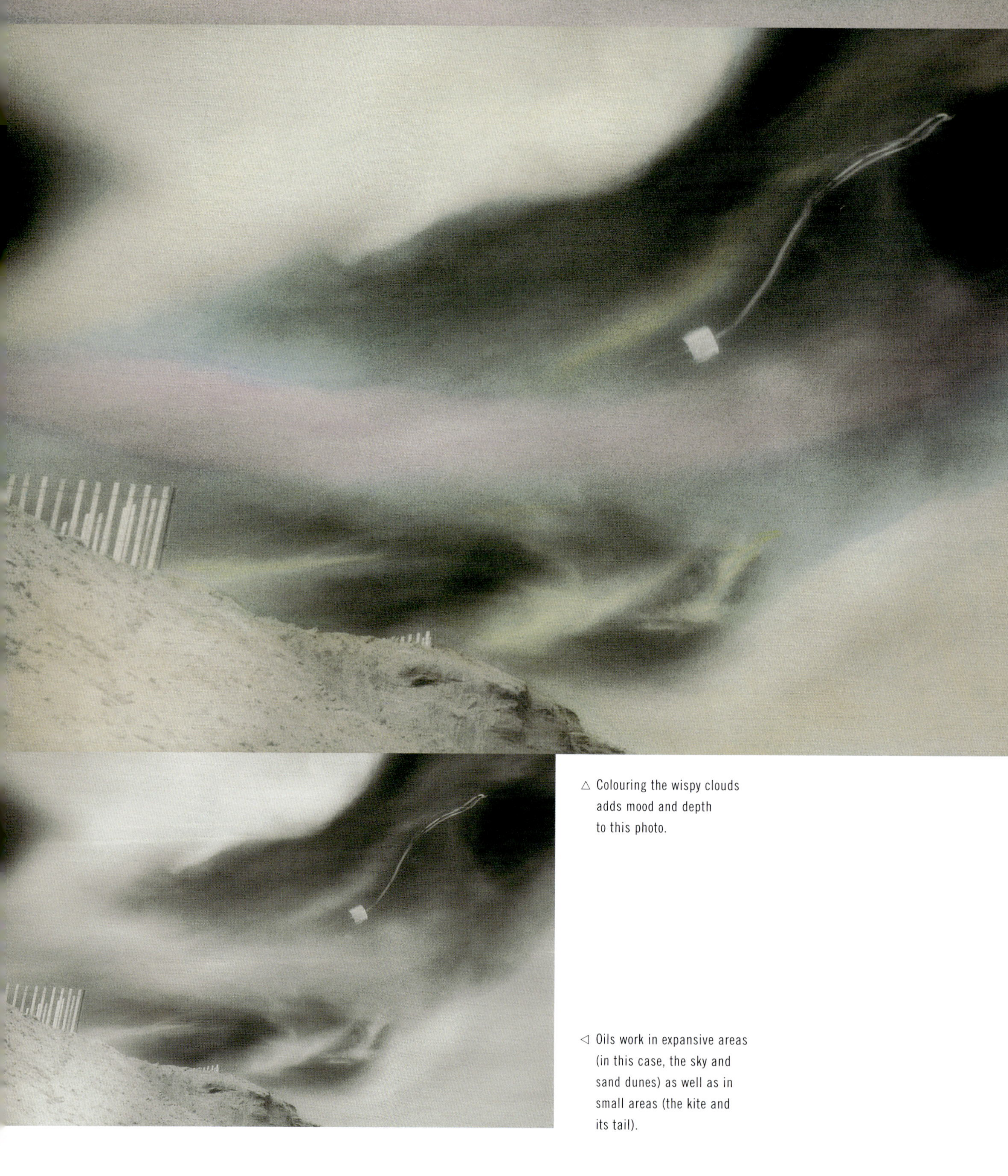

△ Colouring the wispy clouds adds mood and depth to this photo.

◁ Oils work in expansive areas (in this case, the sky and sand dunes) as well as in small areas (the kite and its tail).

Hand Colouring Expansive Areas with Oils

GETTING STARTED

Prepare the print surface with either mineral spirits or the turpentine-and-oil solution, which is also used with coloured pencils. (It's very important to use very small amounts of these solutions and to coat the print evenly.) Squirt a small amount of the oil colours that will be used to hand colour the image onto a palette. You will be using the colours directly from the palette.

MATERIALS

- black-and-white print on matte-surface paper
- oils: sepia, ultramarine blue, cadmium orange, magenta, lemon yellow, crimson red, cadmium green, pink
- cotton balls
- toothpicks
- cotton swabs
- turpentine-and-oil solution
- blender
- artist's palette
- transparent tape

SEPIA

LEMON YELLOW

ULTRAMARINE BLUE

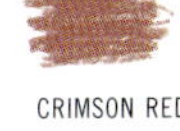

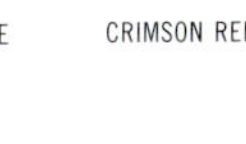

CRIMSON RED

CADMIUM ORANGE

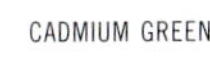

CADMIUM GREEN

MAGENTA

PINK

▷ **1**

Use a cotton swab to dab the sepia oil onto the dunes. With a fresh cotton swab, smooth the colour in. Do not allow colour to collect in areas. Keep using fresh cotton swabs until you have a smooth layer of colour. If necessary, add more layers of colour later for greater saturation.

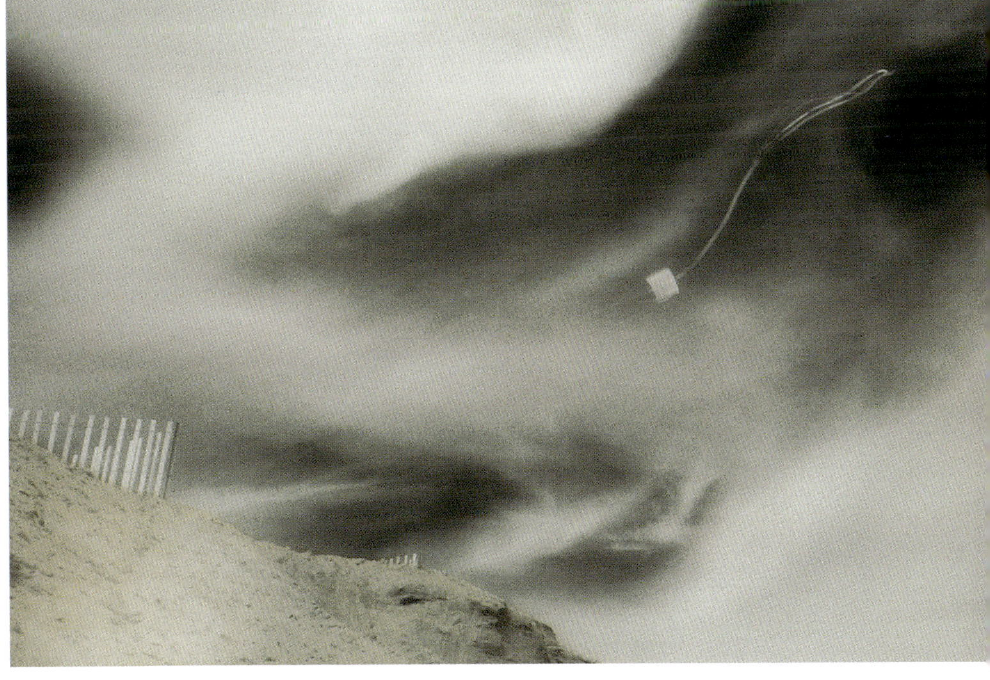

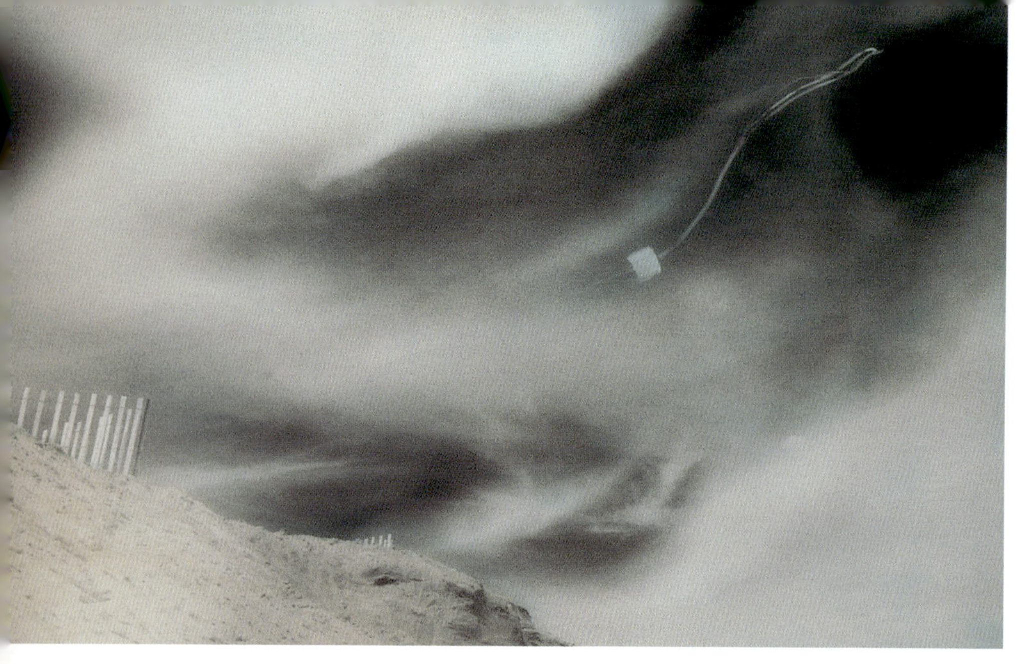

◁ 2

With a cotton swab, colour the entire sky area and kite with ultramarine blue. Use circular motions to smooth it in. Don't worry about colour bleeding into the clouds, fence, or kite.

TIP

- Use the blender to erase unwanted colours.

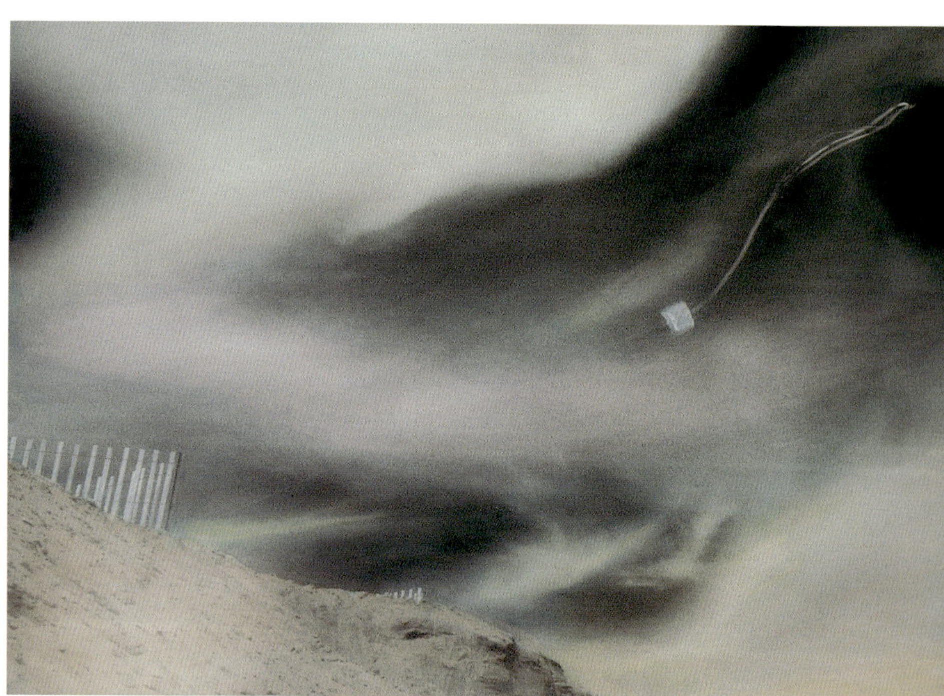

△ 3

Use a cotton swab to colour the clouds in the upper-left portion of the photograph with cadmium orange, and smooth it in. For balance, use the same colour for the clouds in the lower right. Use magenta for the cloud in the middle of the picture, applying the colour with a cotton swab. For the wisps of clouds near the dunes, use lemon yellow applied with a toothpick wrapped in a small amount of cotton.

▷ 4

After the paint has dried, go back into the clouds with the same colours and add another layer of colour for a deeper, richer look. Gently run a toothpick dipped in water along the fencing to erase the blue colour. Be careful not to scratch the print's surface. With a clean toothpick, do the same in the tail of the kite. Dip a clean toothpick wrapped in cotton in a small amount of water. With your fingers, squeeze out any excess water. Erase the blue in the kite. Notice that, without colour, the kite and fencing stand out more.

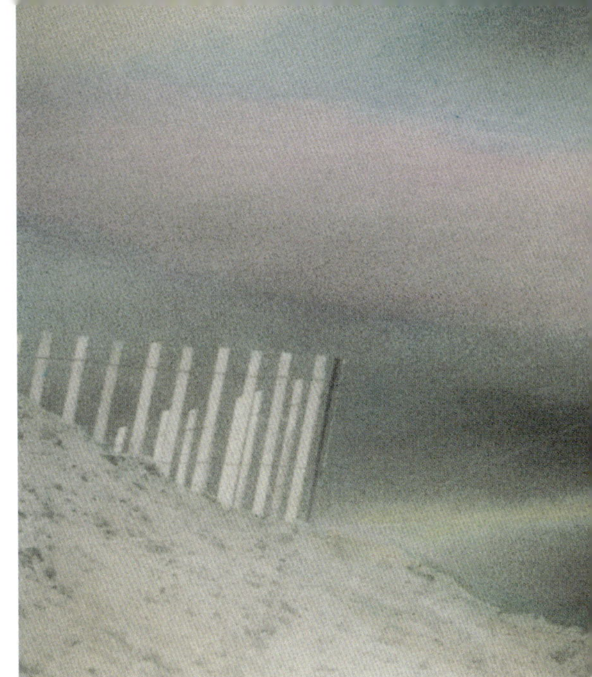

VARIATION

Oil paints are ideal for textured detail work.

1. Prepare the print's surface by applying the turpentine-and-oil solution with a toothpick wrapped in a small amount of cotton. Use the solution very sparingly.
2. Prepare your palette.
3. Apply a small amount of lemon yellow to the kite with a toothpick wrapped in cotton. Apply crimson red with a fresh toothpick (not wrapped in cotton). Apply crimson red to one section of the kite's tail. Then, using the same procedure, add cadmium green and pink to the other sections of the tail.

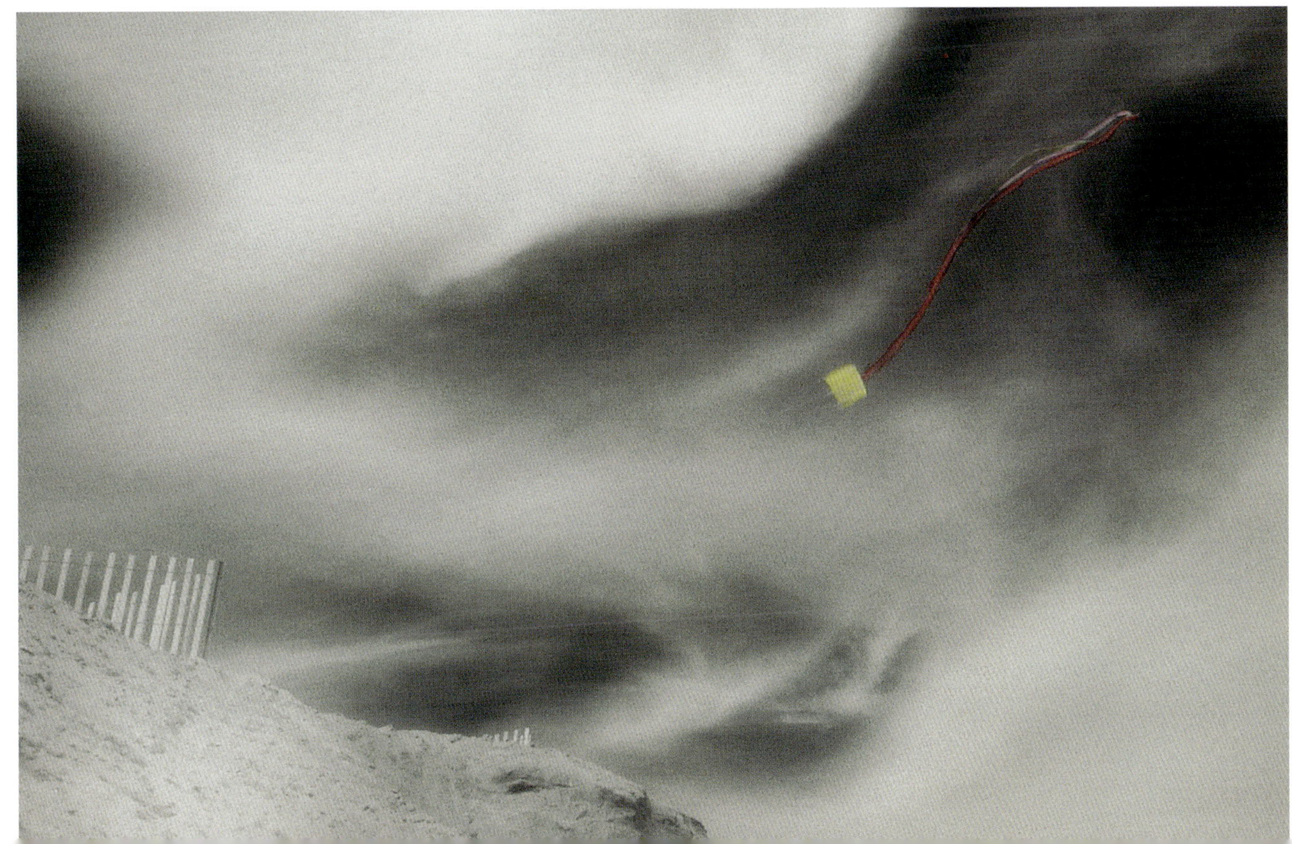

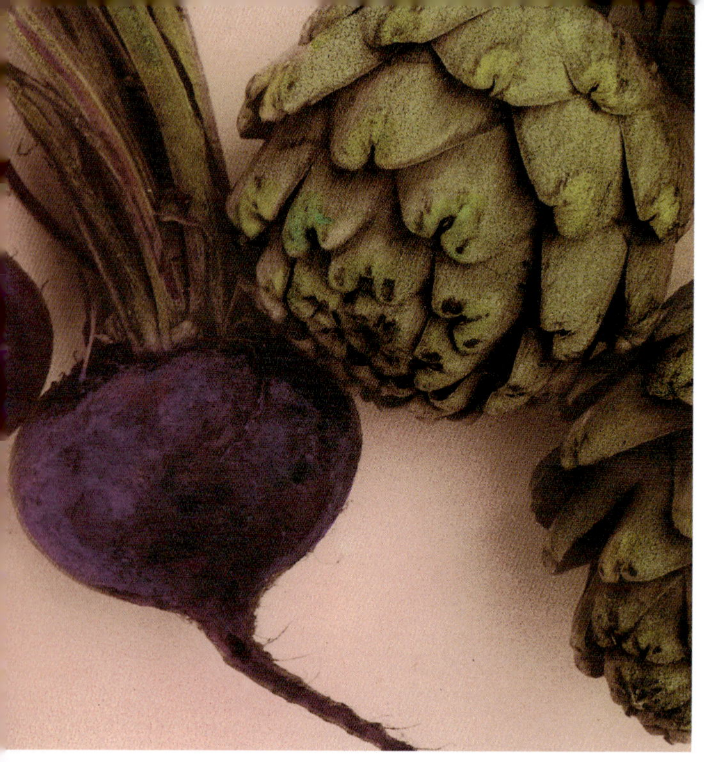

CREATING SPECIAL EFFECTS

Now it's time to experiment and really play. You have a basic understanding of hand colouring and have learned with materials that are very forgiving, will erase easily, and are easy to apply to a print. This is your foundation. Now try mixing various mediums to create textures or even to totally obscure the image. Continue to avoid glossy paper. Remember that many mediums can be applied to a semimatte surface, but in order to use pencils, matte paper is still required. Most materials are either water-based (watercolour paints, retouching dyes, tempera, gouache, acrylics, pen and ink) or oil-based (oil paints, photo oils, oil sticks, oil pastels, oil-based markers). Other options include coloured pencils, crayons, and markers. Some are transparent, and some are opaque. Different materials can be mixed, but be careful: The water-based materials can erase or dissolve pencils and oils, and the solvent used with pencils and oils can erase or dissolve watercolours. The gallery sections that follow offer many examples of different hand-colouring techniques—everything from using markers to making collages. No two look the same!

▽ Mix mediums to balance a textured background painted with acrylics and delicate subject matter coloured with markers.

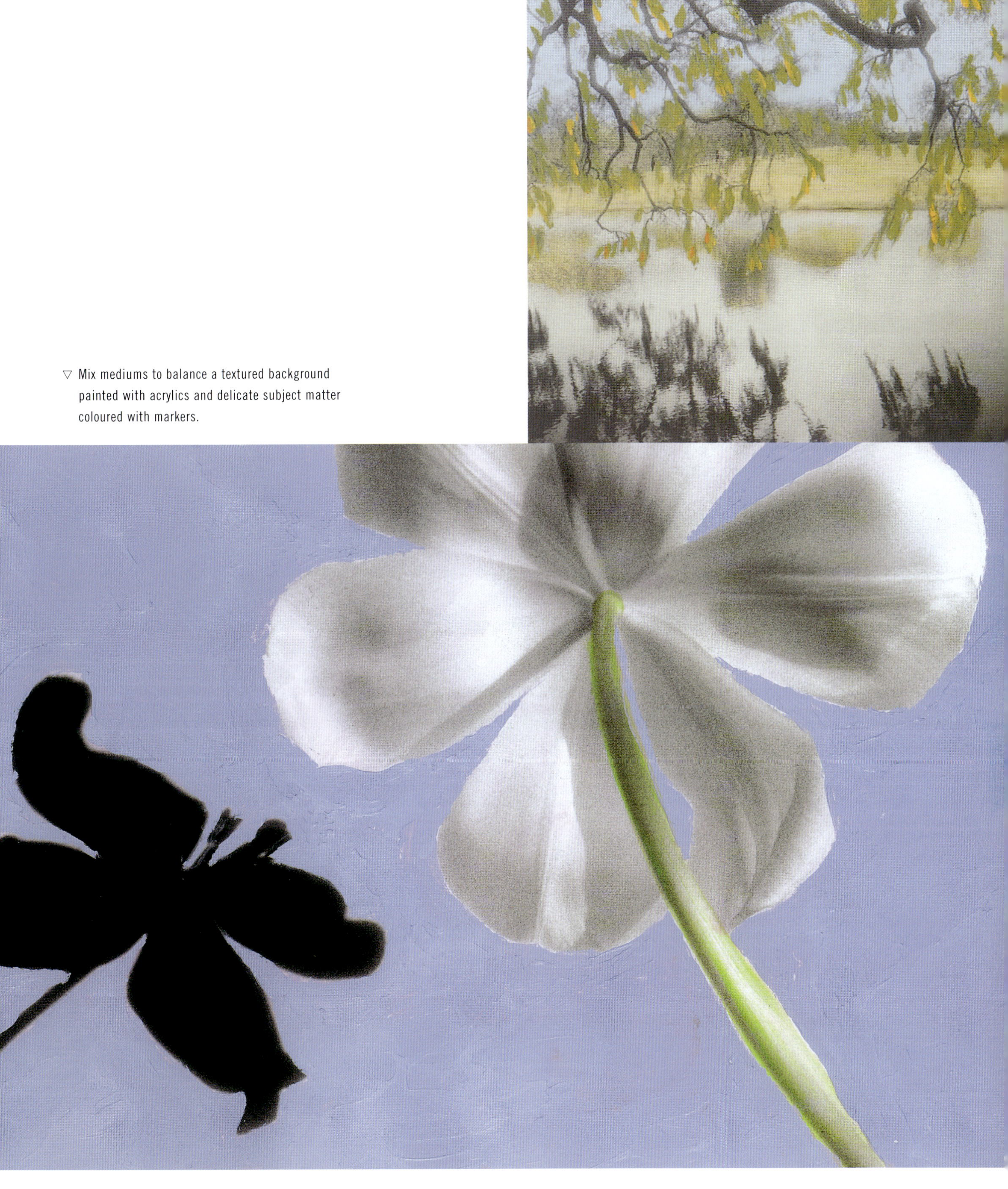

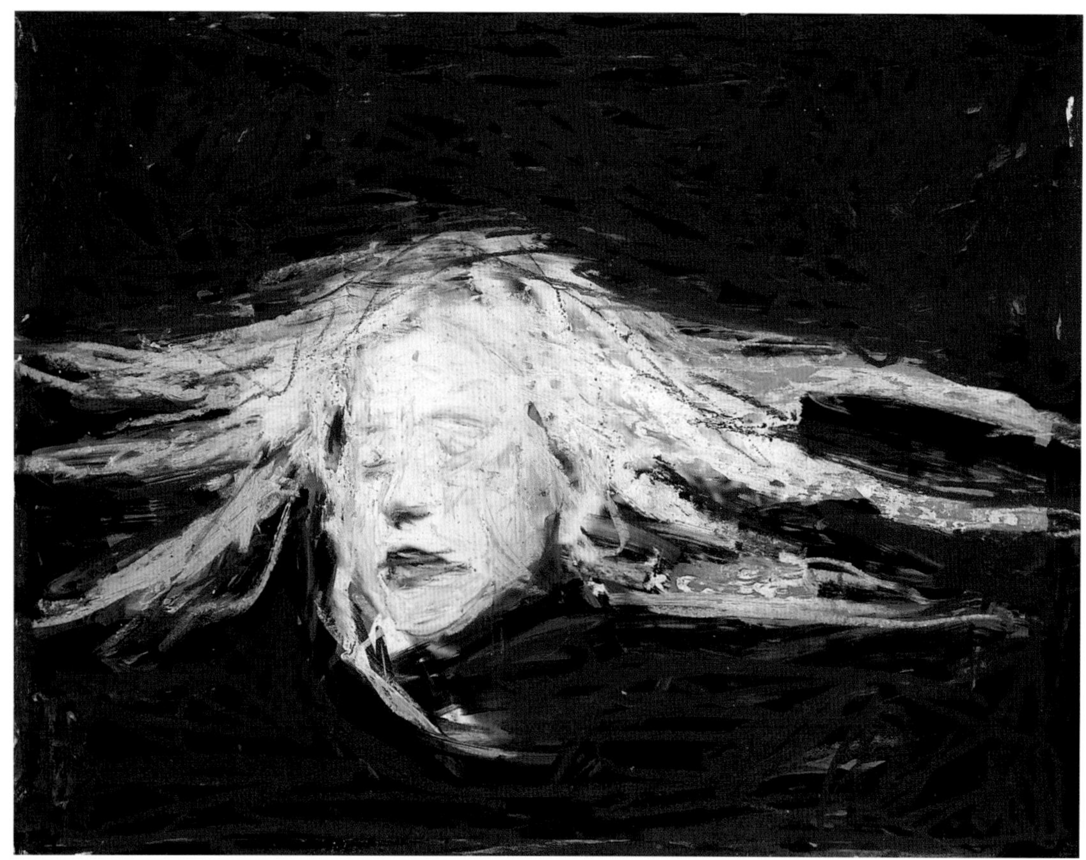

◁ *Katie*
by Amy Jean Rowan
Here, Rowan used permanent markers, oil sticks, oil pastels, and charcoal.

Markers

Markers are great fun to work with, and there are lots of varieties to choose from. There are water-based, solvent-based, or oil-based markers, and there are many colours and point ranges (from fine tip to broad tip). Markers are fairly permanent, so be sure that what you put down on paper is what you want. To thin the markers and make them easier to apply, try using a clear blender marker, which most art-supply stores carry. The blender also extends the ink's drying time, makes it somewhat transparent, and makes it possible to mix colours. Without the blender, the marker acts as an opaque medium and dries immediately. Rarely are markers used exclusively to hand colour a photograph. Instead, they're usually used in just a section or two.

▽ *Bus Stop*
by Amy Jean Rowan
Rowan used oil pastels and a paint pen to colour this image.

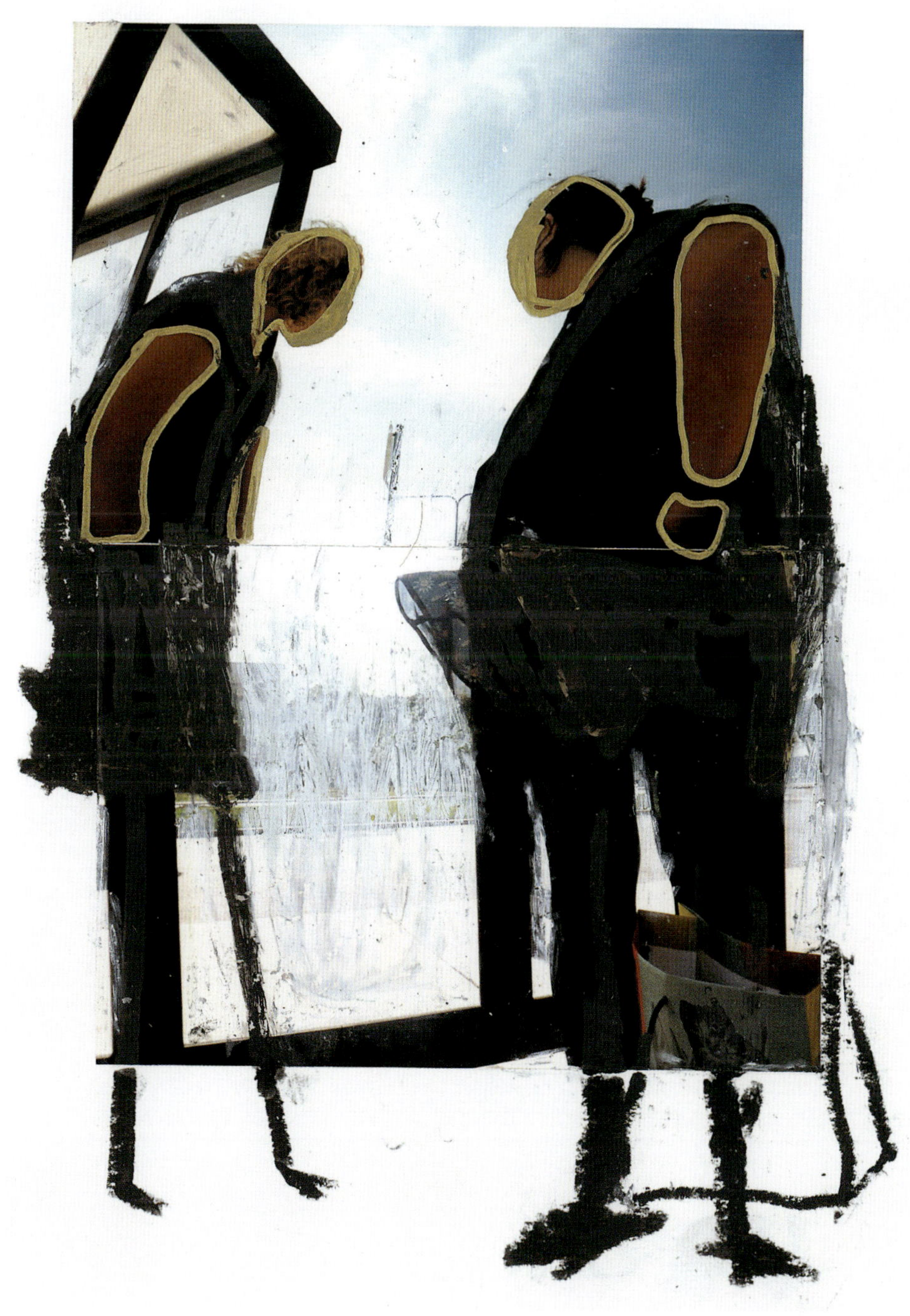

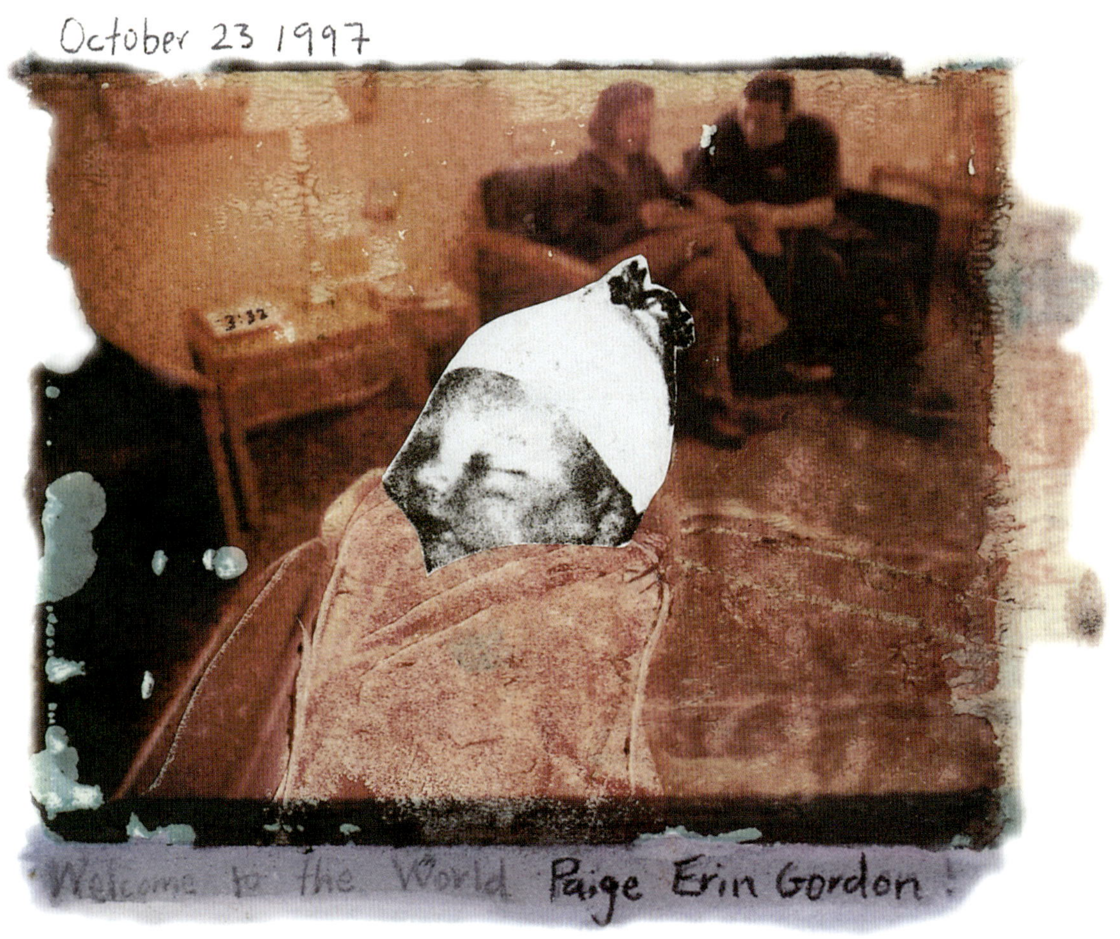

△ *October 23, 1997*
by Amy Jean Rowan
Rowan made a photocopy of a Polaroid transfer and coloured it with markers.

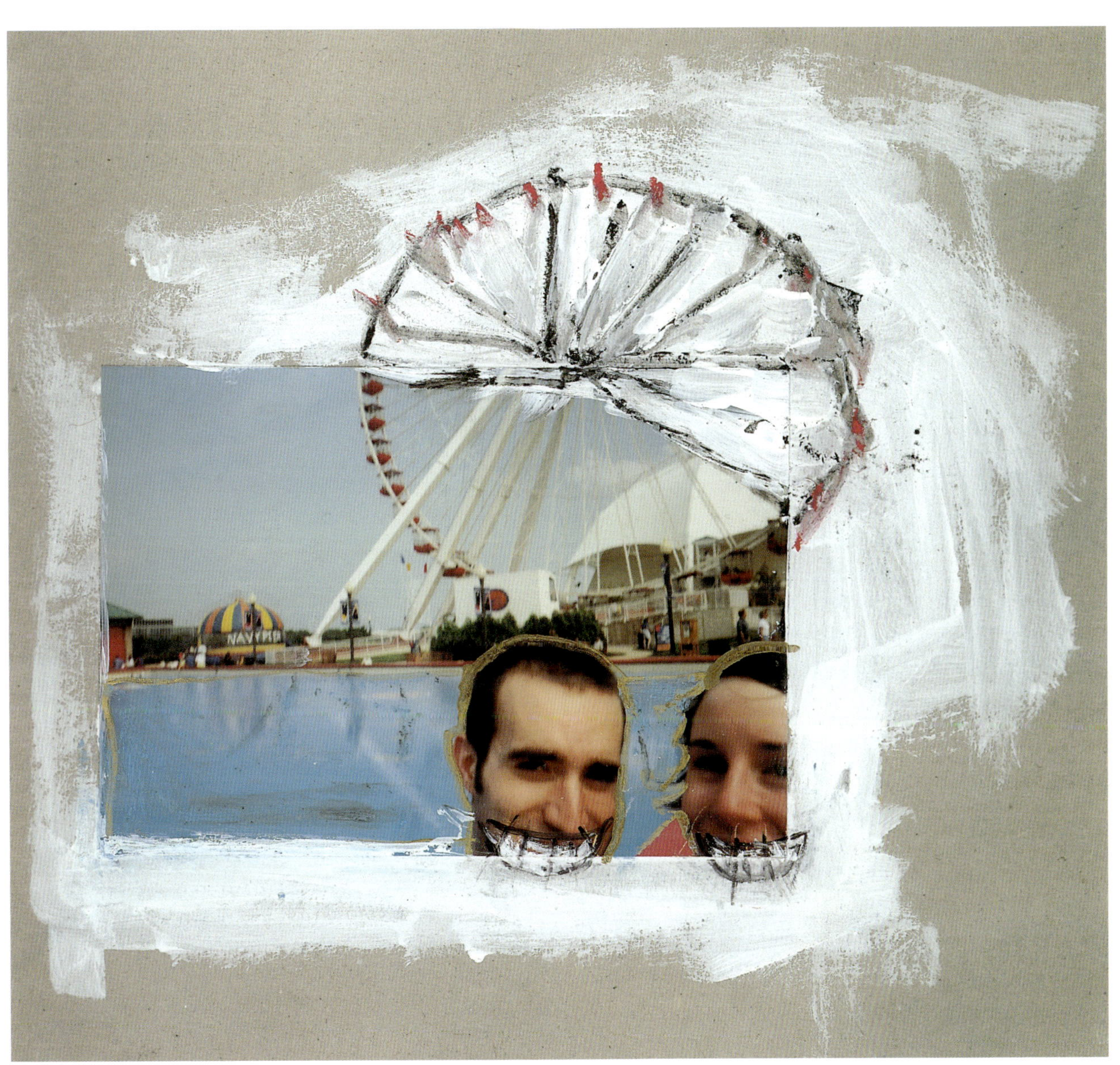

△ *Ferris Wheel*
by Amy Jean Rowan
Rowan used a combination of gesso, oil pastels, pastels, Conté crayons, and a paint pen on this colour photograph.

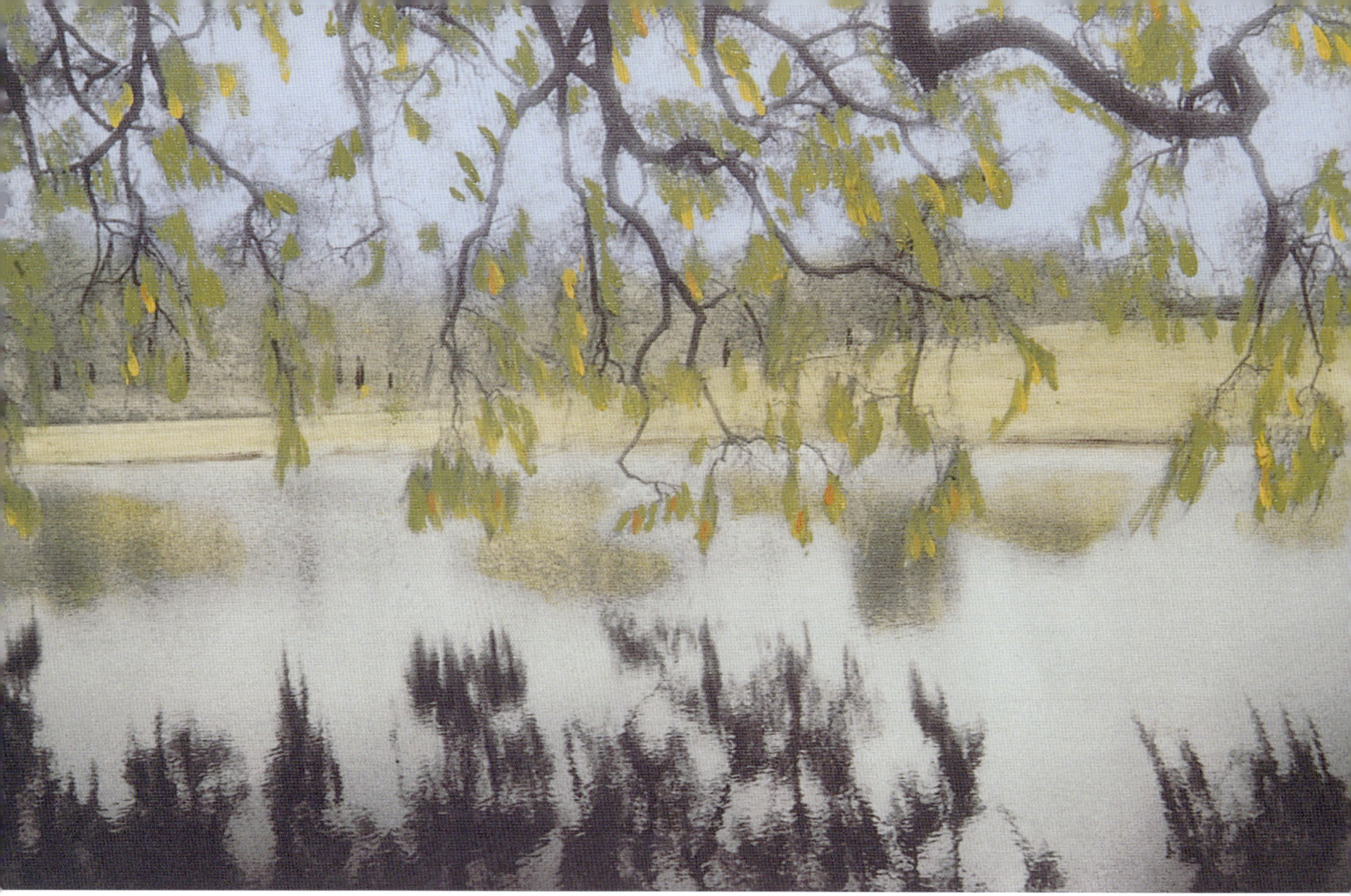

From *Pastoral Interludes* series
by Kate and Geir Jordahl
The photographs in this series were hand coloured with coloured pencils and acrylics.

Acrylics

Although acrylics come in a variety of bold and vibrant colours, they can have a flat appearance on a print. To avoid dull colour, thickly apply substantial amounts of paint to create texture, or add another medium on top of the acrylics. Before they dry, acrylics are easy to remove with water, but once dry (and they dry very quickly), they're very durable. Normally, acrylics are very opaque, but since they're water-based, they can be combined with water for a more transparent look.

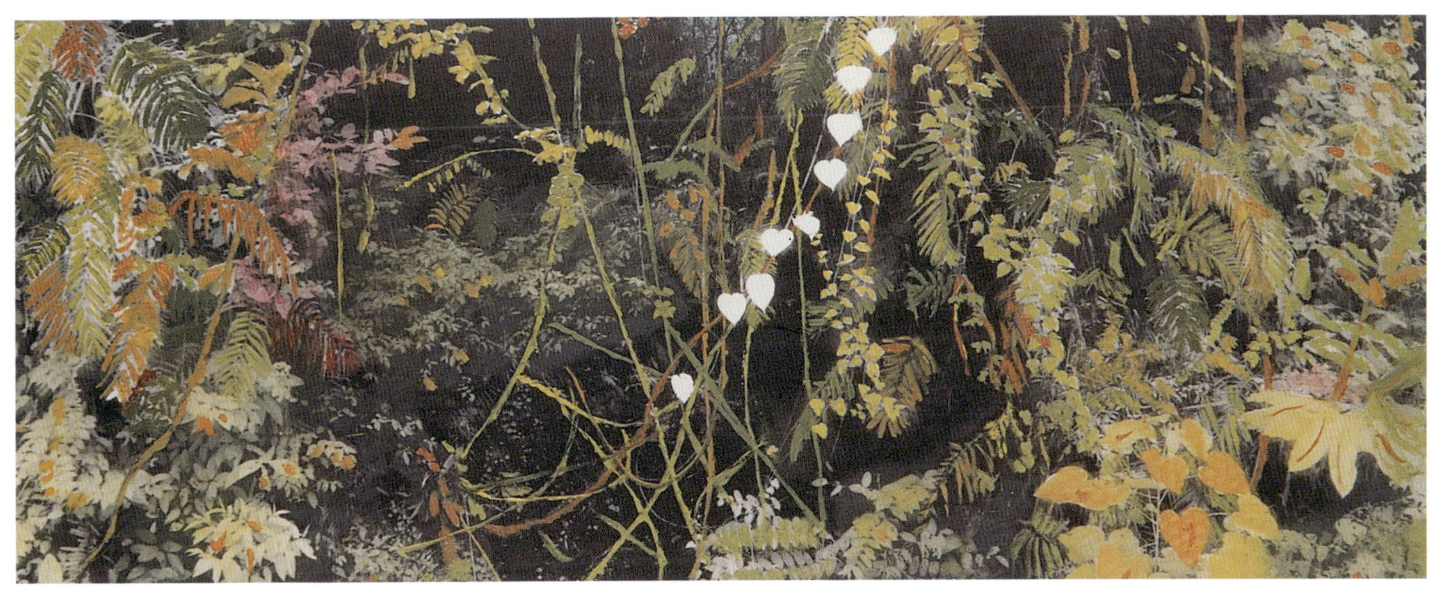

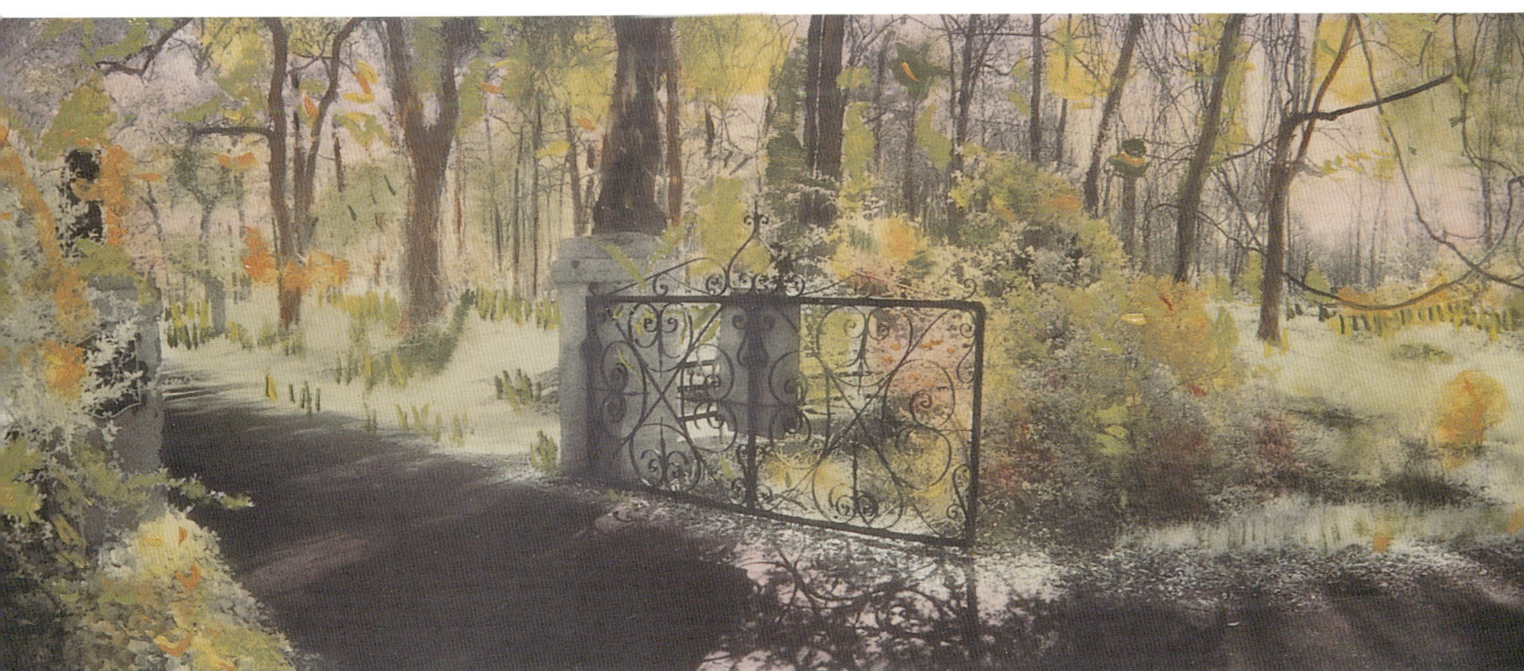

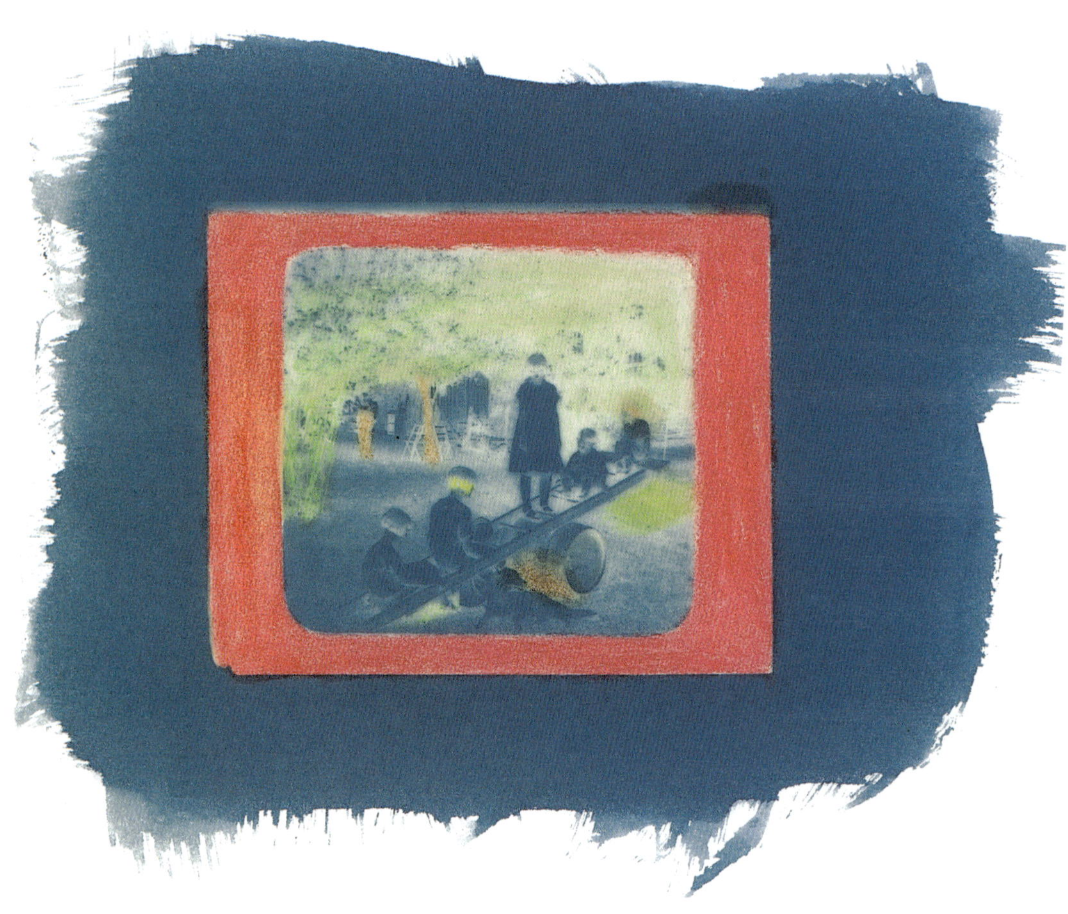

◁ *Untitled*
by Laurie Klein
This cyanotype was made from a glass positive found at a flea market. A contact print of it was made and hand coloured with watercolour pencil.

Watercolours

Watercolours are popular with hand colourists because they're translucent and can be used to create delicate washes of colour. Tube watercolours produce deeper colour than watercolour cakes, are easier to apply, and can be erased with small amounts of water. Liquid watercolours are very hard to remove and fade quickly, but they're incredibly vibrant in colour. Watercolours in general work best on fibre-based paper. Apply watercolours with paintbrushes or cotton swabs, and prepare the colours on a palette. Also available are water-based crayons and pencils. These can be applied directly to a print and smoothed in with a cotton swab (or not smoothed in if texture is desired). Watercolours can often appear subtle, but layers can be added for greater intensity. Be sure to let each layer dry before adding another.

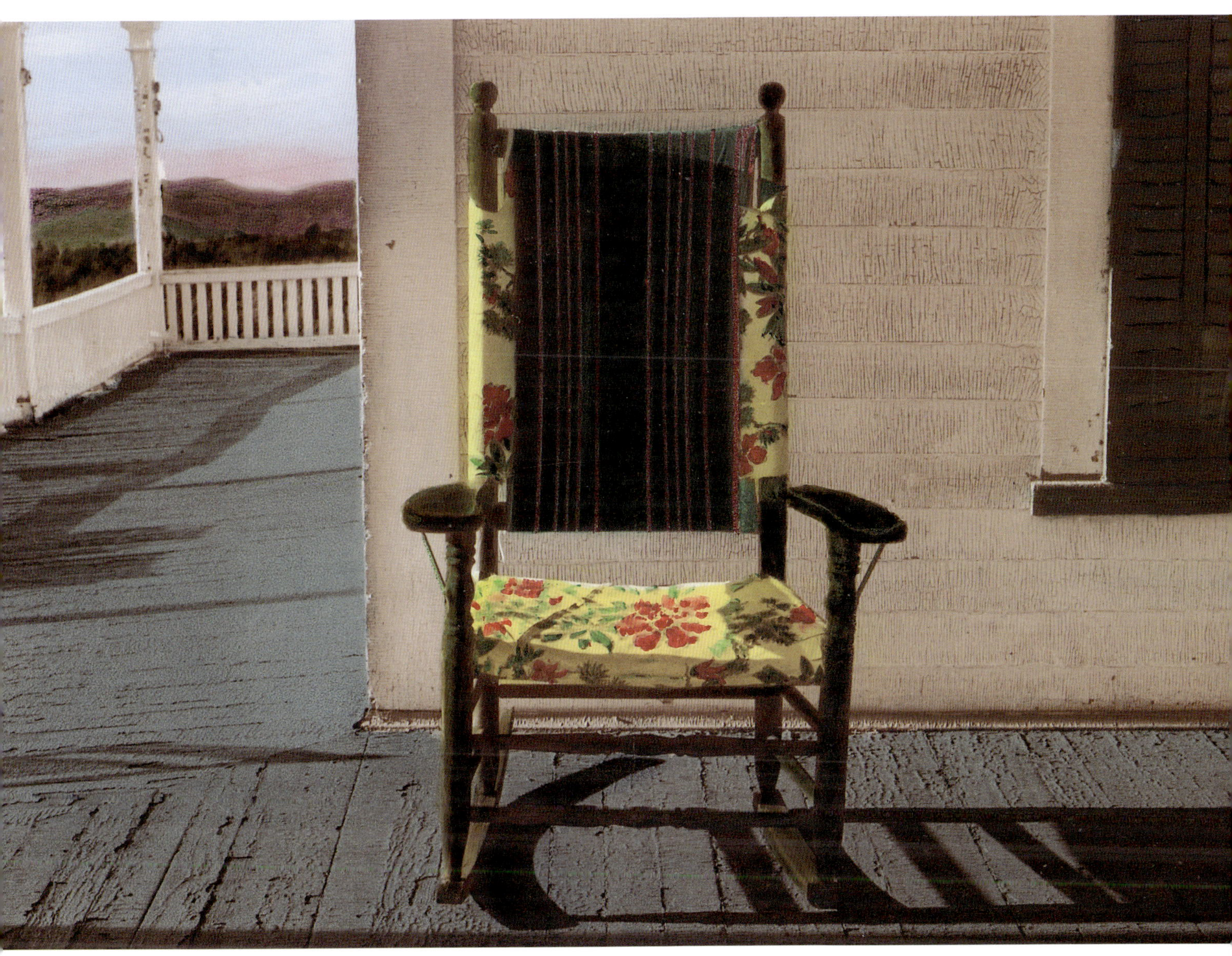

△ *Untitled*
by Jane Page-Conway
The artist first tones her photographs and then hand colours them with watercolours.

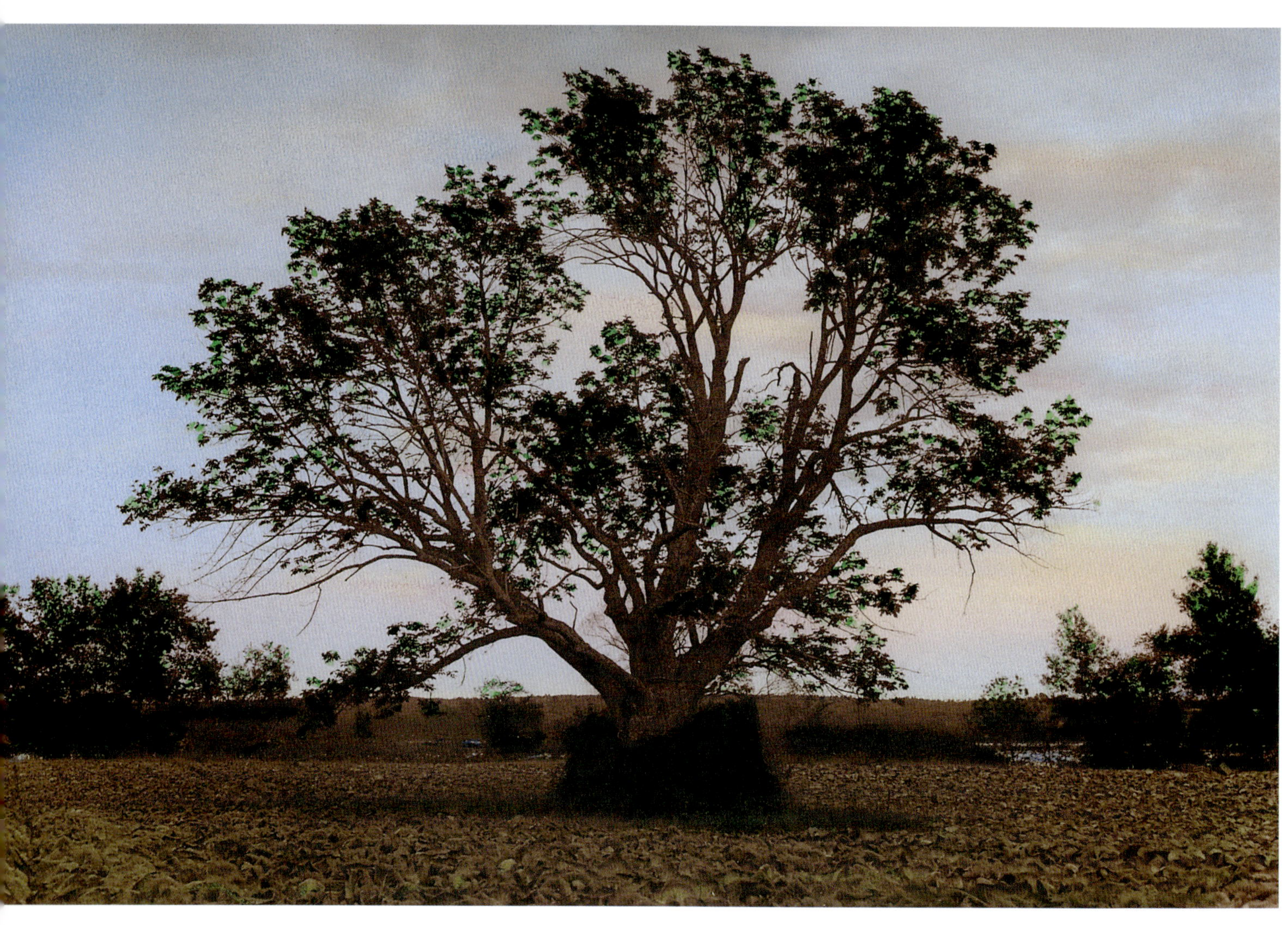

△ *Untitled*
by Jane Page-Conway
The artist first tones her photographs and then hand colours them with watercolours.

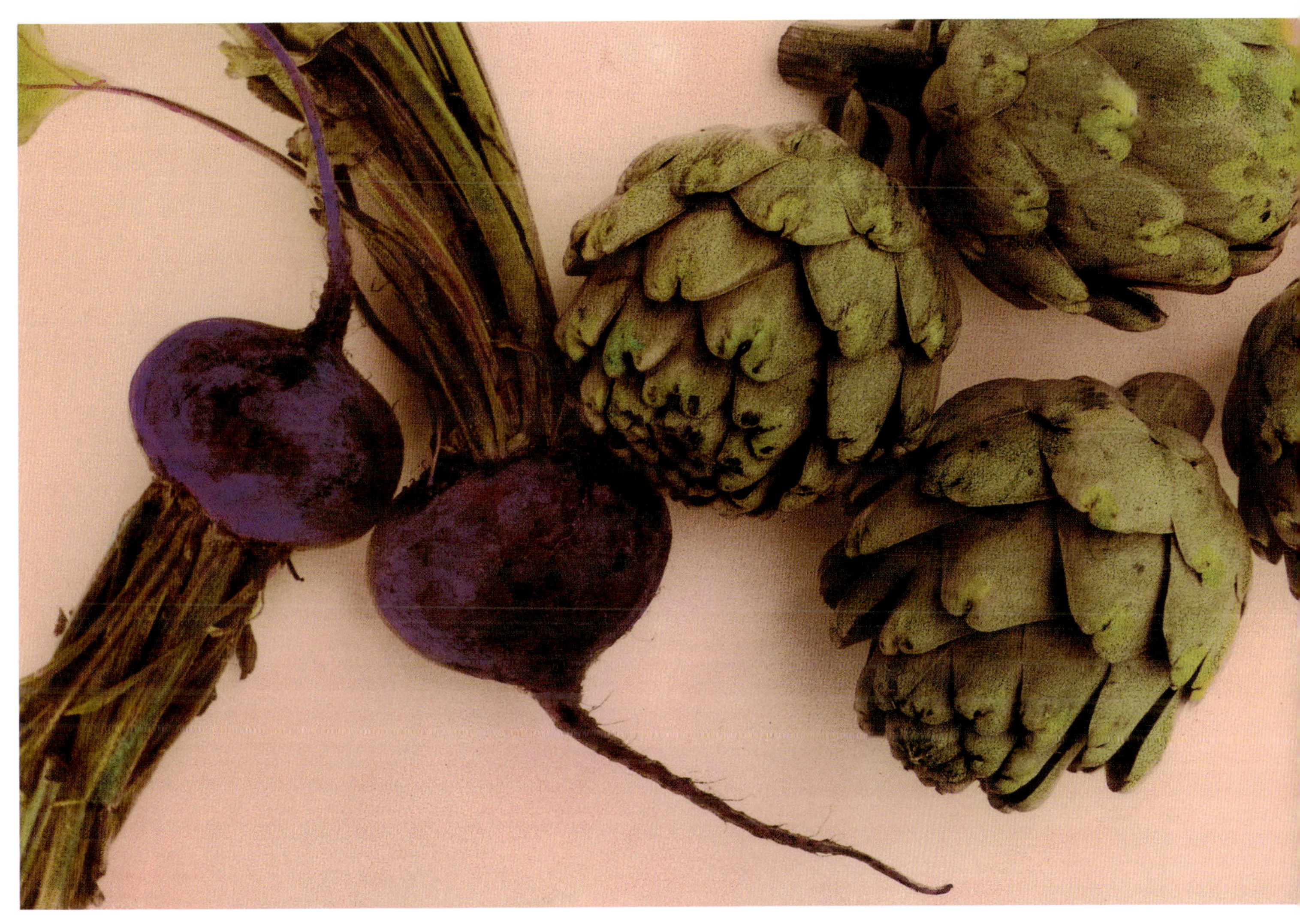

△ *Untitled*
by Jane Page-Conway

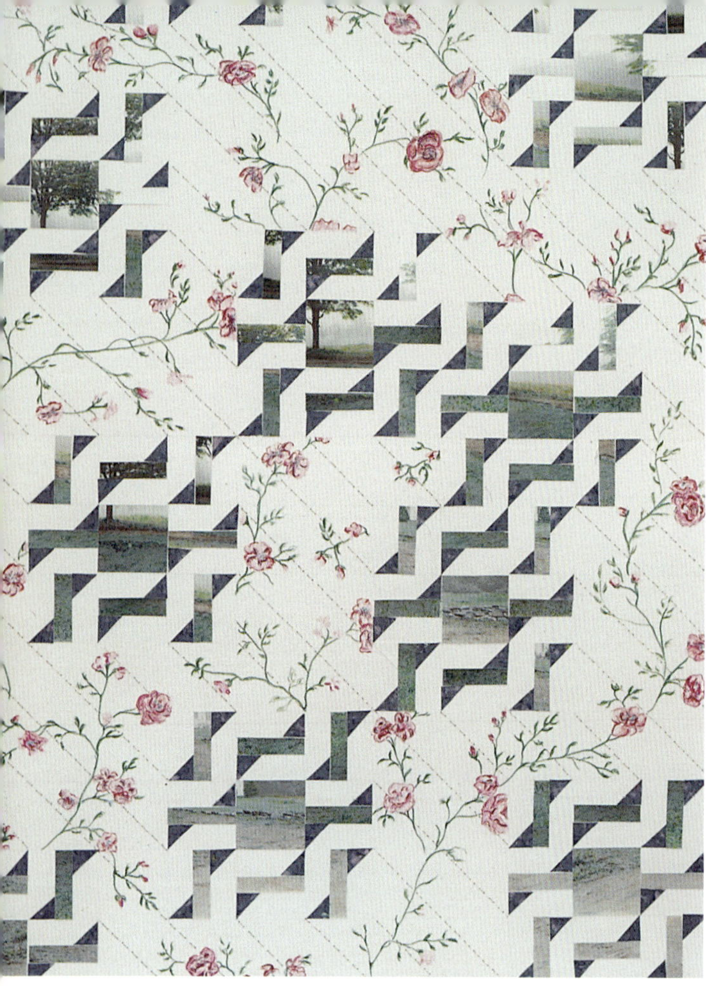

◁ *Home*
by Mary McCarthy
McCarthy cut up a hand-coloured black-and-white photograph and collaged the pieces into a "quilt."

Mixed Media

Many hand colourists use alternative film processes. Instead of making a silver photographic print, many make their own emulsions or buy pre-made emulsion and paint or coat a piece of paper with it. This process gives the print a handmade, tactile look, but the negative needs to be the size of the image you want to produce. Palladium and platinum printing are also quite popular. These prints have a silvery quality. Van Dyke prints are brownish in colour, and cyanotypes are like blue prints. Very popular these days are Polaroid or image transfers that are transferred onto cold- or hot-pressed watercolour paper and then hand coloured. Many artists create collages and integrate hand colouring into the piece. Collages can be created using a variety of materials, such as photocopies of old family snapshots, pictures cut out from magazines, old postcards, images that have been sewn together, or hand-made paper or fabric.

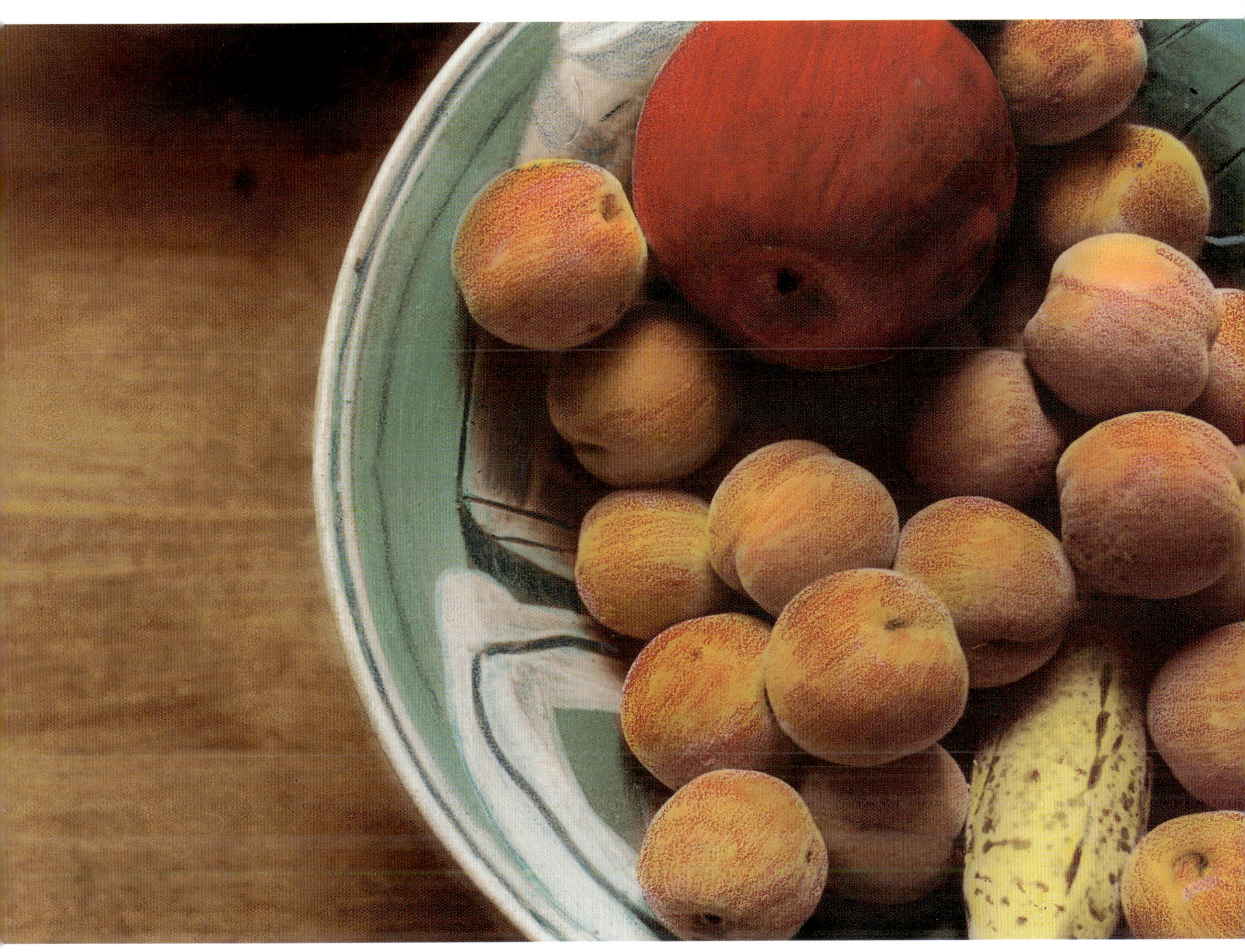

△ *Untitled*
by Jane Page-Conway
This image was toned with a mix of acrylics, oils, and pastels.

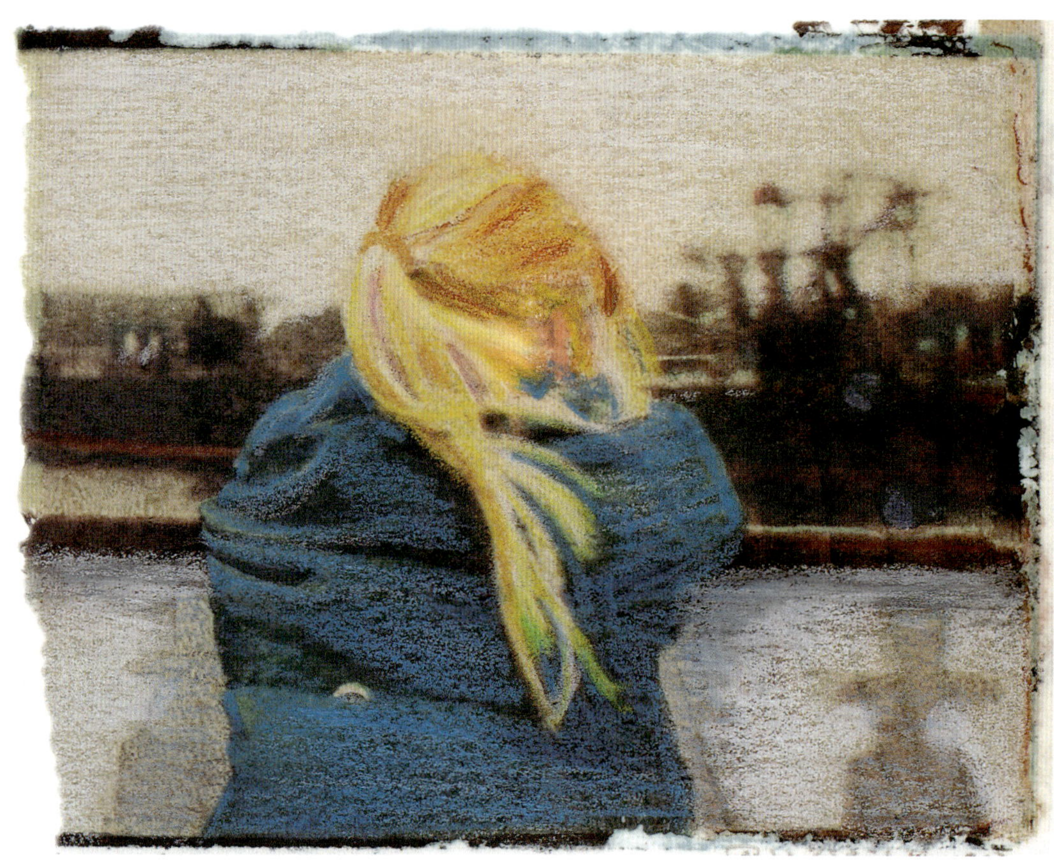

△ *Alyssa*
by Bobi Eldridge
Eldridge made a Polaroid transfer and then hand coloured it with coloured pencils and tempera.

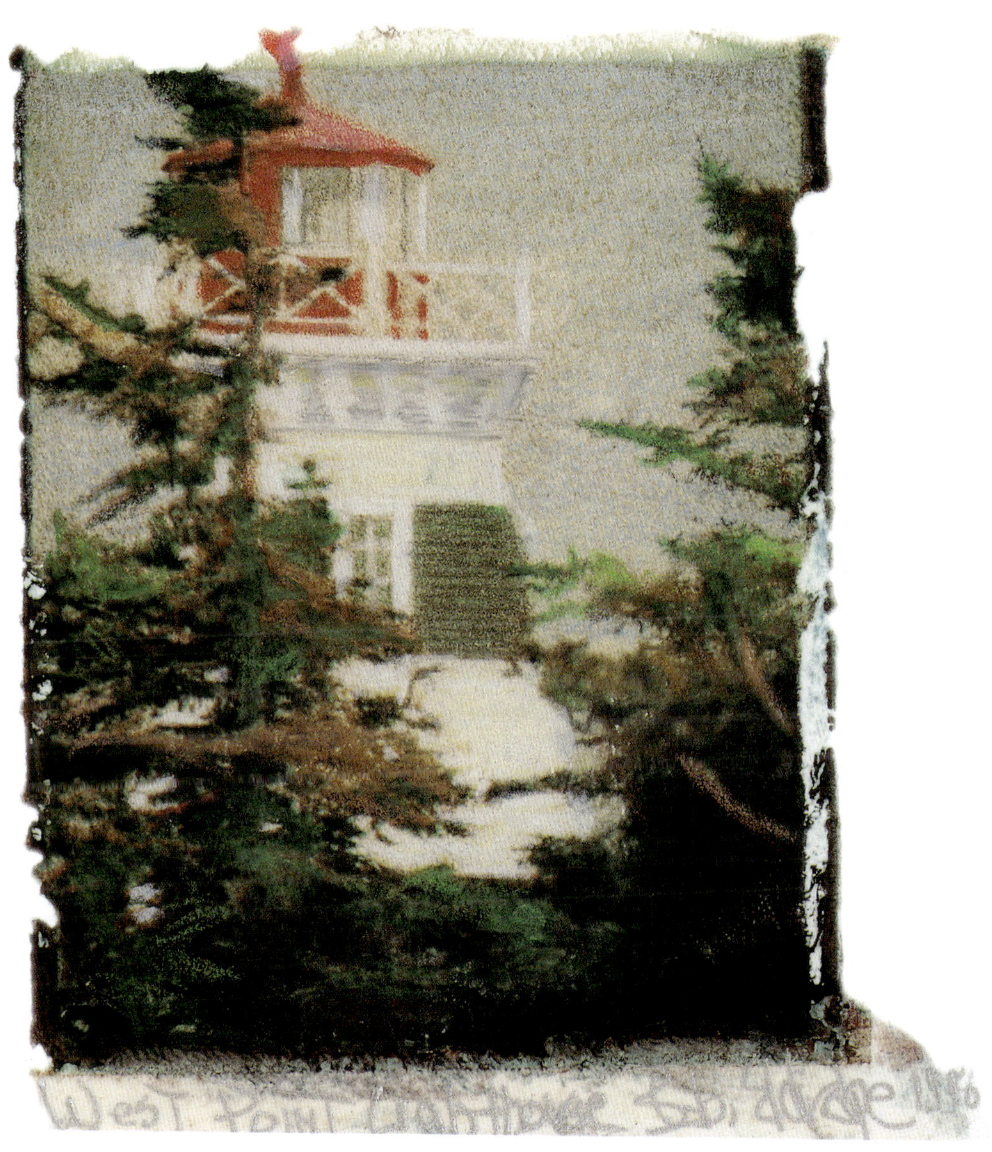

△ *West Point Lighthouse*
by Bobi Eldridge
Eldridge made a Polaroid transfer and then hand coloured it with coloured pencils and tempera.

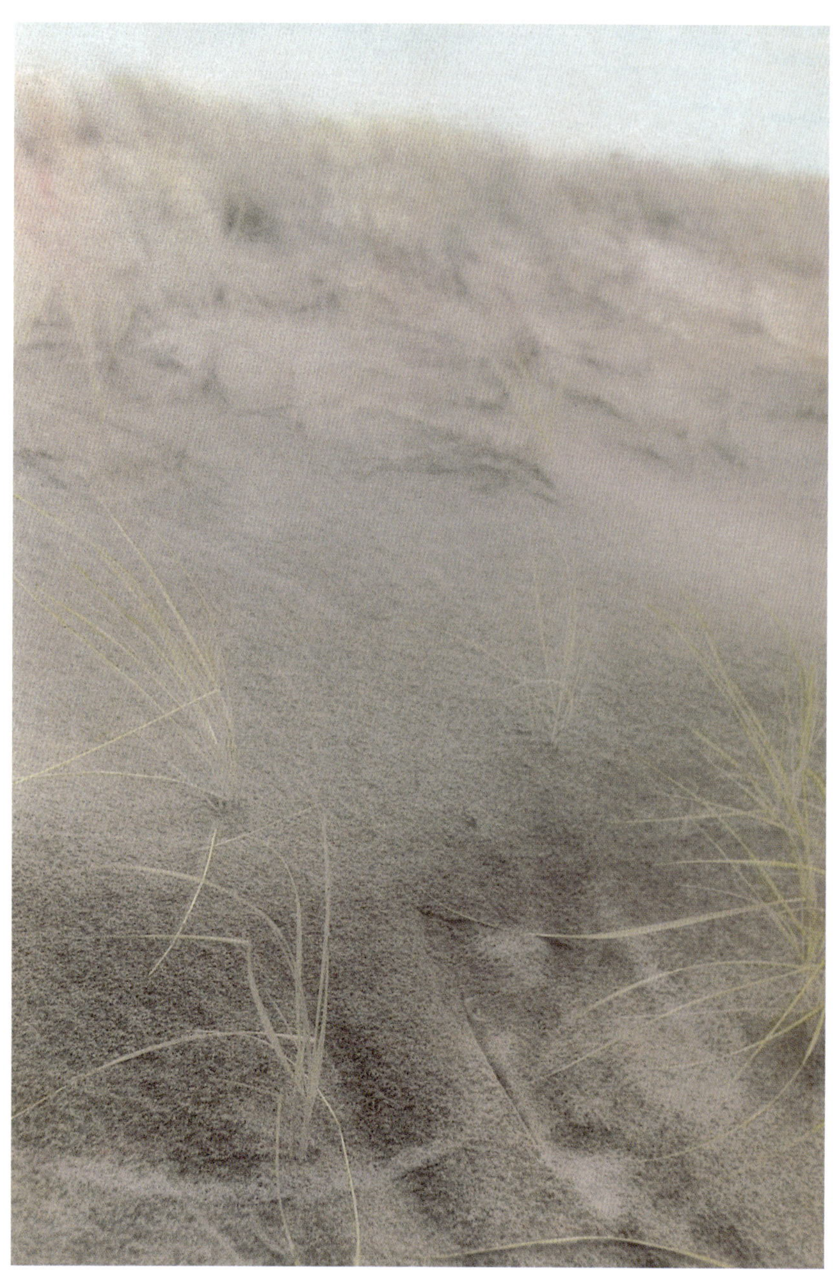

Directory of Artists

Bobi Eldridge
P. O. Box 1702
Orleans, MA 02653

Kate and Geir Jordahl
144 Medford Avenue
Hayward, CA 94541

Laurie Klein
Laurie Klein Gallery
290 Federal Road
Brookfield, CT 06804

Mary McCarthy
249 A Street, No. 25
Boston, MA 02210

Jane Page-Conway
13 Wildes Road
Bowdoinham, ME 04008

Amy Jean Rowan
52 Blueberry Lane
Bridgewater, CT 06752

Index

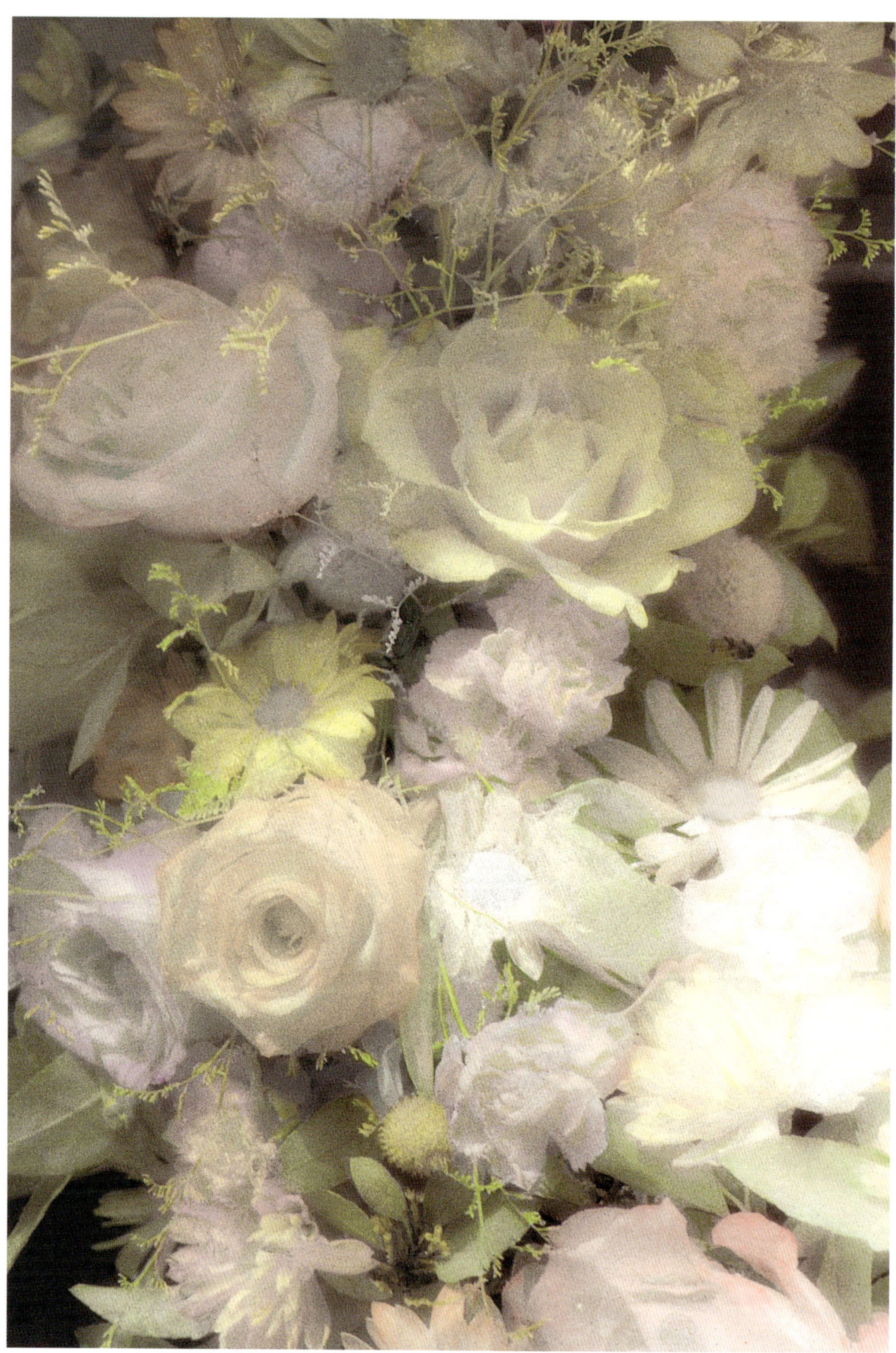

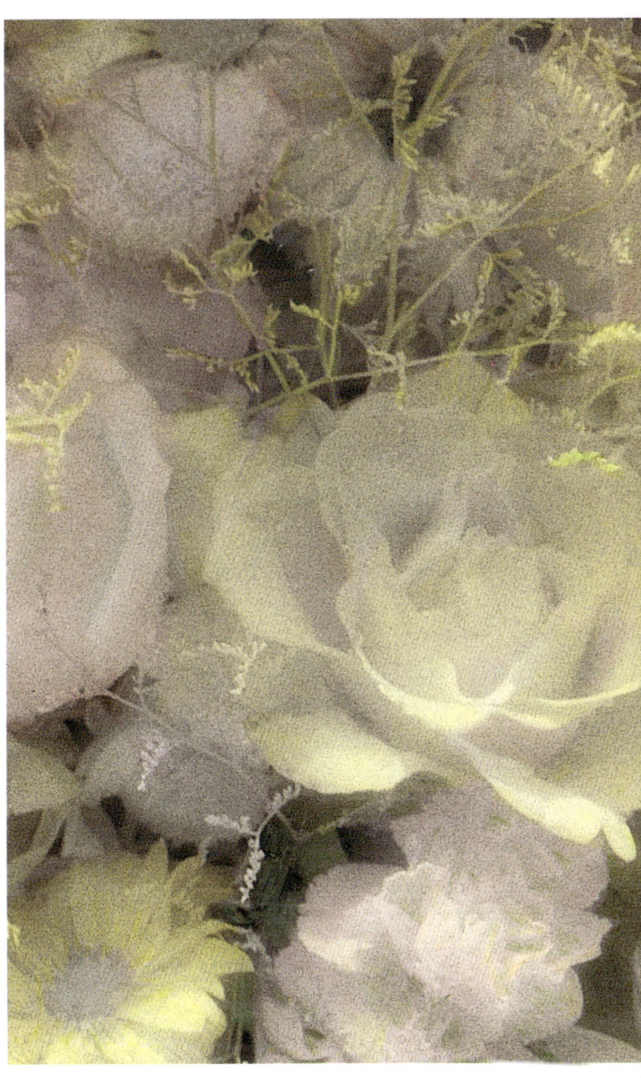

Acknowledgments

I would like to thank all of my family, who have always told me there isn't anything I can't do. Many of the photographs in this book are pictures of them. I especially want to thank my sons, Kyle and Bryce, for their patience and support. Thank you also to my clients, who not only gave permission but encouraged me to use their photographs for this book. I received much assistance from the women who work with me at the Laurie Klein Gallery: Ellen and Amy helped me put my thoughts on paper (Ellen also organized much of the material and was there when I needed an extra hand), and Jennifer kept the Laurie Klein Gallery running smoothly while I was occupied with this project; and Fred, a friend and my accountant, looked out for me and the bottom line. Thank you Mary McCarthy for helping me find Rockport and to all at Rockport, especially Kristina, Shawna, and Martha. Lastly, I want to thank my companion, Gordon, who helps me enjoy and make sense of my journey and encourages me to be all that I am, including the author of this labour of love. Much love to you all.

—LJK

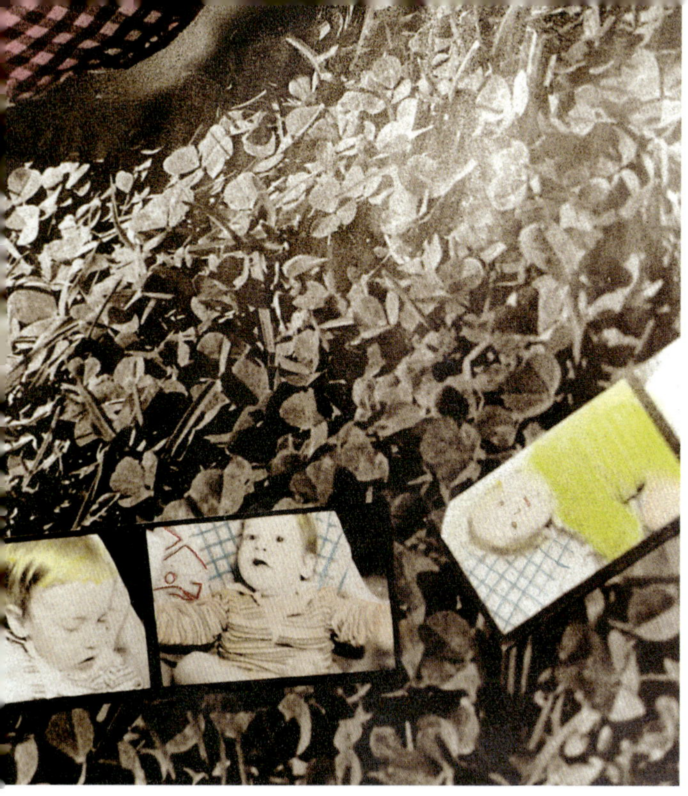

About the Author

Laurie Klein lives in Brookfield, Connecticut, where she operates the Laurie Klein Gallery. Laurie specializes in portrait and wedding photography. She shoots predominantly in black and white and then hand colours the photographs. Laurie has traveled throughout the country for her work. She is a protégée of Ansel Adams and has taught photography to amateur and professional photographers for eighteen years. Her method for hand colouring her creative compositions was recently featured on Lifetime's *Our Home* show. Laurie's lovely images have also been featured in numerous magazines and books and in a line of greeting cards, and her fine-art work has been exhibited internationally. Sanford Corporation, which makes the coloured pencils she uses, has sponsored Laurie for a number of years.

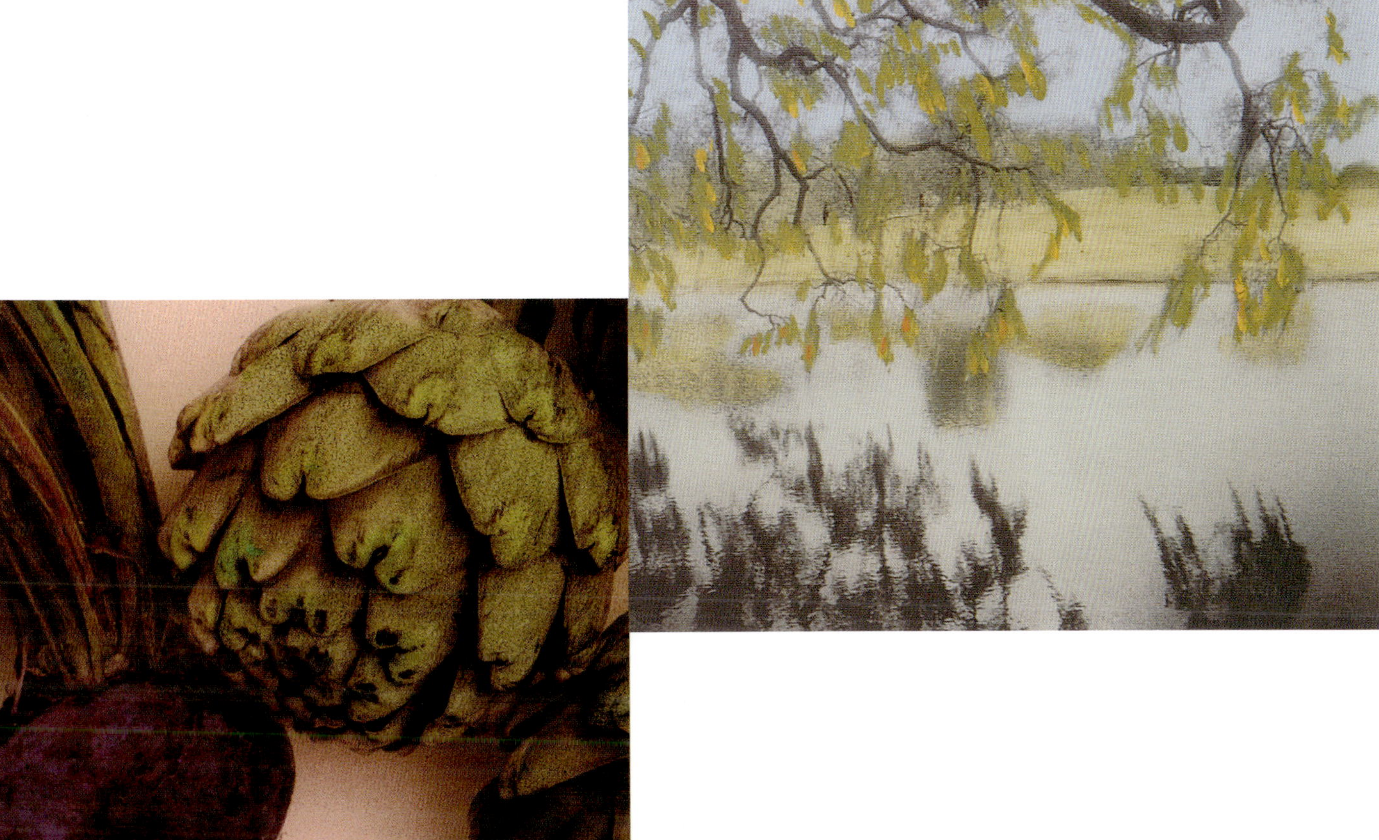